The Scarecrow Author Bibliographies

JACK KEROUAC:
An Annotated Bibliography
Of Secondary Sources,
1944-1979

by
ROBERT J. MILEWSKI

with the
assistance of
JOHN Z. GUZLOWSKI
and
LINDA CALENDRILLO

*The Scarecrow Author
Bibliographies, No. 52*

The Scarecrow Press, Inc.
Metuchen, N.J., & London
1981

Frontispiece by Bill Van Nimwegen

Library of Congress Cataloging in Publication Data

Milewski, Robert J   1948-
    Jack Kerouac : an annotated bibliography of secondary
sources, 1944-1979.

    (The Scarecrow author bibliographies ; no. 52)
    Includes index.
    1. Kerouac, John, 1922-1969--Bibliography.
I. Guzlowski, John Z., joint author. II. Calendrillo,
Linda, joint author.
Z8463.4.M54   [PS3521.E735]   016.813'54   80-24477
ISBN 0-8108-1378-5

ACKNOWLEDGMENTS

I would like to thank the following people who either helped me gather information (by giving both their time and then leads to important materials) or gave me their support: Steve Allen, Richard Ardinger, Jim Burns, William Burroughs, Carolyn Cassady, Marshall Clements, Malcolm Cowley, Andy Darlington, Al Gelpi, Allen Ginsberg, Douglas Hill, Richard Hill, John Clellon Holmes, Arthur & Kit Knight, Lloyd Leipzig, Dennis McNally, John Montgomery, Dan Propper, Kevin Ring, Jonas Sjöström, Stanley Twardowicz, and Joy Walsh.

Also, many thanks to the following librarians who helped with my information gathering needs over the years: Bob Daugherty, Ron Fark, Vern Frudd, Bill Gargan, Michele Ann Kapecky, Charles S. Longley, Bob McLeod, Russell Maylone (and the Special Collections Department staff of Northwestern University), Jim Scofield, Elmer Thogersen, and Bill Thrasher.

The following publishers of Kerouac's books also helped greatly by opening their review clippings files to me for inspection: Farrar, Straus & Giroux; Harcourt Brace Jovanovich; Ithaca Press; New Directions; and Viking Press.

I am indebted to those who granted me permission to reprint or reproduce materials, to all those who are unnamed, and to the few who listened to hours and hours of my rambling on about Jack Kerouac and this book.

Special thanks to Linda Calendrillo and John Z. Guzlowski who helped during the most important time of this work by sharing the job of reading hundreds of pages of articles and annotating them. And to Bill Van Nimwegen, for his shared enthusiasm toward Jack Kerouac and his frontispiece to this book.

CONTENTS

PREFACE

I became interested in Jack Kerouac while reading
The Subterraneans in 1966. A friend had introduced me to
the book. From then on I was a Kerouac fan. I read his
works and collected reviews of them. He affected my life in
many ways. I even acted out parts of On The Road.

Kerouac's death in October 1969 struck home. I had
wanted to meet him for several years (although not with a
"Dharma Bums"-stencilled jacket and the "Let's-go-out-and-
get drunk" attitude of many others) and had even been on the
East Coast near where he lived several times (but lost the
nerve to hunt him up). He was only three years older than
my father (and somewhat of a father and a teacher to me
through his writing).

In 1973, soon after reading Ann Charters' biography
of Kerouac, I decided to do something for him. I was fed
up with people's attitudes toward him and his work. My college literature teachers gave him lip service and thought him
a third-rate writer. Most book reviewers picked away at
him like vultures.

My tribute to the man would take the form of a critical bibliography. Since that time I have worked on and off
and on this book: traveled to archives, publishers, and libraries which had Kerouac materials files; spent long hours
on research, compilation, and annotation; and corresponded
with many people for information. This work is a product of
my effort. A bibliography lovingly worked on yet out-of-
date before it is even printed; a work hardly finished when
it seems completed.

Jack Kerouac: An Annotated Bibliography of Secondary
Sources, 1944-1979 gives information on articles written
about or related to the Beat author Jack Kerouac; his life and
his work. These take the form of book reviews, literary
criticism, comparative literature pieces, interviews, biographies, personal reminiscences, and newspaper reportage,

published from 1944 through 1979, on Kerouac's private, public, and literary life.

The book is subdivided into various topical categories and, in some cases, cross-referenced in the Index for easy access. In general, most articles were annotated except for book and film reviews (unless containing noteworthy information). Titles of books and articles were listed, for the most part, as they were printed, as far as capitalization and punctuation are concerned.

The particular bibliographic style used here is culled from and is a combination of all the major works, as such: the University of Chicago Press's A Manual of Style, the Modern Language Association's MLA Handbook, Kate L. Turabian's A Manual for Writers, and the American Library Association's Anglo-American Cataloging Rules. It seemed that no one work could fully answer the situations brought up by some of the works listed.

What has not been included here are short reviews that were mainly plot summaries, text quotations, or (those which I term) "notices of publication"; pieces which contained only a passing reference or two to Kerouac; and most newspaper wire service--UPI, AP, etc.--reviews, obituaries, and such, after an initial citing. In other words, included are those articles and reviews that had literary and documentary significance, and those that a Kerouac researcher would find useful, in some way, for continuing or further scholarship on the man and his work.

The appendixes serve to expand on the bibliographic, historic, and literary research already done on Jack Kerouac.

R. J. M.

INTRODUCTION

Sidelong Glances at Jack Kerouac

The ghost of Jack Kerouac wants to take its rightful and earned place in American literature, in American history, and in the American landscape. He appears almost to have achieved what he wants. With the release of a half dozen serious biographies, including the 1980 film version of Carolyn Cassady's Heart Beat, Kerouac is on the threshold of achieving true cultural status and lasting literary credentials. He is gaining a significant voice and position in the troubled, coast-to-coast, literary free-for-all that has existed since the Beat generation first claimed attention.

But Kerouac's ghost has a serious adversary: his public image, that mask imposed on him ever since those early attention-getting days of the Beat generation. The literary critics, the news media, the book reviewers, the general public--almost everyone, it seems--have never been able to figure out a way to treat Kerouac. Unable to regard him straight on, they have taken the image they have of him as the thing itself, as Kerouac himself. They shaped him into the King of the Beats; he even started to act as this caricature of himself. As the unwillingly-dubbed leader of the Beats and their bastard progeny, the beatniks (a term coined by San Francisco newspaper columnist Herb Caen), Kerouac achieved fame but was never taken seriously as an artist. His writing was not given much more than footnote literary attention. Kerouac rose fast and quickly for what he said rather than how he said it: his legend, growing larger-than-life, hurt his work; people saw a media star before they saw a shelf full of books. Everything flowing from or following Kerouac received more attention.

What follows attempts to off-set much of the hype that surrounds Kerouac's ghost. It attempts to overview his considerable achievement as a writer in America and to define his treatment by and retreat from society.

* * *

As a writer, Jack Kerouac is important in several ways. First, he was the founder of a new spontaneous prose. In three weeks during April and May 1951, Kerouac wrote On The Road. It was typed on one long roll of paper and described by a critic as the longest sentence in the English language. It was a novel about the adventures of a young man (or young men) in America. It was written according to theories which Kerouac had been developing since writing The Town And The City. 1*

In October 1951, through the encouragement and suggestion of Denver pal Ed White, Kerouac started to "sketch" his ideas like a painter, using words instead of paint. White was a catalyst by focusing Kerouac's theories and giving them concreteness. Later, Allen Ginsberg and William Burroughs asked Kerouac to "write a little brochure of instruction about how to write like you do. "2 The outcome of this was "Essentials of Spontaneous Prose"3 and later, "Belief and Technique for Modern Prose. "4 Published about the same time as On The Road, "Essentials" was a manifesto and, in a sense, a declaration of war on the "accepted style of writing at that time [the 1950's], or the traditional artifice of novel-writing then. "5 Ginsberg was so impressed with it that he even hung a copy in his Berkeley apartment for all to see.

Kerouac's writing theories impacted on the world of the New Critics, the high teacup school of literary criticism, and helped set in motion the machinery of its eventual downfall. As one critic notes, Kerouac "rescued mid-century prose from the flat dull cadence of the 1950s and set sentences exploding in the air. "6

Kerouac's prose broke through literary boundaries for structure, content, and feeling. Helen K. Taylor, On The Road's in-house editor at Viking Press, said that his "bold writing talent ... is almost always effective [and its] effectiveness ... builds an energy of its own that is all-pervasive.... The writing, " she adds, "is a torrential force that comes directly out of the material, instead of being applied to it.... [On The Road] is a piece of raw sociology [portraying] the hipster generation [which is] constantly forced to think of the why of [itself]. "7 Evelyn Levine, one of On

---

*Notes for the Introduction begin on page 9.

The Road's prepublication readers (for Viking) described
Kerouac as "a fresh, new (and fascinating) talent ... the
novel must be published even if it is a literary and financial
failure."[8]   And Anaïs Nin said that

> In Kerouac's On The Road, the lyrical passages
> have a primitive beauty.   All of them are alive.
> The basic research in American writing does not
> lie in surrealism, or in the flat dull realism of
> middle-class novels, but in this original language
> born of jazz, which has the tempo of American life,
> its rhythm, its vitality and colorfulness.   The re-
> sistance to it, to its artistry, its uniqueness, only
> comes from a fear of freedom, the fear of indi-
> viduality which has tried to make writing an anony-
> mous, functional utility. [9]

On The Road is a novel written in a straight, quasi-
documentary, story-telling fashion.   Within its structure, the
narrator, Sal Paradise, is able to digress and reflect on the
events he is involved in, to either push or pull his conclu-
sions/opinions/observations into the past, the future, or the
present (the immediacy of the act of writing). [10]   The book's
long, sweeping, poetic lines have been referred to as Whit-
manesque and as being more than able to describe the various
landscapes of America.   Also, the lines, conceived without
punctuation (in the correct, grammatical sense), serve to il-
lustrate that thought and feeling don't need external structure,
only rhythm and cadence. [11]

Kerouac's writing can be seen as being in an essentially oral tradition, spontaneous yet self-effacing, written
down yet meant to be read out loud in a flurry, in a frenetic
outpouring of feeling. [12]   It is not limited to the page and
the strictures of punctuation or literary etiquette.   He opened
new ground for both the novelist and the nonfiction writer,
yet his methods--being new, exciting, and different--lead to
his being both loved and applauded and lambasted and feared
by the critics and other writers (who were not so original or
experimental).

Gilbert Millstein was one of On The Road's greatest
supporters.   In his review in the New York Times (5 September 1957, p. 27) he said:

> [T]he fact is that "On the Road" is the most beau-
> tifully executed, the clearest and the most important

utterance yet made by the generation Kerouac himself named years ago as "beat," and whose principal avatar he is.

Just as, more than any other novel of the Twenties,
"The Sun Also Rises" came to be regarded as the
testament of the "Lost Generation," so it seems
certain that "On the Road" will come to be known as
that of the "Beat Generation...." [It] is a major
novel.

Another supporter, K. Peyton Johnson, wrote in the Savannah
Morning News (8 September 1957, p. 35):

On the Road ... is not only important because it
is well, sometimes beautifully and movingly, written by a man who has something to say, but also
because it explores a movement that has long wanted
the attention of an author of depth and talent....
Kerouac's heroes are rebels against the cult of con-
formity, "togetherness," "social adjustment," and
"the organization man...." Perhaps the strongest
element in the book is the tortured, but very strong,
almost haunted, love of America.

Others did not like On The Road and time after time
they either attacked it thoroughly or gave it some points while
taking away many others. One critic from Bestsellers (15
September 1957, p. 186) said:

The book is hardly a novel. The only plot consists
in detailing the dubious adventures of an amoral,
thrill-crazy group.... After fifty pages of ...
lickety-split feverish narrative told in bop-lingo, in
which words are used in connotations that not only
distort but pervert their meaning, the reader grows
bored, then annoyed, then angry. A farrago of
dope addiction, fornication, adultery, drunken brawls,
thievery and psychotic sweats, the only value this
might have would be to a student of abnormal psychology.... Adults will be almost nauseated.

Jack Kerouac saw himself as a spy in someone else's
body; saw himself as an observer in/of the world recording
through the "keyhole of his eye," as Jack Duluoz, everything
around him. [13] In this, he can be seen as a precursor of
the "new journalism"[14] which turned traditional news reportage

into a high art, into a type of literary documentation somewhere between fiction and nonfiction. His thinly disguised
autobiographical fiction-reporting, such as in On The Road,
is closely followed (in form and idea) by works like Tom
Wolfe's "experimental nonfiction novel"[15] The Electric Kool-
Aid Acid Test (in which Kerouac appears very briefly), and
Hunter S. Thompson's Fear and Loathing in Las Vegas.

Like Wolfe's and Thompson's narrators, Kerouac's
narrators are involved intimately with the action at hand in
his books. They are both observer and participant, and yet
seem to report the story accurately.[16] As opposed to the
hackneyed reporter on the sidelines documenting everything play-
by-play, the narrator's involvement is the key to the telling
of the story; it is enhanced by his participation.

Kerouac lived what he wrote about. His assignment:
His life in and impressions of America.

Jack Kerouac is important, secondly, because he is
a social historian of the first order. He documented a generation seeking a realignment of values during a crucial
transition period in the twentieth century. He noted the
changing attitudes of a social order that had fallen apart in
1929 and then went through successive convulsions every
decade from the 1930's to the 1960's; from New Deal to
World War Two to McCarthyism and the Korean and cold
wars to Viet Nam and massive anti-war demonstrations; from
the old wobbly-hoboes to the Lost Generation to the Beats and
the beatniks to the hippies. In post-War America (up through
the 1950's), during which time Kerouac wrote most of his
major work, it was a time of short hair, bobby soxers, 3-D
glasses, rock 'n' roll, Billy Graham, the Big Ten, apple
pie, Dwight "Ike" Eisenhower, and the Bomb. And Kerouac
was there.

In his travels, Kerouac met up with people from
nearly all walks of life--cowboys, hoboes, writers, farmers,
Mexicans, blacks, hipsters, jazz musicians, junkies, busi-
nessmen, grandmothers, and housewives--and he would try to
figure out the why of them, the whole story of their lives.[17]
Also, he described the American landscape along the road
(primarily from behind the window of a car, bus, train, railroad hotel, or flophouse) and conjured up images as clear and
meaningful as those of photographic pioneers such as Edward
Weston (who had gone across the country on a Guggenheim
fellowship in the late 1930's documenting similar experiences

visually) or Ansel Adams (famous for his landscape pictures, especially of Yosemite).

The Beats developed as a group, albeit small and very loosely organized, during the 1940's and 1950's. Kerouac, as de facto historian, reported his unwillingness--and that of his friends and those he met on the road--to live according to society's strictures, to the rules of the game. One reviewer said that the Beats rebelled not against their fathers, as had the previous generation of the twenties, but against their very own generation: "against the ivy league suit, the philosophy of 'being well adjusted' and 'good public relations' that [their] generation in large part [had accepted] as its own. "[18]

For Kerouac it was a time of hoboing and hitchhiking and a succession of odd jobs to finance the traveling (and his life-style, in general). It was lumberjack shirts instead of grey flannel suits. It was move, Move, MOVE: an unrootedness bred from the pioneer spirit that had taken hold of people and kept Americans on the go, searching for opportunity and change. Conversely, it was also a running away from the everyday life that both bored and frightened Kerouac; the headlong rush into another kind of life, a living in experience and worldliness.

> "Whee. Sal, we gotta go and never stop going till
> we get there. "
> "Where we going, man?"
> "I don't know but we gotta go. "[19]

It was noncommitment to politics in an age of stand-taking and blacklisting. It was also Jack Kerouac in love with America; an America of an earlier, a more innocent age. [20]

*　*　*

Jack Kerouac, through his writing, exerted a force (or influence) on the outside world. The life-style of the Beats was emulated by the beatniks. They had their pads, poetry readings, beards, dark clothing, hot and cool jazz, chicks, slangs, parties, wine, marijuana, etc.; and all this borrowed, largely, in itself from the bohemians, hipsters, and jazz musicians Kerouac knew and wrote about. (Later, the hippies of the sixties would adopt or transform some of these for their own use.) Also, the young of each generation since Kerouac have gone "on the road, " across the country, ex-

ploring his America. On The Road, that Baedeker of beat-
ism, became the traveler's guide of the penniless set, America's second and third generation "dharma bums." Kerouac
became the "hero of the alienated."[21]

Several of Kerouac's novels metamorphosed his friend,
Neal Cassady (that real-life odd, adolescent, eccentric, criminal, Denver streetwise punk), into the bigger-than-life "Beat
saint" and "Holy Goof," Dean Moriarty, a. k. a. Cody Pomeray.[22] Cassady became the unequalled, endlessly energetic
and frantic, cult and drug hero of the beatniks and the hippies; the bus driver for Ken Kesey and his Merry Pranksters. (It is ironic that many young people only know Kerouac through his association with Cassady, who in turn was
associated with Kesey.) And whether or not Cassady was
critical of Kerouac's portrayals of him, he lived out his
life as the ultimate underground superman.

As Kerouac affected the world, it also pushed in on
him. His rise to fame was brief and much similar to his
fabulous roman candles image in On The Road: a bright,
fast swoosh to the top and then exploding across the sky (and
never to be heard from again in quite the same way). On
the way up (and down) his ability to handle the pressures ac-
companying this long sought after notoriety became fragmented. He could not adjust to it and was quickly left in
despair; he could neither play the literary nor the celebrity
game. His insecurity and confusion in the tinsel world he
had entered, the treatment of his timely and unique work, and
the running commentaries and railings on his personal affairs
contributed to his inability to defend himself or to deal with
his life in any logical way. Kerouac was consequently mis-
interpreted by those who did not know or understand him.[23]

In general, the news media treated Kerouac as an
anomaly and his works as either sensationalism or boredom.
On The Road was a book for the tongue-waggers, the sooth-
sayers, and the cocktail party set. It might have been taken
more seriously and accepted as a legitimate literary work if
it had not been hinted that the life-style, attitudes, and characters presented in it were based in reality. Kerouac was
the "King of the Beats" (bestowed in January 1959 by Seymour
Krim), the beatnik king, or the Beat spokesman--among others; all titles he was loath to carry. Popular book reviewers could easily mix-up the events in a book with real life
and criticize both. As a result, Kerouac would get drunk before going into an interview, one which he did not want to

attend, and grunt answers (displaying a combination of shyness and belligerence) to questions from an unknowledgeable or unsympathetic host. [24]

Kerouac was essentially conservative and religious; and this was noted early on in his career, or legend (before the publication of On The Road), by Kenneth Rexroth:

> Kerouac calls himself a Buddhist, but he is certainly the most excited Buddhist I have ever heard of. Sometimes he lapses into pages of terrifying gibberish.... At its best his prose is what they call a smashing indictment. Kerouac may be a member of the "beat," but he is far from being a member of the "cool" generation. He is too frantic at times for even my middle-aged taste. Behind all the jive he is really an outraged Puritan, an angry Hebrew Prophet, Elisha sicking on the bears. [25]

Disenchanted with the non-acceptance of his art and of his seriousness as a legitimate writer by the literary critics and his peers, Kerouac saw early on that he was not getting the kind of support he needed to develop his theories, to grow into the great and accepted writer he wanted to become. Norman Podhoretz cruelly attacked him as one of the know-nothing bohemians, lashing out at his primitivism, spontaneity, and style as well as calling the Beat generation regressive, criminal, and brutal. Truman Capote called Kerouac's writing nothing more than typing. John Updike wrote a short parody of On The Road peopled by Beat-like pre-schoolers.

Some of Kerouac's long time friends deserted him (gradually and to varying degrees). They could not identify with the man who, having grown older and more conservative, even reactionary, in his politics (endorsing, for example, the opinions of William Buckley), became verbose, aggressive, and perhaps even abusive in his criticism of them. Allen Ginsberg could only smile while sitting in a studio audience listening to Kerouac denounce the Jews. [26] There is the story that he had had a door slammed in his face when he tried to visit his friend in Lowell. [27] (Perhaps Ginsberg was one of the few people who could understand and empathize with Kerouac; and recognize the forces which, over the years, determined his personality deterioration.) While William Burroughs suggested that Kerouac perhaps cut down his drinking (because of his genuine concern for the other's health), other friends could only grimace at Kerouac's drunken threats or theatrics; especially of waiting in the trees with a shotgun for any "commies" or "pinkoes. "

As much as Kerouac may have missed his friends, he also closed himself off from them (and others) because of his disillusionment with the world's treatment of him. He could have seen his friends' successes reflected bitterly in his own seeming failures. (Ginsberg was criticized for having made his transition from the Beats to the hippies, in effect becoming one of their many gurus, by using the writing skills Kerouac had taught him, though in poetry rather than fiction. Yet this was a survival tactic which Kerouac himself had not learned. Others pulled ahead using his techniques while he mired in his old guard, though once avantgarde, writing theories.) Alcoholism, long a problem, tore at him more than ever. He became a lonely, unwilling exile in St. Petersburg, Florida, thinking more of his mother's welfare than his own by guiltily fulfilling a deathbed promise to his father to care for Mémère.

Kerouac's life could be seen, in a Catholic sense, as a hell on earth, purgatorial fires of guilt, doubt, and recrimination burning in him. His suffering never faded. Living was the penance to youthful dreams of a joyous life, his only rewards being those promised in heaven.

In the end, perhaps Kerouac was closer to occupying Proust's sick bed than he thought. The "long shelf full of books, " the Duluoz Legend, has survived him, as he had hoped it would. (Yet it remains incomplete without the publication of the remainder of his body of work.) Poor Ti Jean's life formed "one enormous comedy" in a "world of raging action and folly. " It is doubtful, however, that it was one of "gentle sweetness, " as envisioned in his short preface to Big Sur, or that he died happy. The "keyhole of his eye" was part of something that both opened and closed America and the rest of the wondrous world to Jack Kerouac.

NOTES

1. The Town And The City (1950), Kerouac's first published book, had been written years before On The Road (1957) but in a straighter literary fashion, in a style more akin to Thomas Wolfe and other early influences.

He gained small notoriety as a promising young first novelist.

2. A quote by Kerouac from Ann Charters' A Bibliography of Work by Jack Kerouac (citation 741), p. 53.

3. Jack Kerouac, "Essentials of Spontaneous Prose," Black Mountain Review, No. 7 (1957): 226-228. In this work Kerouac defines nine essentials for spontaneous writing: 1) set-up, 2) procedure, 3) method, 4) scoping, 5) lag in procedure, 6) timing, 7) center of interest, 8) structure of work, and 9) mental state.

4. Jack Kerouac, "Belief & Technique For Modern Prose," Evergreen Review, No. 8 (1959): 57. In this work Kerouac lists thirty essentials for writing.

5. Letter received from John Clellon Holmes, 29 March 1980. To go on about this point, Mr. Holmes further states that Kerouac had great respect and affection for the act of writing, much more so than those who neatly wrote in the established patterns, styles, and mores; or those who would have us think that Kerouac was attacking the craft of writing itself. Kerouac wasn't a barbarian, a "natural," a primitive or anything like that. He could write sentences, build characters, dramatize situations. He elected not to do these things in the ways they had been done before, because of a conscious spiritual and aesthetic decision. He felt the prose of the early 50's going dead under his hand; he went to work very concertedly to revivify it. He knew that the reality of the time couldn't be reflected, created, in that sort of writing. Craftiness, he abhorred; craft, he had a great respect for. But he built the craft into his nerves, his senses, and his mind & heart. He wanted, like Lawrence, to preserve the living core of experience ... he wanted to get it down without having to kill it first. He was, above all else, an artist who was dedicated to the age-old artist's credo: to be truthful, to have reverence for life, to see it large and with forgiveness.

6. Stanley Reynolds, "Jack, back on the road," Guardian (London), 10 November 1979, p. 12.

7. A complete reading of Taylor's remarks appears in Appendix C.

8. A complete reading of Levine's remarks appears in Appendix C.

9. Gunther Stuhlmann, editor, The Diary of Anaïs Nin: 1955-1966 (New York: Harcourt Brace Jovanovich, c1976, 1977), pp. 114-115.

10. Kerouac wrote the majority of his work as well as al-
    most all of his major published books and poetry be-
    fore the publication of On The Road in September 1957.
    With The Dharma Bums, written as a follow-up to
    OTR, at the urgings of one of his publishers, who
    could see the advantage of a sequel, Kerouac's style
    and focus changed, as Massud Farzan has noted:
    > Dharma Bums marked the end of ... the first
    > phase of Kerouac's work, a period of being hip, of
    > experience and experimentation, and more of hope
    > than disillusionment. Kerouac the narrator ...
    > seems to live his happiest days in The Dharma
    > Bums: Kerouac the writer presents ... his most
    > satisfying work, writes his best prose, and re-
    > veals his highest level of narrative skill. Fol-
    > lowing this phase, up until 1961, there is a period
    > of discontinuity in the Duluoz-Legend saga during
    > which assorted publishers put out such titles as
    > Dr. Sax ... Maggie Cassidy ... Visions of Cody
    > ... and Tristessa.
    >   In 1962 was published Big Sur. Much of the
    > book reads and feels like a hangover ... [and al-
    > though a lesser novel] it is a work in which the
    > loneliness and despair are seen and felt on the
    > printed page.... [O]f his next book Satori In
    > Paris ... everything ... is shoddy and scanty.
    > It is not an anti-novel but ... an anti-anti-novel.
    > The hero is ... a spoofy anti-hero not unlike a
    > Malamud schlemiel on a drinking spree.... [O]ne
    > feels a little sad for [Kerouac] ... or even em-
    > barrassed, but one never fails to understand him.
    >   The Vanity of Duluoz (1968) has all the charac-
    > teristics of Kerouac's fiction before it, plus a dis-
    > tinguishing feature--a curious new tone of disil-
    > lusionment, resignation and bitterness, mixed with
    > the warm relaxed voice of a gifted raconteur of
    > old-fashioned realistic novels.... [H]e seems to
    > have added a new dimension to the Proustian tech-
    > nique by writing a book about himself-in-the-past
    > ... and at the same time being in it here and now
    > .... [He] has succeeded in becoming an integral
    > part of the story, moment by moment, in the very
    > process of writing. The result is a living spatial-
    > temporal development rather than a linear unfolding
    > in chronological time. (Massud Farzan, "The
    > Bippie in the Middle; Jack Kerouac [1922-1969],"
    > London Magazine, New Series, 9, No. 11 [1970]:
    > 65-67.)

11. John Clellon Holmes was the first to read On The Road
after Kerouac wrote it. Here are his impressions:
"the style is straight-forward, genuine, simple, still
as lyric, but not as curlicue as it once was. ... The
writing, with only occasional, minor exceptions, doesn't
need any alteration. ... The descriptions are fine,
clean things, filled with Jack's old power. ... He has
made a decided improvement here, I believe, and now
has his own style ... [which] is simple, moving,
evocative, and filled with real perceptions ... a fine
straight narrative that moves with incredible rapidity,
has scenes of unusual power ... and has straight-forward clean American writing and a new recognition of
the depth of the American experience that should set
the critics squabbling." (John Clellon Holmes, "First
Reader of On the Road in Manuscript: An Excerpt
from the Journal of John Clellon Holmes," Moody
Street Irregulars: A Jack Kerouac Newsletter, No. 5
[1979], p. 11.)

12. After listening to Kerouac reading his works, it might
be said to have a revivalist quality to it, especially
in passages from On The Road and Visions of Cody.

13. An example of this is the story about Kerouac position-
ing himself in a room full of people and giving the
impression that he is too drunk to either interact or
pay attention to anyone at all. But, all the while, he
is really seeing, hearing, and recording everything
happening.

14. The "new journalism" can be defined as "descriptive
reporting that employs the techniques of fiction in nonfiction articles by such writers as [Tom] Wolfe, [Jim-
my] Breslin, [Gay] Talese, [Norman] Mailer, and
[Truman] Capote." (John Hollowell, Fact & Fiction:
The New Journalism and the Nonfiction Novel [Chapel
Hill: University of North Carolina Press, 1977], p.
154.) Gay Talese says that "the new journalism,
though reading like fiction, is not fiction. It is, or
should be, as reliable as the most reliable reportage
although it seeks a larger truth than is possible
through the mere compilation of verifiable facts, the
use of direct quotations, and adherence to the rigid
organizational style of the older form. The new journalism allows, demands in fact, a more imaginative
approach to reporting, and it permits the writer to
inject himself into the narrative if he wishes." (Nico-
laus Mills, ed., The New Journalism: A Historical
Anthology [New York: McGraw-Hill, 1974], p. xii.)

15. The passage from which this quote is taken reads:
    In The Electric Kool-Aid Acid Test Wolfe turns
    from the maniacal new fetishes and religions of the
    larger pop culture of the affluent society to those
    of Ken Kesey and the Merry Pranksters, a com-
    mune of beautiful freaks on the ambiguous fringe
    of the future. This book-length story is already
    a classic. Like Capote's In Cold Blood, but in
    an entirely different key, it is really an experi-
    mental nonfiction novel more than anything else,
    and also perhaps the best single work of New Jour-
    nalism to date.... Acid Test is full of psycho-
    sociological insights, but the reader experiences
    the story with a fast-paced involvement that is
    reminiscent of Jack Kerouac's On the Road, a
    book which may have influenced Wolfe. In fact,
    Acid Test is a vision of hippie culture in roughly
    the same way that On the Road was a vision of
    the beat culture of the 1950's, although Wolfe's
    book is better written, and written with a differ-
    ent set of purposes. Although involved with the
    people of his book, Wolfe is also detached, skep-
    tical, and sometimes writes through a broad
    esthetic-historical overview. As a result of his
    shifting point of view, he is more willing to see
    comedy and absurdity than Kerouac was, but both
    books have a vision of the tragedy of their re-
    spective cultures and are closely attuned through
    style to the feverishness of people living out new
    and sometimes desperate life-experiments in order
    to transcend the sickness of their age. (Michael
    L. Johnson, The New Journalism: The Under-
    ground Press, the Artists of Nonfiction, and
    Changes in the Established Media [Lawrence,
    Kansas: University Press of Kansas, 1971], p.
    58.)

16. Hunter S. Thompson, author of Hell's Angels: A
    Strange and Terrible Saga, Fear and Loathing in Las
    Vegas, and other books, took the observer/participant
    concept further along and developed what he called
    "gonzo journalism," a variety of the "new journalism,"
    which is "any frantic form of subjective journalism in
    which the reporter provokes many of the incidents he
    writes about" (Hollowell, Fact & Fiction, p. 158).
    Even though it seems reasonable to assume that Ker-
    ouac provoked some of the events described in his
    books, the real provocateur he reported on was Neal

Cassady, a. k. a. Dean Moriarty and Cody Pomeray.
Cassady's frenetic, undeniably unstructured, and per-
versely illogical, incomprehensible, and explosive/
exploitive life-style led to continuous altercations with
wives, lovers, friends; and constant alterations to
plans and promises never meant to be kept (although
not maliciously).

17. An excellent example of this is Kerouac's description of
a farmer in On The Road:

I heard a great laugh, the greatest laugh in the
world, and here came this rawhide old-timer Nebraska farmer with a bunch of other boys into the
diner; you could hear his raspy cries clear across
the plains, across the whole grey world of them
that day. Everybody else laughed with him. He
didn't have a care in the world and had the hugest
regard for everybody. I said to myself, Wham,
listen to that man laugh. That's the West, here
I am in the West. He came booming into the
diner, calling Maw's name, and she made the
sweetest cherry pie in Nebraska, and I had some
with a mountainous scoop of ice cream on top.
"Maw, rustle me up some grub before I have to
start eatin myself raw or some damn silly idee
like that." And he threw himself on a stool and
went hyawhyaw hyaw hyaw. "And throw some
beans in it." It was the spirit of the West sitting
right next to me. I wished I knew his whole raw
life and what the hell he'd been doing all these
years besides laughing and yelling like that.
"Whooee, I told my soul." (Jack Kerouac, On The
Road [New York: New American Library, c1955.
1957], p. 19.)

18. K. Peyton Johnson, "Young Author Probes Deep Into
the Hipster Psychology," rev. of On The Road, Savannah Morning News, 8 September 1957, p. 35.

19. Jack Kerouac, On The Road (New York: Signet, c1955,
1957), p. 196.

20. Stanley Reynolds has said it similarly: Kerouac "was
a great reporter. He had gone across America as a
hobo writer, the tramp with a notebook like some sort
of American Gorki. In the middle of the grey flannel
suited, Madison Avenue 1950s Kerouac had discovered
a sweat-stained, smokey, dusty, old fashioned America, full of mad characters, pure wild men with fron-
tier visions in their heads but no more frontiers to go
to." (Reynolds, Guardian, p. 12.)

21. Gerald Nicosia, "Kerouac's daughter: The beat goes
    on," Chicago Sun-Times, 21 October 1979, Living sec.,
    p. 5.
22. In the preface to the 1960 New Directions edition of ex-
    cerpts from Visions of Cody, Kerouac had this to say:
    I wanted to put my hand to an enormous paean
    which would unite my vision of America with
    words spilled out in the modern spontaneous meth-
    od. Instead of just a horizontal account of travels
    on the road, I wanted a vertical, metaphysical
    study of Cody's character and its relationship to
    the general 'America.' This feeling may soon be
    obsolete as America enters its High Civilization
    period and no one will get sentimental or poetic
    any more about trains and dew on fences at dawn
    in Missouri. This is a youthful book (1951) and
    it was based on my belief in the goodness of the
    hero and his position as an archetypical American
    Man.
23. Jan Kerouac has been quoted as saying that her father
    "'was doing something more important [than being a
    father]. I knew he was out there bumbling around in
    some kind of very important universe. I realized
    from the beginning that he was kind of a baby, that he
    needed to be protected from all these things--and I
    didn't want to bring the harsh reality of my needs to
    him, and ruin him, because I figured he was some
    very delicate kind of being and that I shouldn't inter-
    fere.'" (Nicosia, Chicago Sun-Times, p. 5.)
24. There are stories of Kerouac having had so much to
    drink that he vomited while performing onstage:
    once at the Village Vanguard and another time on a
    nationally televised program.
25. Kenneth Rexroth, "San Francisco's Mature Bohemians,"
    Nation, 23 February 1957, p. 161.
26. As Kerouac's royalty checks grew smaller, he could
    only lash out at a supposed New York Jewish publish-
    ing house conspiracy against promoting his work, there-
    by denying him of his livelihood. Yet, ironically,
    some of his works have had lasting commercial suc-
    cess, selling an average of 50,000 copies in paperback
    per year.
27. After Kerouac died, his third wife, Stella, is reported
    to have said that he had been a very lonely man be-
    cause his friends had stopped trying to see him. Yet
    it was either Stella or Mémère who barred many peo-
    ple from visiting him, including his friends. Even

Kerouac was suspicious about letting some talk to or interview him. Black author Robert Boles has said that when he tried to visit, instead of answering the door, Kerouac stuck his head out of a window and asked what he wanted. Only after Kerouac had read a manuscript which Boles had given him did he finally let the visitor into his house. There are other stories of Kerouac telling Stella to let people in after she had told them that he was not at home. Kerouac circumvented his lack of visitors, somewhat, by calling his friends on the telephone, usually in drunken states, at all hours of the day or night.

PART I:

REVIEWS OF KEROUAC'S PRIMARY WORKS

A. ENGLISH LANGUAGE REVIEWS

1. Big Sur
    (For additional references, see the Index.)

1. Abrams, Kenneth. "Kerouac: Big Sur," Village Voice, 13 December 1962, pp. 18, 21.

2. "And Other Eyes Seeing (Feeling) Big Sur," Village Voice, 13 December 1962, p. 21.

3. Barker, Richard. "Big Sur," Kulchur, 2, No. 8 (1962): 87-89.

4. Barker, Richard. "Kerouac Stumbles On Truth in Big Sur," San Francisco Examiner, 9 September 1962, Highlight sec., p. 18.

5. "Beat, Beat, Beat," Newsweek, 17 September 1962, p. 99.

6. "Big Sur," Playboy, September 1962, p. 48.

7. "Big Sur," Virginia Quarterly Review, 39 (1963): viii.

8. Bradbury, Malcolm. "New Novels," Punch, 30 October 1963, p. 648.

9. Brooke, Jocelyn. "New Fiction," Listener, 24 October 1963, p. 667.

10. Brownrigg, N. G. "Review & Comment: Epilogue," Contact, 4, No. 2 (1963): 78-79.

11. Carroll, Paul. "Sad Case of Mr. Kerouac--On the Road Down," Chicago Daily News, 22 August 1962, p. 40.

12. Darack, Arthur. "Big Sur," Cincinnati Enquirer, 29 September 1962, p. 10.

13. Davenport, G. "Big Sur," National Review, 23 October 1962, p. 325.

14. DeMott, Benjamin. "Beatnik and James Jones," Harper's, October 1962, p. 92.

15. Donnelly, Tom. "Remembrance of Things Fast," Washington Daily News, 17 September 1962, p. 24.

16. Gold, Herbert. "Squaring Off the Corners," Saturday Review, 22 September 1962, p. 29.

17. Grieg, Michael. "More Beat Than Beatific in a Big Sur Cabin," San Francisco Chronicle, 9 September 1962, This World Magazine sec., p. 28.

18. Jarrett, Thomas D. "Protest Against American Life: Spokesman for the Beatniks On the Road Once Again," Atlanta Journal, 16 September 1962, p. 6-D

19. Jones, D. A. N. "Dharma Daddy," New Statesman, 25 October 1963, pp. 580-581.

20. Lease, Benjamin. "Rover Boy Rides Again," Chicago Sun-Times, 16 September 1962, sec. 3, p. 2.

21. Levine, Paul. "The Season's Difference," Hudson Review, 15 (1962-1963): 598-605.

22. "Lions & Cubs," Time, 14 September 1962, p. 106.

23. Lipton, Lawrence. "Shurning, Schmerning; Come Off It, Jack Kerouac," Los Angeles Times, 9 September 1962, Calendar sec., p. 14.

24. Martin, Ron. "The Road to the Shirshy Sea--Jack Crackerjack's New Kook Book," Detroit Free Press, 9 September 1962, sec. B, p. 5.

25. "New Fiction," Times (London), 24 October 1963, p. 16.

26. "New Fiction," Times Weekly Review, 31 October 1963, p. 13.

27. Nordell, Roderick. "Angry, Beat, and Optimistic," Christian Science Monitor, 4 October 1962, p. 9.

28. O'Brien, John H. "King of the Beatniks on a Binge," Detroit News, 9 September 1962, p. 3-G.

29. Ohmann, Richard M. "The Weary Wild Men," Commonweal, 5 October 1962, p. 49.

30. Osborne, Lynn. "New Kerouac Novel: Breakdown of Beatnik," Miami Herald, 23 September 1962, p. 7-F.

31. Rowland, Stanley J., Jr. "In Search of Mother Love," Christian Century, 26 September 1962, pp. 1170, 1172-1173.

32. Shepherd, Jean. "Amid Dark Spectres, A California Crackup," New York Herald Tribune, 16 September 1962, sec. 6, p. 7.

33. Stocking, David M. "A 'Beat' King Cracks Up," Milwaukee Journal, 30 September 1962, pt. 5, p. 4.

34. Truitt, James McC. "Kerouac? Man, He's Slipping," Washington Post & Times Herald, 16 September 1962, p. G7.

35. "West Coast Madness," Times Literary Supplement, 25 October 1963, p. 868.

36. Wiegand, William. "A Turn in the Road for the King of the Beats," New York Times Book Review, 16 September 1962, p. 4.

2. Book of Dreams
(See also citations 399, 748, and 749.)

37. Gleason, Ralph J. "The Beatific Vision vs. the Beat Scene," San Francisco Chronicle, 5 May 1961, This World Magazine sec., p. 28.

38. Truitt, James McC. "Inside the Beats, and 'Way Out,'" Washington Post, 18 June 1961, p. E7.

3. Desolation Angels
(For additional references, see the Index.)

39. Algren, Nelson. "His ice-cream cone runneth over,"

New York Herald Tribune, 16 May 1965, Book Week sec., pp. 5, 13.

40. "Beatnik Kerouac Returns: New Images of Spirituality," Miami Herald, 16 May 1965, p. 7-F.

41. Bellman, Samuel I. "A Fevered Snowflake," Saturday Review, 12 June 1965, p. 47.

42. "Bumbling Bunyan," Time, 7 May 1965, pp. 110, 112.

43. Burgess, Anthony. "The Big Daddy of the Beats," Observer (London), 22 May 1966, p. 26.

44. Cook, Bruce. "Through Dullsville with Kerouac," Chicago Daily News, 15 May 1965, Panorama sec., p. 8.

44a. Cunliffe, Dave. "Kerouac Prose," Peace News, 22 July 1966, p. 8.

45. "Desolation Angels," Choice, September 1965, p. 387.

46. "Desolation Angels," Playboy, July 1965, p. 25.

47. Gray, Ken. "Out of the Ordinary," Irish Times, 21 May 1966, p. 8.

48. Kirsch, Robert R. "The Quest of Kerouac and Group," San Francisco Chronicle, 23 May 1965, This World Magazine sec., p. 30.

49. "Look Homeward, Hipster," Times Literary Supplement, 26 May 1966, p. 469.

50. Maloff, Saul. "A Line Must Be Drawn," New York Times Book Review, 2 May 1965, p. 4.

51. Mazzocco, Robert. "Our Gang," New York Review of Books, 20 May 1965, pp. 8-9.

52. Miller, William G. "Kerouac's Latest More of the Same," Boston Globe, 27 May 1965, p. 15.

53. Morgan, Edwin. "Passing Through," New Statesman, 27 May 1966, p. 784.

54. "New Fiction," Times (London), 26 May 1966, p. 18.

55. Newman, Charles. "Winsor and Kerouac: Down the Old Road," Chicago Tribune, 2 May 1965, sec. 9, p. 3.

56. Newquist, Roy. "Desolation Angels," New York Post, 2 May 1965, p. 49.

57. Poore, Charles. "An Elegy for the Beat Syndicate of Writers," New York Times, 4 May 1965, p. 41.

58. Price, R. G. G. "A Fitful Backward Glance," Punch, 28 December 1966, p. 970.

59. Price, R. G. G. "New Novels," Punch, 1 June 1966, p. 820.

60. Spender, Stephen. "Literature." In The Great Ideas Today, 1965, pp. 166-211. Chicago: Encyclopaedia Brittanica, 1965.

61. Ward, Bill. "From the Road to a Rocker, Kerouac Finds Destiny in 'Peaceful Sorrow,'" National Observer, 17 May 1965, p. 21.

62. Wilson, John Rowan. "Modern Musketeers," Spectator, 27 May 1966, p. 670.

63. Wordsworth, Christopher. "Dharma-titis," Manchester Guardian Weekly, 2 June 1966, p. 11.

64. Yanitelli, Victor R. "Desolation Angels," Best Sellers, 15 May 1965, p. 90.

4. Dharma Bums
    (For additional references, see the Index.)

65. Adams, J. Donald. "Speaking of Books," New York Times Book Review, 26 October 1958, p. 2.

66. Adams, Phoebe. "Dharma Bums," Atlantic Monthly, October 1958, p. 89.

67. Bellman, Samuel I. "On the Mountain," Chicago Review, 13, No. 1 (1959): 68-72.

68. Bittner, William. "The Yabyum Set," Saturday Review, 11 October 1958, p. 36.

69. Boroff, David. "Dem Bums Back," New York Post, 5 October 1958, p. M11.

70. Bridge, John F. "Keats and The Beats," Wall Street Journal, 2 October 1958, p. 10.

71. Champney, Freeman. "Beat-up or Beatific?" Antioch Review, 19 (1959): 114-121.

72. "Dharma Bums," Best Sellers, 15 October 1958, p. 270.

73. "Dharma Bums," Playboy, October 1958, pp. 9-10.

74. "Dharma Bums," Virginia Quarterly Review, 35 (1959): viii.

75. Enright, D. J. "From Log Cabin to Nirvana," Spectator, 18 September 1959, p. 384.

76. Feldman, Irving. "Stuffed Dharma," Commentary, December 1958, pp. 543-544.

77. Ginsberg, Allen. "The Dharma Bums." In The Village Voice Reader, pp. 311-315. Edited by Daniel Wolf and Edwin Fancher. New York: Grove Press, 1963. First hardback edition: Garden City: Doubleday, 1962. Originally appeared in Village Voice, 12 November 1958, pp. 3-5. Rpt. in German (citation 365).

78. Hogan, William. "Jack Kerouac's Novel About Zen Buddhism," San Francisco Chronicle, 2 October 1958, p. 31.

79. "An Innocent At Home," Times Literary Supplement, 18 September 1959, p. 529.

80. Jackson, Robert P. "The Dharma Bums," American Buddhist, October 1958, pp. 1, 5.

81. "Kerouac Shows Promise: Bums, Bars, and Buddhism," Miami Herald, 19 October 1958, p. 6-H.

82. Klein, Marcus. "Imps from Bottles, Etc," Hudson Review, 11 (1958-1959): 620-625.

83. Leonard, William. "Spokesman of the 'Beat' Cult Matures in 2d Novel," Chicago Tribune, 5 October 1958, Magazine of Books sec., p. 2.

84. Lynn, Kenneth S. "A Kerouac Hero on the Road Once More," New York Herald Tribune Book Review, 4 January 1959, p. 7.

85. Mitchell, Daniel T. "Dharma Bums," Critic, January 1959, p. 62.

86. "Moonstruck Bop-Beater," Newsweek, 6 October 1958, p. 92.

87. "New Fiction," Times (London), 24 September 1959, p. 15.

88. Nichols, Luther. "Kerouac as the Savant of the Religious Beat," San Francisco Examiner, 5 October 1958, Highlight sec., p. 17.

89. Norris, Hoke. "That Kerouac Crowd Is Too Good To Be True," Chicago Sun-Times, 19 October 1958, sec. 3, p. 5.

90. Perrott, Roy. "Life Through the Eyes of the Odd Man Out," Guardian (England), 25 September 1959, p. 7.

91. Poore, Charles. "Books of The Times," New York Times, 2 October 1958, p. 35.

92. Ross, Nancy Wilson. "Beat--and Buddhist," New York Times Book Review, 5 October 1958, pp. 5, 14.

93. Rubin, Louis D., Jr. "Two Gentlemen of San Francisco: Notes on Kerouac and Responsibility," Western Review, 23 (1959): 278-283.

94. Waterhouse, Keith. "New Novels," New Statesman, 19 September 1959, pp. 365-366.

95. West, Anthony. "Young Man Beyond Anger," New Yorker, 1 November 1958, pp. 175-177.

96. Wyndham, Francis. "Dharma Bums," London Magazine, 7, No. 1 (1960): 70-73.

97. "The Yabyum Kid," Time, 6 October 1958, pp. 94, 96.

5. Doctor Sax

98. Adams, Phoebe. "Dr. Sax," Atlantic Monthly, July 1959, p. 83.

99. Bangs, Lester. "Doctor Sax, Mexico City Blues (242 Choruses), Lonesome Traveler," Rolling Stone, 4 March 1971, p. 60.

100. Boroff, David. "Mr. Kerouac Again," New York Post, 3 May 1959, p. M11.

101. Coleman, John. "Perseverance," New Statesman, 19 May 1961, pp. 800-801.

102. Conrad, Barnaby. "Barefoot Boy with Dreams of Zen," Saturday Review, 2 May 1959, pp. 23-24.

103. Corso, Gregory. "Dr. Sax," Kulchur, No. 3 (1961): 96-98.

104. Dempsey, David. "Beatnik Bogeyman on the Prowl," New York Times Book Review, 3 May 1959, pp. 28-29.

105. "Dr. Sax," Reporter, 11 June 1959, p. 48.

106. Gleason, Ralph. "New Kerouac Effort Has Its Moments," San Francisco Chronicle, 15 May 1959, p. 37.

107. "Grooking in Lowell," Time, 18 May 1959, pp. 104, 106.

108. Korn, Eric. "Off the Road," Times Literary Supplement, 22 April 1977, p. 477.

109. Lynn, Kenneth S. "Beatnik King," New York Herald Tribune Book Review, 31 May 1959, p. 11.

6. Heaven & Other Poems

110. "Heaven, and other poems," Choice, January 1978, p. 1497.

7. Lonesome Traveler

111. Bangs, Lester. "Doctor Sax, Mexico City Blues (242 Choruses), Lonesome Traveler," Rolling Stone, 4 March 1971, p. 60.

112. Gieske, Tony. "Kerouac On, Yes, Kerouac," Washington Post, 25 December 1960, p. E7.

113. Haycroft, Colin. "Rake's Progress," New Statesman, 25 May 1962, pp. 766-767.

114. "Lonesome Traveler," Playboy, February 1961, p. 36.

115. O'Gorman, F. E. "Lonesome Traveler," Best Sellers, 15 December 1960, p. 362.

116. "On & On, the Road," Time, 7 November 1960, p. 112.

117. "On the Road Again," Times Literary Supplement, 18 May 1962, p. 359.

118. Shaw, Russell. "Lonesome Traveler," Critic, January 1961, pp. 55-56.

119. Talbot, Daniel. "On the Road Again," New York Times Book Review, 27 November 1960, p. 38.

120. Trevelyan, Raleigh. "On the Bum," Spectator, 18 May 1962, p. 659.

121. Williams, David. "Far Out But Not Beat," Punch, 13 June 1962, p. 919.

8. Maggie Cassidy
(See also citations 477b, 508, and 671.)

122. Ackroyd, Peter. "Mawkish moments," Spectator, 24 August 1974, pp. 246-247.

123. "American drama ... and American dream," Times Literary Supplement, 13 September 1974, p. 971.

124. Boroff David. "Will Kerouac Ever Grow Up?" New York Post, 19 July 1959, p. M11.

125.   Browne, Ray B.   "The Art of the Novel: Veritably, a Tonic, " Washington Post, 19 July 1959, p. E7.

126.   Ciardi, John.   "In Loving Memory of Myself, " Saturday Review, 25 July 1959, pp. 22-23.

127.   Daniel, Frank.   "Kerouac Novel Hailed As Notable, " Atlanta Journal, 19 July 1959, p. 2-E.

128.   Dempsey, David.   "The Choice Jack Made, " New York Times Book Review, 19 July 1959, p. 4.

129.   McLaughlin, Richard.   "First Love in Lowell, " Boston Globe, 19 July 1959, p. A-27.

130.   Podell, Albert N.   "A New Kerouac Novel and A Down Beat Comment, " Chicago Sun-Times, 2 August 1959, sec. 3, p. 5.

131.   Straub, Peter.   "Cold Comforts, " New Statesman, 13 September 1974, p. 355.

9.   Mexico City Blues
     (See also citations 365 and 388.)

132.   Bangs, Lester.   "Doctor Sax, Mexico City Blues (242 Choruses), Lonesome Traveler, " Rolling Stone, 4 March 1971, p. 60.

133.   Creeley, Robert.   "Ways of Looking, " Poetry, 98 (1961):   195-196.

134.   Feinstein, Herbert.   "A Free Poet?" Prairie Schooner, 34 (1960):   100-101, 168.

135.   Hathaway, Baxter.   "Notes, Reviews & Speculations, " Epoch, 10 (1960):   126-128.

136.   Hecht, Anthony.   "The Anguish of the Spirit and the Letter, " Hudson Review, 12 (1959-1960):   593-603.

137.   Nyren, Dorothy.   "Mexico City Blues, " Library Journal, 1 December 1959, p. 3777.

138.   Rexroth, Kenneth.   "Discordant and Cool, " New York Times Book Review, 29 November 1959, p. 14.

10. On The Road
    (For additional references, see the Index.)

139. Adams, Phoebe. "On the Road, " Atlantic Monthly,
     October 1957, pp. 178, 180.

140. Algren, Nelson. "Kerouac Deftly Etches The 'Go'
     Generation, " Chicago Sun-Times, 8 September 1957,
     sec. 3, p. 4.

141. Baker, Carlos. "Itching Feel, " Saturday Review, 7
     September 1957, pp. 19, 32-33.

142. Baro, Gene. "Restless Rebels in Search of - What?"
     New York Herald Tribune Book Review, 15 Septem-
     ber 1957, p. 4.

143. Beatty, Jerome, Jr. "Trade Winds, " Saturday Review,
     28 September 1957, p. 6.

144. Boroff, David. "The Roughnecks, " New York Post,
     8 September 1957, p. M11.

145. Browne, Ray B. "Vocal, the Frantic Fringe, " Wash-
     ington Post, 8 September 1957, p. E7.

145a. Cerulli, Dom. "charivari, " Downbeat, 31 October
      1957, p. 33.

146. Champney, Freeman. "Beat-up or Beatific?" Antioch
     Review, 19 (1959): 114-121.

147. Clay, George R. "A Sleepless Night With the Beat
     Generation, " Reporter, 17 October 1957, pp. 44-45.

148. Cooper, Lettice. "New Novels, " Listener, 29 May
     1958, p. 912.

149. Curley, Thomas F. "Everything Moves, But Nothing
     Is Alive, " Commonweal, 13 September 1957, pp.
     595-597.

150. DeMott, Benjamin. "Cozzens and others, " Hudson Re-
     view, 10 (1957-1958): 620-626.

151. Dempsey, David. "In Pursuit of Kicks, " New York
     Times Book Review, 8 September 1957, p. 4.

152. Feather, Leonard. "Feather's nest," Downbeat, 31 October 1957, p. 33.

153. Fitzgerald, John E. "On the Road," Extension, January 1958, p. 28.

154. "Flings of the Frantic," Newsweek, 9 September 1957, p. 115.

155. Foley, Bernice W. "On The Road," Cincinnati Enquirer, 8 September 1957, p. 42.

156. Frost, Derland. "New Novel for Young Bohemia," Houston Post, 8 September 1957, Now sec., p. 31.

157. "The Ganser Syndrome," Time, 16 September 1957, p. 120.

158. Gleason, Ralph. "Jazz Was the Voice of Kerouac's Generation," San Francisco Chronicle, 1 September 1957, This World Magazine sec., pp. 18, 23.

159. Gleason, Ralph. "Kerouac's Beat Generation," Saturday Review, 11 January 1958, p. 75.

160. Gold, Herbert. "Hip, Cool, Beat--and Frantic," Nation, 16 November 1957, pp. 349-355.

161. Goodman, Paul. "Wingless Wondervogel, 1957," Midstream, 4, No. 1 (1958): 98-101. Rpt. as "Review of On The Road." In Growing Up Absurd, pp. 279-284. New York: Vintage, 1960.

162. Grandsen, K. W. "Adolescence and Maturity," Encounter, August 1958, pp. 83-85.

163. Hannon, Leslie. "The Beat Boys," Sunday Times (London), 25 May 1958, p. 6.

164. Johnson, K. Peyton. "Young Author Probes Deep Into Hipster Psychology," Savannah Morning News, 8 September 1957, p. 35.

165. McLellan, Joseph. "On the Road," Ave Maria, 21 December 1957, p. 27.

166. Millstein, Gilbert. "Books of The Times," New York Times, 5 September 1957, p. 27.

167. Nichols, Luther. "Echoes From the Beat Generation," San Francisco Examiner, 1 September 1957, Modern Living sec., p. 10.

168. Oesterreicher, Arthur. "On the Road," Village Voice, 18 September 1957, p. 5.

169. "On the Road," Best Sellers, 15 September 1957, p. 186.

170. "On the Road," Playboy, November 1957, p. 17.

171. "On the Road," Virginia Quarterly Review, 34 (1958): x.

172. Owen, Patricia. "Three Novels," Tamarack Review, No. 5 (1957): 48.

173. Pickrel, Paul. "On the Road," Harper's, October 1957, pp. 89-90, 92.

174. Redman, Ben Ray. "Living It Up With Jack Kerouac," Chicago Tribune, 6 October 1957, sec. 4, p. 4.

175. Rexroth, Kenneth. "'It's an Anywhere Road for Anybody Anyhow,'" San Francisco Chronicle, 1 September 1957, p. 18.

176. Shapiro, Charles. "The 'Beat' Generation: The Romantic Novel's Last Whimper," Louisville Courier-Journal, 22 September 1957, sec. 4, p. 6.

177. Sigal, Clancy. "Nihilism's Organization Man," Universities and Left Review, No. 4 (1958): 59-63, 65.

178. Steggert, Frank X. "On the Road," Critic, November 1957, p. 27.

179. Tick, Stanley. "America Writes," Meanjin, 18 (1959): 466.

180. Wain, John. "The Beat Generation," Observer (London), 18 May 1958, p. 17.

11. Pic

181. Brockway, James. "Pic/The Subterraneans," Books and Bookmen, July 1973, p. 112.

181a. Burns, Jim. "Kerouac's last road," Tribune (London), 20 April 1973, p. 7.

182. Davies, Russell. "Californians at play," Observer (London), 18 March 1973, p. 37.

183. Paul, Don. "Pic," Rolling Stone, 11 May 1972, p. 68.

184. "Pic," Playboy, February 1972, p. 28.

185. "Pidgin fancier," Times Literary Supplement, 6 April 1973, p. 369.

186. Warner, Jon M. "Pic." In Library Journal Book Review 1971, p. 660. Edited by Judith Serebnick. New York: Bowker, 1972.

187. Wordsworth, Christopher. "Voice of the Turtle," Manchester Guardian Weekly, 24 March 1973, p. 25.

12. Satori In Paris
(See also citations 342, 436, and 440a.)

188. Bartek, Zenka. "Eyeful," Times (London), 18 November 1967, p. 22.

189. Coleman, John. "Off the Road," Observer (London), 19 November 1967, p. 27.

190. Cruttwell, Patrick. "Fiction Chronicle," Hudson Review, 20 (1967): 165.

191. "God Bless Armorica," Time, 23 December 1966, p. 80.

192. Greenfeld, Josh. "Eastern exposures," Chicago Tribune, 5 February 1967, Book Week sec., pp. 4-5. See also New York World Journal Tribune, 5 February 1967, Book Week sec., pp. 4-5.

193. Hendrick, George. "Satori in Paris," Books Abroad, 41 (1967): 345.

194. Kisor, Henry. "A Sampling of Varied Talents," Chicago Daily News, 24 December 1966, Panorama sec., p. 8.

195. Maddocks, Melvin. "Kerouac: still on the road," Christian Science Monitor, 29 December 1966, p. 5.

196. Mara, Maura. "Satori in Paris," Best Sellers, 15 December 1966, p. 350.

197. Montague, John. "Nuggets from the Stein mine," Manchester Guardian Weekly, 28 December 1967, p. 10.

198. Moynahan, Julian. "Twenty Beat Years," Listener, 27 June 1968, pp. 841-842.

199. "Other New Novels," Times Literary Supplement, 1 February 1968, p. 114.

200. Sarris, Andrew. "More Babbitt Than Beatnik," New York Times Book Review, 26 February 1967, p. 5. Rpt. as "Jack Kerouac." In The Primal Screen: Essays on Film and Related Subjects, pp. 282-283. New York: Simon & Schuster, 1973.

201. "Satori in Paris," Playboy, February 1967, p. 24.

13. Scattered Poems

202. Ritter, Jesse. "Scattered Poems," Rolling Stone, 14 October 1971, p. 58.

203. Warner, Jon M. "Scattered Poems." In Library Journal Book Review 1971, p. 363. Edited by Judith Serebnick. New York: Bowker, 1972.

14. The Subterraneans
(For additional references, see the Index.)

204. Adams, Robert Martin. "Fiction Chronicle," Hudson Review, 11 (1958): 289-290.

205. Blakeston, Oswell. "Trial of a Salesman," Time and Tide, 16 July 1960, p. 841.

206. "The Blazing & the Beat," Time, 24 February 1958, p. 104.

207. Boroff, David. "Beatville, U. S. A.," New York Post, 23 February 1958, p. M11.

207a. Brockway, James. "Pic/The Subterraneans," Books and Bookmen, July 1973, p. 112.

208. Champney, Freeman. "Beat-up or Beatific?" Antioch Review, 19 (1959): 114-121.

209. Coleman, John. "Big Gleeful Hood," Spectator, 8 July 1960, p. 73.

210. Dempsey, David. "Diary of a Bohemian," New York Times Book Review, 23 February 1958, p. 5.

211. Hogan, William. "Kerouac Abroad and Two Offbeat Works," San Francisco Chronicle, 2 August 1960, p. 25.

212. Kerridge, Roy. "The Subterraneans," Punch, 27 July 1960, pp. 140-141.

213. Kilby, Clyde S. "Love and Loss," New York Herald Tribune Book Review, 23 February 1958, p. 4.

214. Levin, Martin. "The Cool Crowd," Saturday Review, 22 March 1958, p. 25.

215. Malcolm, Donald. "Child's Play," New Yorker, 5 April 1958, pp. 137-138, 141-142.

216. "Mentality of the Herd," Times Literary Supplement, 8 July 1960, p. 429.

217. "New Fiction," Times (London), 14 July 1960, p. 15.

218. "New World Symphonies," Times Weekly Review, 21 July 1960, p. 10.

219. Nichols, Luther. "Kerouac Roams Bohemia," San Francisco Examiner, 21 February 1958, sec. 2, p. 3.

220. O'Gorman, Frank E. "The Subterraneans," Best Sellers, 1 March 1958, p. 407.

221. Pinck, Dan. "Digging the San Franciscans," New Republic, 3 March 1958, p. 20.

222. Rexroth, Kenneth. "The Voice of the Beat Generation Has Some Square Delusions," San Francisco Chronicle, 16 February 1958, This World Magazine sec., p. 23.

223. Russell, William. "Kerouac's The Subterraneans," Mainstream, 15, No. 6 (1962): 61-64.

224. Wordsworth, Christopher. "Voice of the Turtle," Manchester Guardian Weekly, 24 March 1973, p. 25.

15. The Town And The City
    (For additional references, see the Index.)

225. Bond, Alice Dixon. "Intense Story of a Man, His Wife and Their Clan of 8 Children," Boston Sunday Herald, 19 March 1950, p. 4-C.

226. Brooks, John. "Of Growth and Decay," New York Times Book Review, 5 March 1950, p. 6.

227. Bullock, Florence Haxton. "Overall Account of the Currently Young Generation," New York Herald Tribune Book Review, 5 March 1950, p. 7.

227a. Burns, Jim. "Debut of the Beat Generation," Tribune (London), 16 November 1973, p. 9.

228. Davies, Russell. "One more for the road," Observer (London), 19 August 1973, p. 31.

229. Dedmon, Emmett. "Family Novel Gets Lost on New York Sidewalks," Chicago Sun, 5 March 1950, Book Week sec., p. 4.

230. Hass, Victor P. "Good Story Lost in Flood of Rhetoric," Chicago Tribune, 5 March 1950, Magazine of Books sec., p. 4.

231. Jackson, Joseph Henry. "Breakup of a Family," San Francisco Chronicle, 10 March 1950, p. 20.

232. Jones, Carter Brooke. "John Kerouac's First Novel Reveals Vigorous New Talent," Washington Star, 5 March 1950, p. C-3.

233. Jones, Howard Mumford. "Back to Merrimac," Saturday Review, 11 March 1950, p. 18.

234. McFee, William. "A Family Chronicle of the Thirties," New York Post, 5 March 1950, p. M16.

235. Poore, Charles. "Books of the Times," New York Times, 2 March 1950, p. 25.

236. Revere, Richard H. "Fever Chart for Novelists," Harper's, May 1950, pp. 118, 120.

237. "The Town and the City," Catholic World, 171 (1950): 72.

238. "War and Peace," Newsweek, 13 March 1950, pp. 80, 82.

239. Weiner, Leslie. "The Town and the City," New York Daily Compass, 22 March 1950, p. 21.

16. Tristessa
(See also citation 508.)

240. Balliett, Whitney. "Soft Coal, Hard Coal," New Yorker, 27 August 1960, pp. 97-98.

241. Lea, George. "For Those Who Dig Kerouac," Chicago Sun-Times, 2 August 1960, sec. 3, p. 4.

242. Leonard, William. "Kerouac - As Always," Chicago Tribune, 4 September 1960, Magazine of Books sec., p. 6.

243. Mitchell, Adrian. "Lyndhurst," New Statesman, 23 October 1964, p. 622.

244. "Sentimental Sainthood," Times Literary Supplement, 29 October 1964, p. 973.

245. Talbot, Daniel. "Beat and Screaming," New York Times Book Review, 19 June 1960, p. 4.

246. "Tristessa," Mexican Life, 36, No. 7 (1960): 35-36.

17. Vanity Of Duluoz
    (See also citations 386 and 440a.)

247. Bannon, Barbara A. "Vanity of Duluoz," Publishers Weekly, 27 November 1967, p. 42.

248. "Be your age," Times Literary Supplement, 27 March 1969, p. 317.

249. Carruth, Hayden. "An ex-Beat in search of his past," Chicago Daily News, 3 February 1968, Panorama sec., p. 9.

250. Dollen, Charles. "Vanity of Duluoz," Best Sellers, 15 February 1968, p. 442.

251. Haworth, David. "On the Roadwork," New Statesman, 21 March 1969, p. 416.

252. Hemmings, John. "On to Brighton," Listener, 10 April 1969, p. 503.

253. Holmes, John Clellon. "There's an Air of Finality to Kerouac's Latest," National Observer, 5 February 1968, p. 25.

254. Lanier, Sterling. "The new Jack Kerouac," Boston Globe, 11 February 1968, p. A37.

255. Lask, Thomas. "Road to Nowhere," New York Times, 17 February 1968, p. 27.

256. Maddocks, Melvin. "Hit the space bar and GO!" Christian Science Monitor, 21 March 1968, p. 13.

257. Richardson, Jack. "Prop Art," New York Review of Books, 11 April 1968, pp. 34-36.

258. Rosofsky, Herman L. "Vanity of Duluoz," Library Journal, 15 February 1968, p. 772.

259. "Sanity of Kerouac," Time, 23 February 1968, p. 96.

260. Schaap, Dick. "The pre-hippie hippie pulls off the road," Chicago Sun-Times, 4 February 1968, Book Week sec., p. 2.

261. Sourian, Peter. "One-Dimensional Account," New York Times Book Review, 18 February 1968, p. 4.

262. Tytell, John. "Vanity of Duluoz," Catholic World, 207 (1968): 92.

18. Visions of Cody
      (For additional references, see the Index.)

262a. Bannon, Barbara A. "Visions of Cody," Publishers Weekly, 13 November 1972, p. 41.

263. Blakeston, Oswell. "Visions of Cody," Books and Bookmen, 19, No. 7 (1974): 89.

264. Bowering, George. "Visions of Cody," Open Letter, Second Series, No. 5 (1973): 95-98.

265. Broyard, Anatole. "Maunder in the Cafeteria," New York Times, 9 January 1973, p. 37.

265a. Burns, Jim. "Forties roller-coaster," Tribune (London), 30 November 1973, p. 11.

266. Christy, Jim. "Fact - the man could write," Globe and Mail (Toronto), 20 January 1973, p. 29.

267. Cook, Bruce. "Brilliant Moments - and Others - in 'Lost' Kerouac," National Observer, 20 January 1973, p. 21.

268. Coyne, J. R., Jr. "Visions of Cody," National Review, 30 March 1973, p. 377.

269. Cross, Leslie. "The 'Beat King' Returns," Milwaukee Journal, 28 January 1973, pt. 5, p. 4.

270. Davis, Marc. "Kerouac novel reaffirms his importance as major writer," Chicago Sun-Times, 7 January 1973, Book Week sec., p. 16.

271. "Hobo concerto," Times Literary Supplement, 2 November 1973, p. 1333.

271a. Kamstra, Jerry. "An Early Chaotic Kerouac Novel," San Francisco Chronicle, 11 February 1973, This World sec., p. 39.

272. LaSalle, Peter. "Sad Jack Kerouac without the myths: A man of heart who worked and suffered," Chicago Daily News, 24 March 1973, Panorama sec., p. 4.

273. Latham, Aaron. "Visions of Cody," New York Times Book Review, 28 January 1973, p. 42-43.
      See also citation 475.

274. Mungo, Raymond. "Manly Love," Village Voice, 1 February 1973, p. 23.

275. Noble, Donald R. "Visions of Cody," Southern Humanities Review, 9 (1975): 333-334.

276. Ravitz, Alec C. "Dreamer in leather jacket," Cleveland Plain Dealer, 7 January 1973, p. 10-G.

277. Rhodes, Richard. "Kerouac in perspective: beating a path to the sixties," Chicago Tribune, 11 February 1973, Book World sec., pp. 1-2.

278. Rogers, Michael. "Kerouac & Ginsberg: On the Road Again," Rolling Stone, 12 April 1973, p. 68.

279. Salzman, Jack. "End of the Road," Washington Post, 8 April 1973, Book World sec., p. 3.

280. Sheppard, R. Z. "Sweet Jack Gone," Time, 22 January 1973, p. 71-72.

281. Solomon, Albert J. "Visions of Cody," Best Sellers, 1 February 1973, p. 488.

282. Solomon, Carl. "Visions of Cody." In The Beat Book, p. 72. Edited by Arthur Winfield Knight and Glee Knight. California, Pennsylvania: 1974.

283. Straub, Peter. "One More For the Road," New Statesman, 23 November 1973, p. 782.

284. Taylor, Robert. "Back to Kerouac," Boston Globe, 23 January 1973, p. 17.

285. Tytell, John. "Revisions of Kerouac," Partisan Review, 40 (1973): 301-305.

286. "Visions of Cody," Choice, May 1973, p. 458.

287. "Visions of Cody," Kirkus Reviews, 15 October 1972, p. 1214.

288. "Visions of Cody," New Yorker, 17 February 1973, p. 110.

289. "Visions of Cody," Playboy, January 1973, p. 28.

290. "Visions of Cody," Prairie Schooner, 48 (1974): 88.

291. Warner, Jon M. "Visions of Cody," Library Journal, 15 September 1972, p. 2860.

292. Yaryan, Bill. "Kerouac Revisited: The Beat Goes On," Coast, June 1973, pp. 28-30.

19. Visions of Gerard
(For additional references, see the Index.)

293. Barrett, William. "Beat and Beatified," Atlantic Monthly, September 1963, pp. 122-124.

294. "Children Should Be...," Newsweek, 9 September 1963, p. 93.

295. Curley, Thomas. "Chapters from Kerouac Gospel," Commonweal, 27 September 1963, pp. 19-20.

296. Druckner, Don. "Kindly Kerouac," Chicago Sun-Times, 29 September 1963, sec. 3, p. 2.

297. Flint, R. W. "Cosmic Comics," New York Review of Books, 28 November 1963, p. 5.

298. Foote, Irving F. "Romantics Indicted: Kerouac's 'Visions' Rates As Moving Book," Atlanta Journal, 8 September 1963, p. 8-D.

299. Grumbach, Doris. "Visions of Gerard," Critic, October-November 1963, p. 84.

300. "Kerouac's Small Saint," Time, 6 September 1963, p. 86.

301. Lucey, Beatus T. "Visions of Gerard," Best Sellers, 1 October 1963, p. 226.

302. Maloff, Saul. "A Yawping at the Grave," New York Times Book Review, 8 September 1963, pp. 4-5.

303. Marchand, LaFayette L. "Jack Kerouac Is Kerouac, Still Kerouac," Boston Globe, 29 September 1963, p. A-63.

304. Mitchell, Adrian. "Lyndhurst," New Statesman, 23 October 1964, p. 622.

305. Phelps, Robert. "Tender Kerouac: Spontaneity Is Not Enough," New York Herald Tribune, 8 September 1963, sec. 6, p. 3.

306. Roy, Gregor. "Visions of Gerard," Catholic World, 188 (1963): 132-133.

307. "Sentimental Sainthood," Times Literary Supplement, 29 October 1964, p. 973.

308. Stanley, Donald. "Saintly Memories," San Francisco Examiner, 6 September 1963, p. 33.

309. Sullivan, Richard. "A Tale Worrying Over Life's Old Question," Chicago Tribune, 8 September 1963, Magazine of Books sec., p. 4.

310. "Visions of Gerard," Playboy, October 1963, p. 44.

311. "Visions of Gerard," Virginia Quarterly Review, 40 (1964): viii.

20. Other Works
(For references to the following works, see the Index.)

"The Beginning of Bop"

"The Essentials of Spontaneous Prose"
"Old Angel Midnight"
"The Origins of Joy in Poetry"
"The Origins of the Beat Generation"
The Scripture of the Golden Eternity

B. FILMS, INCLUDING MOTION PICTURE ADAPTATIONS
    AND REVIEWS OF PRIMARY WORKS,
    AND RELATED PIECES

1. Pull My Daisy
    (For additional references, see the Index.)

312. "Endsville: Zen-Hur," Time, 14 December 1959, p.
      66.

312a. Feinstein, Herbert. "Passion on the San Francisco
       Screen," American Quarterly, 12 (1960): 205-210.

313. Hatch, Robert. "Films," Nation, 18 June 1960, p.
      540.

314. Kauffmann, Stanley. "Art and the Merely Arty," New
      Republic, 6 June 1960, pp. 22-23.

315. Knight, Arthur. "The Far Out Films," Playboy, April
      1960, p. 46.

316. MacDonald, Dwight. "Amateurs and Pros," Esquire,
      April 1960, pp. 26, 28, 32. Rpt. in Dwight Mac-
      Donald On Movies, pp. 341-342. New York: Berk-
      ley Medallion, c1969, 1971.

317. Mekas, Jonas. "Cinema of the New Generation," Film
      Culture, No. 21 (1960): 13-15, 18. Rpt. as "Free
      Cinema and the New Wave." In The Emergence of
      Film Art: The evolution and development of the mo-
      tion picture as an art, from 1900 to the present,
      pp. 400-419. By Lewis Jacobs. New York: Hop-
      kinson and Blake, 1969.

318. Mekas, Jonas. "New York Letter: Towards a spon-
      taneous cinema," Sight and Sound, 28 (1959): 120.

319. Mekas, Jonas. "Pull My Daisy and the Truth of Cinema." In Movie Journal; The Rise of the New American Cinema, 1959-1971, pp. 5-6. New York: Collier Books, 1972. Appeared originally as "Movie Journal," Village Voice, 18 November 1959, pp. 8, 12.

320. "Pull My Daisy," New York Times, 10 April 1960, sec. 2, p. 1.

321. "Pull My Daisy," Times Literary Supplement, 27 October 1961, p. 778.

322. Selz, Thalia. "The Beat Generation," Film Quarterly, 13, No. 1 (1959): 54-56.

322a. "Study of 'Beats' in Action," Times (London), 11 July 1960, p. 3.

323. Tyler, Parker. "For 'Shadows,' Against 'Pull My Daisy,'" Film Culture, No. 24 (1964): 28-33.

323a. Winsten, Archer. "'Pull My Daisy' Bows," New York Post, 10 April 1960, p. 19.

2. The Subterraneans

324. Alpert, Hollis. "One Down, Two Up," Saturday Review, 9 July 1960, p. 24.

325. Arden, Doris. "Beatnik Love Conquers All," Chicago Sun-Times, 27 March 1961, sec. 2, p. 14.

326. Beckley, Paul V. "The Subterraneans," New York Herald Tribune, 7 July 1960, p. 16.

327. Cameron, Kate. "Movie Based on Story of Beatniks," New York Daily News, 19 June 1960, sec. 2, p. 3.

328. Fitzpatrick, Ellen. "The Subterraneans," Films In Review, 11, No. 7 (1960): 430-431.

329. "'Good-By, Sweet Song...,'" Newsweek, 18 July 1960, p. 88.

330. Hartung, Philip T. "The Screen: Novels-Into-Films, " Commonweal, 5 August 1960, p. 403.

330a. MacDonald, Dwight. "Films, " Esquire, September 1960, pp. 152, 154-156.

331. Masters, Dorothy. "Beekman Shelters Kerouac's Beat-niks, " New York Daily News, 7 July 1960, p. 66.

331a. Mekas, Jonas. "Movie Journal, " Village Voice, 18 May 1960, p. 11.

332. "The Subterraneans, " Film Facts, 2 September 1960, pp. 190-191.

333. "The Subterraneans, " Film Quarterly, 14, No. 1 (1960): 62.

334. "The Subterraneans, " Green Sheet, July 1960, p. 3.

335. "The Subterraneans, " Motion Picture Herald, 25 June 1960, p. 749.

336. "The Subterraneans, " Time, 20 June 1960, p. 64.

337. Tube. "The Subterraneans, " Variety, 22 June 1960, p. 6.

338. Weiler, A. H. "Subterraneans, " New York Times, 7 July 1960, p. 26.

C. FOREIGN LANGUAGE REVIEWS AND RELATED ARTICLES

1. Flemish

339. Bierkens, J. G. "Aanvullende Nota's bij de KEROUAC-studie, " Labris, 4, No. 1 (1965): 81-98.

340. Bierkens, Jozef. "Desolation Angels, " Labris, 5, No. 1 (1966): 76-86.

341. Bierkens, Jozef. "Jack Kerouac Old Angel Midnight 1, " Labris, 5, No. 3 (1967): 85-95.

342. Bierkens, Jozef. "Satori in Paris, " Labris, 5, No. 3 (1967): 79-84.

343. Kazan, Max. "The Scripture of the Golden Eternity, " Labris, 4, No. 2 (1966): 73-78.

344. Raes, Hugo. "Jack Kerouac: Nieuwe Literaire Schok in America, " De Vlaamsche Gids, 42, No. 10 (1958): 637-638.
      Review of The Subterraneans.

345. Schumacher, Huub. Jij bent een engel. Rotterdam: Leminiscaat, 1972.
      Booklength study on Kerouac.

2. French

345a. Amette, Jacques-Pierre. "Jack Kerouac, " La Nouvelle Revue Française, No. 231 (1972): 93-96.
      A short study on Kerouac.

346. Astre, Georges-Albert. "Beatniks, Nouveaux 'Saints', 'Nouveaux' Barbares?" Critique; Revue Generale Des Publications Francaises Et Etrangeres, September 1960, pp. 693-704.
      Kerouac's On The Road is reviewed, along with Lawrence Lipton's The Holy Barbarians and Lawrence Ferlinghetti's A Coney Island of the Mind.

347. Beaulieu, Victor-Levy. Jack Kerouac, Essai-Poulet. Montreal: Editions du Jour, 1972. Rpt. in France as Jack Kerouac. Paris: Editions de L'Herne, 1973. Later, translated into English (citation 423).

347a. Burroughs, William S. "Epitaphe pour un beatnik, " Le Nouvel Observateur, 3 November 1969, p. 40. Rpt. in Jack Kerouac (citation 348), p. 91.
      Obituary.

348. Burroughs, William S.; Kerouac, Jack; and Pélieu, Claude. Jack Kerouac. [Paris]: L'Herne, 1971.
      To best describe this work is to list its contents:

      Burroughs, William S. "Jack Kerouac, " pp. 13-15, 17-20. (For English translation see citation 429a.)
      Aranowitz (sic), Alfred G. "Interview avec Jack Kerouac, " pp. 23-51.

Kerouac, Jack. "Notes" (from Ann Charters' A Bibliography of Works by Jack Kerouac), pp. 53-61.

Pélieu, Claude. "mosaïques électriques indigo off soft zoom Jack Kerouac et la radio-nuit-de-l'enfance," pp. 67-80.

Pélieu, Claude. "chun cromlrech moruah!" pp. 81-86.

"Jack Kerouac, Beat Novelist, Is Dead at 47," New York Daily News, 22 October 1969, p. 88. (Reprint; see citation 722.)

Pélieu, Claude. "Epilogue," pp. 89-90.

Burroughs, William S. "Epitaphe pour un beatnik," p. 91. (Reprint; see citation 347a.)

Ginsberg, Allen. "Jack Kerouac est mort le 21 october 1969," pp. 93-95.

Plus photos and illustrations. See also citation 747a.

349. Dethy, Claire. "Les nouveaux chemins de l'ouest Jack Kerouac," Revue Nouvelle, No. 2 (1970): 207-210.
      General article on Kerouac.

350. Dommergues, Pierre. "L'Art De La Béatitude." In Les Ecrivains Américains D'Aujourd'Hui, pp. 69-86. Paris: Presses Universitaires de France, 1965.
      General article on the Beats with a section on and references to Kerouac.

351. Dommergues, Pierre. "Le Dernier Roman de Jack Kerouac," Les Langues Modernes, 58, No. 2 (1964): 77-80.
      General article on Kerouac with special mention of Visions of Gerard.

351a. Dupeyron-Marchessou, Hélène. "Beat Generation et Hippies: Les Mythes et les Dieux," Les Langues Modernes, 70, Nos. 2-3 (1976): 197-208.
      A study of the Beats and the Hippies with references to Kerouac throughout.

352. Gresset, Michel. "Les Clochards célestes ou l'Amérique en auto-stop," Mercure de France, 349 (1963): 620-621.
      Review of The Dharma Bums.

353. Keineg, Paol, editor. Bretagnes: Revue littéraire et

politique trimestrielle, No. 4 (1976). Morlaix,
France: 1976.
　Kerouac issue; one half of the number is devoted
to the author. Listing of contents follows:

Kerninon, Michel. "Jack Kerouac ou Noël sur la
　terre, " pp. 6-8.
Keineg, Paol. "Etats D'Urgence, " p. 9.
Gwernig, Youenn. "J'Ai Retrouvé Mon Frère..., "
　pp. 10-11.
"Trois lettres de Jack Kerouac à Youenn Gwernig, "
　pp. 12-17.
Chentier, Marc. "Ti Jean L'Canuck: Notes sur les
　idées politiques de Kerouac, " pp. 18-22.
"Lettre à Pierre Le Bris de Jack Kerouac, " p. 23.
Le Pellec, Yves. "Quand s'éveilla l'Amérique
　Ginsberg Temoigne, " pp. 24-29.
"Bibliographie, " p. 30.

354.　Kyria, Pierre. "Le Monde Américain " Revue De
　　　Paris, March 1967, pp. 120-125.
　　　　General article on American writing with references
　　　to Kerouac.

354a. Le Pellec, Yves, editor. "Beat Generation, " Entre-
　　　tiens, No. 34 (1975).
　　　　The entire issue of this French literary magazine
　　　(288 pages) is devoted to the Beats. It includes
　　　articles about, interviews with, and works by the
　　　Beat writers. A section from Kerouac's Visions of
　　　Cody is reprinted. Translations of John Clellon
　　　Holmes' "The Great Rememberer" and Warren Tall-
　　　man's "Kerouac's Sound" appear. There is also a
　　　short piece entitled "Avec Ti-Jean et Mémère" by
　　　Michel Mohrt.

355.　Le Pellec, Yves. "Visions of Cody ou Jack Kerouac,
　　　voyeur de l'Amérique, " Caliban, No. 12 (1975):
　　　81-92.
　　　　Scholarly study of Visions of Cody.

356.　Levesque, R. Dion. "Jean-Louis KEROUAC, ROMAN-
　　　CIER, " La Patrie, 11 May 1951, p. 26.
　　　　Review of The Town and the City.

357.　Mekas, Jonas. "Le Nouveau Cinéma Américain: Ten-
　　　dances et Climat, " Cahiers du Cinéma, June 1960,

pp. 23-33.
Article mentions Pull My Daisy.

358.	Terrier, Michel.	"Béatitude Et Emerveillement Dans
'On The Road' De Jack Kerouac," Etudes Anglaises,
29 (1976):	468-477.
Study of On The Road.

359.	Van Den Haag, Ernest.	"Jack Kerouac et la 'Beat
Generation,'" Temps Modernes, 15, No. 163 (1959):
568-576.
General article on Kerouac and the Beats.

3.	German

359a.	Betz, Gertrude.	Die Beatgeneration als literarische
und soziale Bewegung: Untersucht am Beispiel von
Jack Kerouac; "The Subterraneans," "The Dharma
Bums" und "Desolation Angels." Kasseler Arbeiten
zur Sprache und Literatur, Vol. 2.	Edited by Jo-
hannes Anderegg, Manfred Raupach, and Martin
Schulze.	Frankfurt am Main: Peter Lang, 1977.
Book-length social and literary study of Kerouac's
works and the Beat Generation.

360.	Enzensberger, Hans Magnus.	"Die Dummheit unter-
wegs," Neue Deutsche Hefte, 6, No. 64 (1959):
758-759.
Review of On The Road.

361.	Gebhardt, Eike.	"Jack Kerouac." In Amerikanische
Literatur der Gegenwart, pp. 248-267.	Edited by
Martin Christadler.	Stuttgart: Alfred Kröner, 1973.
Long scholarly study on Kerouac.

362.	Hansen-Love, Friedrich.	"Die weissen Neger Ameri-
kas," Hochland, 51 (1959):	521-533.
General article on the Beats with references to
Kerouac.

363.	Hasenclever, Walter.	"Zornig--aber nicht jung:
Amerikas 'Beat Generation,'" Der Monat, 2, No.
121 (1958):	74-76, 78.
General article on the Beats with references to
Kerouac.

364. Kraus, Wolfgang. "Ohne Ankunft unterwegs," Die Bucher-Kommentare, 8, No. 4 (1959): 7.
Review of On The Road.

364a. "Die Legende Des Duluoz: Jack Kerouac oder amerikanische Literatur auf dem Weg." Radio-essay/Studio für Neue Literatur. Süddeutsche Rundfunk. 7 May 1976.
This item is a transcript of a German radio program on Kerouac and the Beats.

365. Paetel, Karl O., editor. Beat: Eine Anthologie. Hamburg: Rowohlt, 1962.
An anthology of Beat writings and articles/criticisms on the Beats. It includes translations of the following works by Kerouac:

"Beat-Glückselig: Über den Ursprung Einer Generation" (The Origins of the Beat Generation), pp. 24-32.
"Der Ursprung der Freude in der Poesie" (The Origin of Joy in Poetry), pp. 48-57.
"Mexico City Blues" (Choruses nos. 14, 34, 50, 52, 59, 208, 216-b, 227, 240), pp. 96-102.
"Zupf mein Blümchen" (Pull My Daisy), with Allen Ginsberg and Neal Cassady, pp. 124-125.
Excerpts from On The Road, pp. 145-151.
Excerpts from The Dharma Bums, pp. 151-165.
"Ein Beatnik-Dialog," p. 249. (Correspondence to and from Kerouac.)

Also includes the following (which are listed elsewhere in this work):

Holmes, John Clellon. "Die Philosophie der Beat Generation," pp. 231-236.
Miller, Henry. "Vorwort zu 'The Subterraneans,'" pp. 236-237.
Ginsberg, Allen. "Die Dharma-Bums; Ein Rezension," pp. 238-241.

This work also contains a large bibliography of critical writings on the Beats from the German and American press.

366. Possin, Hans-Joachim. "Jack Kerouac: On the Road." In Amerikanische Erzahlliteratur, 1950-1970, pp. 49-56. Edited by Frieder Busch and Renate Schmidt-

von Bardeleben. Munchen: Wilhelm Fink, 1975.
Scholarly study of On The Road.

4. Hungarian

367. Pal, Darabos. "Zen, Salinger, Kerouac," Helikon
Vilagrodalmi Figyelo, 12, No. 3 (1966): 315-331.
Study of Zen in the writings of Kerouac and J. D.
Salinger.

5. Italian
(See also citations 455 and 482.)

368. Amoruso, Vito. "Jack Kerouac - La Parabola Del
Buon Ribelle. " In La Letteratura Beat Americana,
pp. 35-88. Bari, Italy: Editori Laterza, 1969.
Long study of Kerouac's works.

369. Barilli, Renato. "Il Problema Della Letteratura 'Beat':
Tre Americani alla ribalta: Mailer, Selby jr. e
Kerouac," Corriere Della Sera, 91, No. 284 (1966):
11.
This piece includes a review of Kerouac's Big Sur.

370. Bisol, Gaetano. "Jack Kerouac: I 'beats': Fatto Di
Costume E Fenomeno Letterario, " Letture, Rassegna
critica del Libro e dello Spettacolo, 22, No. 4 (1967):
251-270. Rpt. in Profili Di Scrittori, No. 8, pp.
129-150. Milan, Italy: Edizioni "LETTURE", 1968.
Rpt. also in Scrittori Americani, pp. 79-111. Milan,
Italy: Edizioni "LETTURE", 1970. And again, rpt.
as a pamphlet with the title, "Jack Kerouac e le orgini
del movimento beats. " Milan, Italy: LETTURE, n. d.
A long study on Kerouac with sections on On The
Road, The Subterraneans, The Dharma Bums, and
Big Sur. Includes bibliographical materials.

371. Bulgheroni, Marisa. "Jack Kerouac: il cronista della
'beat generation. '" In Il Nuovo Romanzo Americano,
1945-1959, pp. 175-181. Milano, Italy: Schwarz
Editore, 1960.
This work contains a chapter on the Beats and a
section on Kerouac, plus other references to him in
the text. Includes a translation of Kerouac's "The
Origins of the Beat Generation. "

372. Bulgheroni, Marisa. "Kerouac A Big Sur." In Il
Demone Del Luogo: Letture Americane, pp. 87-90.
Milano, Italy: Istituto Editoriala Cisalpino, 1968.
This work contains a review of Big Sur, plus
other references to Kerouac in the text.

373. Castelli, Ferdinando. "La desolata corsa di Jack Kerouac verso la morte," La Civilta Cattolica, 122, No.
1 (1971): 34-47.
General study on Kerouac.

374. Cimatti, Pietro. "Su Pericoli della Celebrita: Jack
Kerouac: scrittoreo divo?" La Fiera Letteraria,
1 October 1961, p. 4.
General article on Kerouac.

375. Filippetti, Antonio. Kerouac. Firenze: La nuova
Italia, 1975.
Small book-length study on Kerouac.

376. Gebbia, Alessandro. "La letteratura beat americana."
In Studi Americani, Nos. 19-20, pp. 361-399. Rome:
Edizioni Di Storia E Letteratura, 1973-1974.
This is an extensive bibliography of, firstly, the
primary works in English of the Beat writers and,
secondly, Italian translations and criticisms of these
works. Much on Kerouac.

377. Gebbia, Alessandro, and Sergio Duichin, editors.
Kerouac Graffiti. Roma: Arcana Editrice, 1978.
To best describe this work is to list its contents:

Duichin, Sergio, and Alessandro Gebbia. "Se prima
eravamo in pochi...," pp. 5-22.
Gebbia, Alessandro. "A la recherche du Kerouac
perdu," pp. 23-43.
Duichin, Sergio. "Italian Kerouac graffiti," pp. 45-
67.
"Bibliografia," pp. 68-69.
"Chiave all'indentità dei personaggi," pp. 70-71.
Le Pellec, Yves. "La nuova conscienza (intervista
con Allen Ginsberg)," pp. 73-95.
Kerouac, Jack. "Lettera a John Clellon Holmes,"
pp. 97-106.
Burroughs, William. "Jack Kerouac," pp. 107-114.
Krim, Seymour. "L'eredità di Kerouac," pp. 115-
135.
Amram, David. "In memoria di Jack Kerouac,"

pp. 137-140.
Montgomery, John. "Da Kerouac West Coast; un pilota bohemien - dettagliate istruzioni per la navigazione, " pp. 141-147.
Saijo, Albert. "Un viaggio con Jack da San Francisco a New York, " pp. 149-152.
Adkins, Carl. "Jack Kerouac ha abbandonato la strada per sempre, " pp. 153-161.
McGrady, Mike. "Jack Kerouac: beat perfino a Northport, " pp. 163-168.

378. Gorlier, Claudio. "La Beat Generation: Rivolta E Innocenza, " Terzo Programma, No. 1 (1963): 109-184.
Long work on the Beats with references to Kerouac throughout.

379. Miller, Henry. Preface to I sotteranei [The Subterraneans]. Milano, Italy: Feltrinelli, 1965.
Translation from English (citation 476).

380. Pivano, Fernanda. "La Beat Generation, " Aut Aut; Revista di Filosofia di Cultura, No. 49 (1959): 1-15.
General article on the Beats with references to Kerouac.

381. Pivano, Fernanda. "La 'beat generation.'" Preface to Sulla Strada [On The Road]. Milano, Italy: Mondadori, 1959. Rpt. as "Kerouac E La 'Beat Generation.'" In La Balena Bianca E Altri Miti, pp. 423-454. [Milano, Italy]: Mondadori, 1961.

382. Pivano, Fernanda. Beat Hippie Yippie; Dall' Underground alla Controcultura. Roma: Arcana Editrice, 1972.
This work contains several sections devoted to both Kerouac and Neal Cassady.

383. Pivano, Fernanda. C'era Una Volta un Beat; 10 anni di ricera alternativa. Roma: Arcana Editrice, 1976.
A book on the Beats with several short sections on Kerouac, references to him throughout, including pictures of him and reproductions of letters and postcards from him to Pivano.

384. Pivano, Fernanda. "Gli Americana Bruciati, " Successo, 2, No. 4 (1960): 38-43. Rpt. as "Come nacquero i cosiddetti 'beat.'" In America Rossa E Nera,

pp. 278-290. [Firenze, Italy]: Vallecchi, 1964.
General article on the Beats with references to
Kerouac throughout.

385. Pivano, Fernanda. Preface to I Sotterranei [The Sub-
terraneans]. Milano, Italy: Feltrinelli, 1960. Rpt.
as "Kerouac Scittore Del 'Bop.'" In La Balena Bianca E Altri Miti, pp. 463-482. [Milano, Italy]:
Mondadori, 1961.

386. Pivano, Fernanda. Preface to Vanita di Duluoz: Un'-
educazione avventurosa, 1935-1946 [Vanity of Duluoz:
An Adventurous Education, 1935-1946]. Milano,
Italy: Bompiani, 1970.

387. Pivano, Fernanda. Preface to Visioni di Cody [Visions
of Cody]. Roma: Arcana, 1974.

388. Pivano, Fernanda. "I Ritornelli Di Kerouac," L'Euro-
pa Letteraria, 1, No. 1 (1960): 165-168. Rpt. as
"Kerouac Poeta." In La Balena Bianca E Altri Miti,
pp. 455-461. [Milano, Italy]: Mondadori, 1961.
Review of Mexico City Blues.

389. Van Den Haag, Ernest. "Gli eroi di Kerouac: Appunti
sulla letteratura della 'beat generation,'" Tempo
Presente, 11 (1958): 863-866.
A general article on Kerouac and the Beats.

390. Zaninetti, Teresio. "Sulla strada di Kerouac," Alla
Bottega (Brianza), 8, No. 1 (1970): 12-14.
A review of On The Road.

6. Japanese
(See citation 478.)

7. Norwegian

391. Sorensen, Roald. "Den tolvte bok om Jack," Arbeider-
bladet, 28 February 1963, p. 8.
A review of Big Sur.

8. Polish

392. [Baranowska, A.] "Nowinki Z San Francisco,"

Tworczosc, 7 (1958): 193-195.
General article on the Beats with references to
Kerouac throughout.

393. [Baranowska, A.] "Z Frontu 'Beatnikow,'" Tworczosc,
8 (1959): 190-191.
General article on Kerouac's works.

394. Elecktorowicz, L. "Nobel Becketta i zgon Kerouaca,"
Zycie Literackie, No. 45 (1969): 14.
Obituary on Kerouac.

395. Krdrynski, Juliusz. "Koniec dragi," Dziennik Polski,
25, No. 261 (1969): 4.
Obituary on Kerouac.

396. Mamon, Bronislaw. "Budda prozy amerykanskiej,"
Tygodnik Powszechny, 23, No. 45 (1969): 4.
Obituary on Kerouac.

397. Sachs, Viola. "Wedrujaca Granica a Literatura
Amerykanska," Przeglad Humanistyczny, 10, No. 1
(1966): 43-57.
General article with references to Kerouac and the
Beats.

398. Slomainowski, Andrzej. "Na Drodze," Kultura: Tygodnik Spoleczno-Kulturalny, 7, No. 47 (1969): n. p.
Obituary.

9. Russian
(See also citation 746.)

399. Anastas'ev, N. "Dva porazheniia," Molodaia Gvardiia,
No. 10 (1962): 304-309.
An article on Book of Dreams.

400. Levidova, I. "Neprikaiannye dushi. (Geroi knig Dzhek
Keruaka, Dzheimsa Selindzhere, Trumena Kapote i
Ivena Konnella)," Voprosy Literatury, No. 10 (1960):
108-131.
Translation of article title: "Uneasy spirits.
(The heroes of the books of Jack Kerouac, James
Salinger, Truman Capote and Evan Connell)." This
article examines the social misfit as a common theme
in the works of the above authors.

401. Mendel'son, M. "Literature dukhovnogo krizisa ...
     'Bitnik' i ego geroi (Dzh. Keruak)," Literatura i
     zhizn', 7 December 1960, n. p.
     Translation of article title: "Literature of a
     spiritual crisis ... The "beatnik" and his heroes
     (J. Kerouac). "

402. Nedelin, V. [In the Gloom of Psychoanalysis: Freud-
     ism and the Seekers of Anti-Idealogy], Inostrannaia
     Literatura, No. 10 (1963): 196-216.
     General article with references to Kerouac.

403. Nedelin, V. "Piligrimy nikuda, " Instrannaia Literatura,
     No. 9 (1959): 262-263.
     Review of The Dharma Bums.

404. Orlova, R. (Is Rooted in Human ... (On the Develop-
     ment of the American Novel)), Voprosi Literaturi,
     No. 8 (1961): 97-122.
     General article with references to Kerouac.

405. Tugusheva, M. "'Razbitoe pokolenie' Ameriki," Liter-
     aturnaia Gazeta, 20 December 1958, p. 4.
     General article on the Beats with references to
     Kerouac.

406. "'Verter' iz 'podzemel'ia. ' (Luidi podzemel'ia')," Lit-
     eraturnaia Gazeta, 5 September 1954, p. 4.
     Review of The Subterraneans.

10. Spanish

407. Coy, Francisco Javier. "Sentido Y Alcance De La
     'Beat Generation,'" Filologia Moderna, 4 (1963):
     109-121. Rpt. in Sic; Revista Venezolana de Orien-
     tación, 29, No. 287 (1966): 335-338, 340. Appeared
     also as "Jack Kerouac, Profeta De La 'Beat Genera-
     tion,'" Punta Europa, 8, No. 82 (1963): 56-67.
     Long article on Kerouac's works.

408. Diaz De Cespedes, Ignacio. "Jack Kerouac: Los vaga-
     bundos del Dharma," Sur, No. 273 (1961): 62-63.
     Review of The Dharma Bums.

409. O'Neill, Ana. "Kerouac 'Generación Castigada' Y
     Literatura, " Sur, No. 264 (1960): 71-72.

An article on On The Road and The Subterraneans.

410. Peltzer, Federico. "En el camino," Senales, No. 120
(1960): 17.
Review of On The Road.

411. Soto, Pedro Juan. "En el camino," Asomante, 18,
No. 2 (1962): 88-89.
Review of On The Road.

412. Trujillo, Manuel. "Jack Kerouac o la generación
vencida," Revista Nacional De Cultura, 23, No. 144
(1961): 149-154.
General article on Kerouac.

413. Umbral, Francisco. "Requiem Por La 'Beat Generation' (En La Muerte De Jack Kerouac, Alcohólico Y
Pionero)," La Estafeta Literaria, No. 433 (1969):
18-20.
Obituary on Kerouac.

414. Villar, Arturo del. "Balance de la literatura 'beat,'"
Arbor: Revista General de Investigación y Cultura,
No. 353 (1975): 109-113.
Review of Bruce Cook's The Beat Generation.

11. Swedish
(See also citation 855.)

415. Fremer, Bjorn. "The Beat Generation," Orkester
Journalen; tidskrift for jazzmusik, December 1958,
p. 19.
Article on Kerouac's influence by bop and jazz
music.

415a. Sjöström, Jonas. "Helt nya perspektiv på Kerouacs
'luffande,'" Dagens Nyheter (Sweden), 2 May 1977,
p. 4.
This is a review of a fictitious lost novel by
Kerouac titled "Tortured Angel." (Sjöström was
later interviewed about his hoax.)

PART II:

GENERAL REVIEWS AND ARTICLES ON KEROUAC

A. GENERAL, LITERARY STUDIES AND REVIEWS

416. Allen, Eliot D. "That Was No Lady--That Was Jack Kerouac's Girl." In Essays In Modern American Literature, pp. 97-102. Edited by Richard E. Langford. Deland, Florida: Stetson University Press, 1963. Rpt. in Jack Kerouac, On The Road: Text and Criticism (citation 438).
    Allen thinks that Kerouac is perfectly good informant about Western scenes from freight cars, cross-country travel, jazz, and Beat parties; but this virtuosity ends when he talks about American women. His picture is strangely distorted: all of the women are physically attractive yet nonrepresentative. They are inarticulate, having no ideas or no mind; and/or they are uninhibited: willing to undress without conscience, drink excessively, take drugs, love freely. Allen thinks Kerouac should start regarding women as people.

417. Allsop, Kenneth. Hard Travellin', The Hobo and His History. London: Hodder and Stoughton, 1967.
    Allsop feels that the ideas which Kerouac displayed in On The Road express a restlessness similar to that of the hobo: a search for freedom in a past, idyllic America. Through frenetic lunges across the continent the Beats/hobos/wobblies/other discontents retreat from mass America - which they find repulsive - into a nonexistant garden of Allah; but the men inhabiting this place - the space between the cities - are not about to let the wanderers have this freedom at their expense. On The Road, to Allsop, becomes a 20th century equivalent of The Pilgrim's Progress.
    See also citations 441, 491, 515, and 609.

418. Ardinger, Richard. "Long-awaited, But Worth It," Moody Street Irregulars: A Jack Kerouac Newsletter, No. 3 (1979): 10.
    This piece is a review of the reprint edition of John Clellon Holmes' Go. This work was the first

book published to characterize the Beat generation.
It deals more with the philosophical side of the movement than the visionary, Kerouacean, experience aspect. Ardinger recommends the work and encourages
several readings of it--to learn about craft--as well
as comparisons with some of Kerouac's novels. In
Go, Gene Pasternak represents Jack Kerouac.

418a. Aronowitz, Alfred G. "The Yen For Zen," Escapade,
October 1960, pp. 50-52, 70.
This article examines the interest in Zen Buddhism
by the Beat writers. Both Alan Watts and Gary Snyder are quoted; but the longest quote is by Kerouac
who talks about first discovering it for himself. He
also relates a story about visiting D. T. Suzuki after
the publication of The Dharma Bums.

419. Ashida, Margaret E. "Frogs and Frozen Zen," Prairie Schooner, 34 (1960): 199-206.
In this article, Japanese or traditional Zen is con-
trasted with American or Beat Zen (in the figure of
Jack Kerouac). The author feels that "spontaneous
prose" does not achieve the revelatory communication
which it hopes for, but instead is so confusing and
undisciplined as to breed its own confusion. The division of the world by Kerouac into Hipster and enemy
is seen as socially destructive and un-Zen. Although
the author appreciates the attempt of Americans to
follow the literary style of true Zen, she believes
the Beat writers fail to achieve an emotional or ethi-
cal understanding of traditional Zen.
See also citations 473 and 509.

420. Askew, Melvin W. "Quests, Cars, and Kerouac,"
University of Kansas City Review, 28 (1962): 231-
240. Rpt. in Jack Kerouac, On The Road: Text
and Criticism (citation 438).
Askew describes On The Road in not very flatter-
ing terms but concedes it is involved with and has
evolved from two literary traditions: independence
and expansion. It is an expression of the mobile
and free American character; and it also depicts the
search/quest for the father. But Askew feels that
the book is troubled by a lack of human experience
and human values; the characters are machine-like
and, as a result, the work suffers as literature.

421. Balakian, Nona. "The Prophetic Vogue of the Anti-
heroine, " Southwest Review, 47 (1962): 134-141.
Rpt. in Critical Encounters: Literary Views and Reviews, 1953-1977. Indianapolis: Bobbs-Merrill,
1978.
Balakian discusses the treatment of the woman as
heroine/anti-heroine in modern fiction. To her,
Kerouac's women/chicks affect nothing so much as
purposeful brainlessness.

422. "The 'Beat' Generation, " Current Affairs Bulletin
(Australia), 7 December 1959, pp. 35-48.
This article spends time defining the Beat generation. Besides being approached from the social,
psychological and behavioral aspects, it is also analyzed through its language and literature. Kerouac
is referred to and quoted throughout the piece, and
he is regarded as the spokesman of this new generation. Nonetheless, he is criticized as lacking artistic discipline and having too few good ideas.

423. Beaulieu, Victor-Lévy. Jack Kerouac: a chicken-essay.
Translated by Sheila Fischman. Toronto: Coach
House Press, 1976. For original French-language
editions, see citation 347.
Beaulieu, a French-Canadian novelist, contends
that Kerouac invariably tries to recapture his French-
Canadian heritage through his writing. The author
supports this thesis with Kerouac's fears of women,
death and sex, his mother-worship, his rebellion
against his father, and his angst toward the universe.
See also citation 751.

423a. Beckett, Larry. "Old Angel Kerouac: A Deathblow
Putdown, " Evergreen Review, No. 34 (1964): 11-12.
In this letter to the editor, Beckett criticizes
Kerouac's Old Angel Midnight (which had been pub-
lished in the previous issue of Evergreen Review).
He calls the piece "wearying and imbecile, " "incom-
prehensible, " and "phoney. "

423b. "The 'Bop Letters' Contest, " Escapade, October 1959,
pp. 58-59.
The editors of Escapade offered $100 each to the
best pro and the best con letters about Kerouac's
article "The Beginning of Bop" (which appeared in

the April 1959 issue). The two winning letters are
printed here as well as a handful of the runners-up.

424. Bowering, George. "On the Road: & the Indians at the
End, " Stony Brook, Nos. 3/4 (1969): 191-201.
Bowering feels that On The Road has had an im-
pact on both living styles and writing styles since it
was published. It can offer ideas that are literary,
if not philosophical. He attempts to refute the de-
meaning criticisms given to Kerouac by Melvin Askew
(citation 420) and Norman Podhoretz (citation 483).

424a. Brouillette, Paul. "An Evaluation of Jack Kerouac's
Duluoz Legend, " Moody Street Irregulars: A Jack
Kerouac Newsletter, No. 4 (1979): 9-11.
Brouillette sees Kerouac as being aware of the
ups and downs of literary reputation; that his later
writing revealed his real melancholic nature (which
had been covered over earlier because of his enthusiasm); that his writing would remain youthful as he
grew older. Kerouac's Duluoz Legend was an affir-
mation of faith in himself and in life; a mythology
encompassing fantasy, popularization, romance, ex-
aggeration, and emotion. It went a full circle from
optimism to bitterness; from self-pity to recrimination and sarcasm.

425. Bryant, Jerry H. The Open Decision: The Contemporary American Novel and Its Intellectual Background.
New York: Free Press, 1970.
The figure of Cain in the "hip" novel is discussed.
Kerouac is one of a group of writers whose work is
analyzed. These writers recognize a repressiveness
in an industrialized, middle-class and technological
society. They see that spontaneity is an important
response by which an individual--Cain--can fight any
restraints. The individual becomes the rebel/outlaw
as a result of this defense. The writers' styles as
forms/means of presenting this rebellion are examined.

426. Burdick, Eugene. "The Innocent Nihilists Adrift in
Squaresville, " Reporter, 3 April 1958, pp. 30-33.
Burdick defines the Beat generation and the hipsters who inhabit it. He sees there being few real
hipsters but many who are living on its fringes.

Kerouac is referred to several times and is seen as
one of the original Beats. He is thought of as a bad
writer, even though he had sensitive perception.

427. Burns, Jim. "Jack Kerouac, " Second Aeon, No. 11
      (n. d.): 73-76.
          In this short piece, Burns generally defends (and
      would like others to respect) Kerouac's attitudes
      about everything, including himself: his views being
      human rather than legendary. Burns sees Kerouac
      as being a chronicler of the ordinary, a talent who
      could make the pictures he created seem real.

428. Burns, Jim. "Jazz & the Beats, " Jazz Monthly, Janu-
      ary 1971, pp. 17-22.
          Burns goes into the use/place of jazz in the writ-
      ing/lives of the Beats. Kerouac is referred to
      throughout.

429. Burns, Jim. "Jivin' with Jack the Bellboy, " Palantir,
      No. 3 (1976): 19-23. Rpt. in Moody Street Irregu-
      lars: A Jack Kerouac Newsletter, No. 3 (1979): 3-5.
          Burns discusses the references to jazz and big-
      band music in Kerouac's work. He is enthusiastic
      about bop and the musicians that influenced Kerouac's
      life and writing and the Beat generation.

429a. Burroughs, William. "Kerouac, " High Times: The
      Magazine of High Society, No. 43 (1979): 52-55.
      Appeared earlier in altered and shorter form in
      Soft Need (West Germany), No. 8 (1973): 16-21.
      (In English.) This earlier version was translated
      from the French one titled "Jack Kerouac" which
      appeared in Jack Kerouac (citation 348). For a
      later version, with the final cut-up paragraph re-
      stored, see citation 742a.
          In this article, Burroughs talks more about him-
      self than Kerouac. He speaks about writers and
      writing: his, Kerouac's, and others. He relates
      Kerouac's role in his (Burroughs) road to writing
      and remembers experiences with and quotes Kerouac
      on writing.

430. Butler, Frank A. "On the Beat Nature of Beat, "
      American Scholar, 30, No. 1 (1960-1961): 79-92.
          Butler sympathizes with the Beats' attitudes but

dislikes their lack of originality, individuality, and respect for personal achievement. He faults Kerouac for being a gifted writer who is lazy and unconcerned about his craft and its lack of traditional novelistic values - "characterization, structure, and conflict."

430a. Campbell, James. "Kerouac & Co." New Edinburgh Review, No. 47 (1979): 11-14.
In this short essay, Campbell examines the writing, life-style, and philosophy of Kerouac (and the Beats, in general). He sorts out some of Kerouac's conflicts of interests and other reversals which happened along the way.

430b. Carlson, Peter. "'Haiku My Eyes!': a night of Kerouac," The News (Boston), 17 January 1974, pp. 6-7.
This short piece, from the Boston University student newspaper, is an introduction to the haikus by Kerouac which follow. It addresses Kerouac generally; but spends some time on his Northport years from 1958 to 1964.

430c. Ciardi, John. "The Book Burners and Sweet Sixteen," Saturday Review, 27 June 1959, pp. 22, 30.
Ciardi addresses the Post Office seizure of Big Table No. 1 on obscenity charges as a blow to intellectual freedom. He sees both Kerouac's Old Angel Midnight and William Burroughs' Naked Lunch (which appeared in the issue and precipitated the seizure) as serious writing; it is the failure of the postal inspectors to discern the writer's intent rather than only four-letter words and the censorship impulse. Ciardi quotes from both works: he jabs at Kerouac while praising Burroughs.

431. Cloves, Jeff. "Some peace flags," Peace News (England), 17 December 1976, pp. 14-15.
More or less a review of Ann Charters' KEROUAC, Cloves finds similarities between Kerouac's writing and that of the English author, Laurie Lee. Cloves also remarks on how he was personally affected by reading Kerouac's work.

432. "Correspondence: The Beat Generation," Partisan Review, 25 (1958): 472-479.
Responses by LeRoi Jones and David Fitelson, and reply to responses by Norman Podhoretz, on Podhoretz's article (citation 483).

433. Dardess, George. "The Delicate Dynamics of Friendship: A Reconsideration of Kerouac's On The Road,"
American Literature, 46 (1974): 200-206. Rpt. in
Jack Kerouac, On The Road: Text and Criticism
(citation 438).
Dardess' theme is that On The Road has a developed sense of the novel and that this work is disciplined, intelligent and honest.

434. Dardess, George. "Jack Kerouac As Religious Teacher," Moody Street Irregulars: A Jack Kerouac Newsletter, 1, No. 1 (1978): 4-6.
Dardess sees Kerouac being a religious teacher
because of his passion in searching for God through
his writing. Kerouac's spontaneous prose is regarded
as the method by which he tries to experience and
sense God: he interrogated all phenomena to yield
their secrets; the inspection of his own soul was particularly minute.

435. Dardess, George. "The Logic of Spontaneity: A Reconsideration of Kerouac's 'Spontaneous Prose Method,'" Boundary 2, 3, No. 3 (1975): 729-745.
Dardess speaks at length and gives specific examples of the tenets of Kerouac's spontaneous prose
method. He also makes comparisons with similar
ideas by Ralph Waldo Emerson and Henry David
Thoreau. Dardess believes Kerouac's prose has a
substance, direction and method that will soon be
recognized instead of attacked.

436. Davis, Wesley Ford. "Jack Kerouac: A Critical Note,"
Father Joe's Handy Homilies, 1, No. 2 (1970): 5.
Davis believes that Kerouac's good books--On The
Road, The Dharma Bums, and Satori in Paris--are
the ones which will be remembered in the future.
The reason being that they give a concreteness to
Kerouac's particular reality and sensitivity, and that
they achieve universality with their imagery.

436a. "Dear Playboy: Kerouac," Playboy, Sept. 1959, pp. 9-10.
Pro and con letters to Playboy on their publication
of Kerouac's "The Origins of the Beat Generation."

437. Dolbier, Maurice. "Beat Generation," New York Herald Tribune Book Review, 22 September 1957, p. 2.
This is a very general recap of Kerouac's involvement in the Beat generation and his writings.

438. Donaldson, Scott, ed. Jack Kerouac, On The Road: Text and Criticism. New York: Penguin Books, The Viking Critical Library, 1979.
    This work contains the text of On The Road and critical articles or otherwise on Kerouac, his work, and the Beat generation. In his introduction, Donaldson recognizes the ambivalent reception that On The Road received - even with several strong and favorable reviews which had come before all others - and feels that serious attention should finally be given to Kerouac, his "romantic naïf" notwithstanding. On The Road breaks new ground. Its style is fresh and it is a very American novel. It calls for the kind of nonconformism advocated by the Transcendentalists.

439. Duffey, B. I. "The Three Worlds of Jack Kerouac." In Recent American Fiction: Some Critical Views, pp. 175-184. Edited by Joseph J. Waldmeir. Boston: Houghton Mifflin, 1963.
    Duffey divided his essay into three sections, each describing a facet of Kerouac's concerns. The first "world" is the Beat generation, and here the author discusses the social and philosophical basis of the movement; the second section describes Kerouac's style of writing, the personal narrative; and the third "world" is devoted to automatic writing or what Duffey calls the process of fiction.

440. Everson, William. "Archetype West." In Regional Perspectives: An Examination of America's Literary Heritage, pp. 207-306. Edited by John Gordon Burke. Chicago: American Library Association, 1973. Rpt. in slightly different form in Archetype West: The Pacific Coast As A Literary Region. Berkeley: Oyez, 1976.
    This work places writers into regional groups and discusses the ramifications of these groupings. Kerouac appears briefly in the section about the "Archetype West" because a few of his novels were first popular in California. But since Kerouac is primarily an East coast writer, he is not discussed in detail.

440a. Farzan, Massud. "The Bippie in the Middle; Jack Kerouac (1922-1969)," London Magazine, New Series, 9, No. 11 (1970): 62-69.
    Farzan wants to correct both the critical and public

misunderstanding and underestimation of Kerouac and his work. Kerouac's death gives him the opportunity to take a serious look/retrospective at the author's work which necessarily must be viewed outside the established, academic Jamesian tenets of literary criticism and the novel. Farzan sees Kerouac as one of the few serious writers of contemporary literature who independently led the technique of fiction in a new direction and who produced a volatile body of creative work. He traces a continuum through The Subterraneans, The Dharma Bums, Big Sur, Satori In Paris, and The Vanity of Duluoz.

441. Feied, Frederick. No Pie In The Sky: The Hobo As American Cultural Hero In The Works of Jack London, John Dos Passos, and Jack Kerouac. New York: Citadel, 1964.

This work is an expanded version of Feied's thesis (citation 609). He avoids a sociological approach to the hobo. Kerouac's treatment is seen as more symbolic than economic: the characters in his books took to the road as a form of protest against society and as a means of searching for the values and beliefs that they gravitated toward. Feied refers to On The Road and The Dharma Bums.

See also citations 417, 491, and 515.

442. Fiedler, Leslie. "Death of the Novel," Ramparts, Winter 1964, pp. 2-14. Appeared in an altered and longer form in Waiting for the End, pp. 138-178. New York: Stein and Day, 1964.

Fiedler's main theme is that society is becoming less literate and intellectual because of the emphasis toward the non-literary arts. As a result, interest in writing, especially fiction and the novel, is dying. He sees symptoms of this trend reflected in contemporary writing and he leads an attack on it. Much time is spent on Beat works; primarily William Burroughs for the novel. Fiedler asserts that Allen Ginsberg - the best writer of the trio of Burroughs, Ginsberg and Kerouac - invented the legend and myth of Jack Kerouac, a legend and myth more interesting than his works: Ginsberg created a fantasy from a life that was really dull and conventional.

442a. Fleischmann, Wolfgang B. "A Look at the 'Beat Generation' Writers," Carolina Quarterly, 11, No. 2

(1959): 13-20. Rpt. in Recent American Fiction: Some Critical Views, pp. 110-118. Edited by Joseph J. Waldmeir. Boston: Houghton\Mifflin, 1963.

Fleischmann sees the Beats as a fairly unorganized group without a unified critical point of view or a specifically defined style of writing. Much of their work is seen as having come from earlier American literary traditions; although they are the heroes of a revolt against the academic control of writing and criticism. He introduces and categorizes all the important Beat writers and examines Kenneth Rexroth's views of the Beat generation. Kerouac and Allen Ginsberg are referred to throughout the piece.

443. Fleischmann, Wolfgang B. "Those 'Beat' Writers," America, 26 September 1959, pp. 766-768.

This is a short introductory piece on Beat writers in which the author describes the literary evolution of the group, its place in the century's scheme of literature, and its failing as a cohesive, experimental literary group. He critiques the works of Kerouac and Ginsberg primarily.

444. Frohock, W. M. "Jack Kerouac and the Beats." In Strangers To This Ground: Cultural Diversity in Contemporary American Writing, pp. 132-147. Dallas: Southern Methodist University Press, 1961.

This author takes the position that the Beats are not an easily definable group because their tenets, their origins, and their members are too evasive to annotate. Taking Kerouac as the central figure for the movement, Frohock takes The Subterraneans and uses it to describe and define the Beat generation's style and sentiments.

445. Fuller, Edmund. "The Hipster or the Organization Man?" In Man in Modern Fiction: Some Minority Opinions on Contemporary American Writing, pp. 133-165. New York: Random House, 1958.

Fuller divides the interest in our culture in conforming to mass culture and behavior as being represented in the two opposing poles of "the hipster" and "the organization man." Kerouac's On The Road epitomizes the first group while Herman Wouk's The Caine Mutiny represents the second. Fuller dislikes the hipster and finally bases his attack on religio-social grounds.

446. Gaffié, Luc. Jack Kerouac: The New Picaroon. New York: Postillion Press, 1977.
   Gaffié examines the picaresque tradition and its elements in three of Kerouac's works: On The Road, The Dharma Bums, and Desolation Angels. He considers Kerouac a forerunner of American writing in his own league and that his success was due to On The Road being published at the right time, to its subject matter and the social character of the 1950's, and to both its timeliness and universality.

447. Ginsberg, Allen. Allen Verbatim: Lectures On Poetry, Politics, Consciousness. Edited by Gordon Ball. New York: McGraw-Hill, 1974.
   This work contains a chapter on Kerouac where Ginsberg talks about his prose with its musical and rhythmical constructions. He sees Kerouac as hearing his writing, of treating it as choruses in jazz songs: Kerouac wrote the music of American speech. Other references abound in the book to Kerouac's writing, his attitudes, and to Ginsberg's love for him.

448. Ginsberg, Allen. "The Great Rememberer." Introduction to Visions of Cody. New York: McGraw-Hill, 1972. Rpt. in Saturday Review: The Arts, December 1972, pp. 60-63.
   Ginsberg remembers the time of the taping that resulted in Visions of Cody. He is Beat historian remembering the "Great Rememberer" Kerouac and Neal Cassady and Beat visions and feelings that accompanied history.

449. Ginsberg, Allen. The Visions of the Great Rememberer: With Letters by Neal Cassady & Drawings by Basil King. Amherst, Massachusetts: Mulch Press, 1974. Appeared earlier (without letters) in Mulch 4, 2, No. 2 (1973-1974): 54-97.
   This memoir takes off from where Ginsberg left off in his introduction to Kerouac's Visions of Cody (citation 448). It is more complex and quotes heavily from Visions of Cody.

450. Glicksberg, Charles I. "The Sexualized World of the Beat Generation." In The Sexual Revolution in Modern American Literature, pp. 143-170. The Hague: Nijhoff, 1971.

In treating Kerouac, Glicksberg presents the sexual scenes in the novels in terms of the psychology of the characters and the tenets of the Beats, and also relates God and Zen to these scenes.

451. Gose, Elliott. "More on 'Kerouac's Sound': To the Editors," Tamarack Review, No. 12 (1959): 76.
Gose feels that Warren Tallman's article on Kerouac (citation 498), rather than being emotionally indulgent or parodying (as much Kerouac criticism has been), is genuinely involved with the subject.

451a. Gribetz, Sid. "Kerouac's Angels," Moody Street Irregulars: A Jack Kerouac Newsletter, No. 4 (1979): 7-8.
Gribetz feels that much of the macho sexism in Kerouac's writing (which he was aware led to male insensitivity) was not really him talking; but rather his America. This treatment was an American stereotype - male domination and aggression; Kerouac was caught in it but he had sensitivity enough to depict the gross dehumanization of women in his books. His work finds him struggling to come to grips with these tensions.

451b. Grunes, Dennis. "The Mythifying Memory: Corso's 'Elegiac Feelings American,'" Contemporary Poetry: A Journal of Criticism, Vol. 2, No. 3 (1977): 51-61.
Grunes examines Corso's poem written for the memory of Jack Kerouac, after his death. He says that it brings to "subdued fruition the Beat cycle which first came of age in the mid-Fifties."
See also citation 849.

452. Hart, John E. "Future Hero in Paradise: Kerouac's The Dharma Bums," Critique: Studies in Modern Fiction, 14, No. 3 (1973): 52-62.
Kerouac's The Dharma Bums is seen as both personal and universal: a journey into ego and self but also a wandering in the world of experience and the sensual; a journey of discovery, recovery and development; a searching down on the ground but also within the self. Hart discusses Kerouac's style - his Zen/meditation/dharma (awakening) orientation, the world he enters/discovers/shares with friends or alone and his ability to function in it.

453. Hassan, Ihab. Radical Innocence: Studies In The Contemporary American Novel. Princeton, New Jersey:
Princeton University Press, 1961.
    Hassan takes various approaches to the contempo-
rary novel. In the section on the Beats, he discusses
the social and philosophical ramifications of the movement. He talks about On The Road and the "auto-
telic" structure of Kerouac's novels.

454. Hazo, Samuel. "The Poets of Retreat," Catholic
World, October 1963, pp. 33-39.
    Hazo first defines the difference between Beat and
beatnik. He then goes on to say that because of
their displacement from society, the Beats will need
perspective in order to create a literature that will
last forever instead of just for the moment. Kerouac
is referred to throughout.

454a. Hentschel, Anthony. "Kerouac Defended," New Statesman, 14 June 1974, p. 839.
    This letter to the editor disagrees with Paul
Theroux's comments on Kerouac (citation 780).

455. Hinchliffe, Arnold P. "The End of a Dream?" In
Studi Americani, No. 5 (1959): 315-323. Rome:
Edizioni di Storia e Letteratura, 1959. (In English.)
    In this short study of the abandonment of the
American dream in three works by Nelson Algren,
Kerouac, and James Gould Cozzens, Hinchliffe sees
On The Road as a picaresque novel which savagely
denies the respectability of the dream. It explores
the search for sensation and for self and belief.
The road functions as a pipeline in the quest for
heaven and kicks; the road provides the means to
move in any direction that one is pointing.

456. Hipkiss, Robert A. Jack Kerouac: Prophet of the
New Romanticism. Lawrence, Kansas: Regents
Press of Kansas, 1976.
    Hipkiss' book is a scholarly and critical study of
Kerouac's works. He explores Kerouac's essential
themes and their treatment and development. He
also compares Kerouac with four other contemporary
writers: J. D. Salinger, James Purdy, John Knowles,
and Ken Kesey.
    See also citations 813-817.

457. Holder, Wayne. "The Road Goes On Forever," Moody
      Street Irregulars: A Jack Kerouac Newsletter, No.
      3 (1979): 6.
           Holder discusses the influence of Neal Cassady on
      Kerouac's writing. He sees the mythic Dean Mori-
      arty as a composite of both Kerouac and Cassady.

458. Holmes, John Clellon. "Existentialism and the Novel:
      Notes and Questions," Chicago Review, 13, No. 2
      (1959): 144-151.
           In this essay, Holmes sees Kerouac's writing as
      dealing mostly with the final phase of Kierkegaard's
      contemporary existentialist equation: at the bottom
      of despair is faith. Kerouac's characters are great
      celebrators of life.

458a. Holmes, John Clellon. "First Reader of On The Road
      in Manuscript: An Excerpt from the Journals of
      John Clellon Holmes," Moody Street Irregulars: A
      Jack Kerouac Newsletter, No. 5 (1979): 11.
           Holmes was the first to read Kerouac's typewriter
      roll of On The Road - even before Kerouac reread
      it. In this piece from his journals, he tells his
      first impressions of the book (although as he admits,
      they are subjective).

459. Holmes, John Clellon. "An Insider's View of Some
      Old Friends," Books, December 1966, p. 5.
           Holmes sees Kerouac as a great writer with a
      large body of work but who remains obscure to most
      people, or who, at the very least, is thought to be
      some wild man in search of kicks.

460. Holmes, John Clellon. Nothing More To Declare.
      New York: Dutton, 1967. Excerpted chapter, "The
      Great Rememberer," reprinted in Jack Kerouac, On
      The Road: Text and Criticism (citation 438).
           Holmes traces his relationship with Kerouac from
      their meeting. He discusses Kerouac's personality
      and his books, and the philosophy of the Beats.
      Holmes writes largely about the impact which the
      movement and the people had on his life.

461. Holmes, John Clellon. "The Philosophy of the Beat
      Generation," Esquire, February 1958, pp. 35-38.
      Rpt. in Nothing More To Declare (citation 460), pp.
      116-126. Also reprinted in The Beats (citation 575)

and Jack Kerouac, On The Road: Text and Criticism (citation 438). Rpt. in German (citation 365).
Holmes articulately explains the attitudes of the Beat generation, the political and social world into which it was born, and the manner in which it attempts to voice itself. References to Kerouac throughout.

461a. Hull, Keith N. "A Dharma Bum Goes West to Meet the East," Western American Literature, 11, No. 4 (1977): 321-329.
Hull's essay is a study of The Dharma Bums' Ray Smith in his philosophical growth: from the self-orientation of solipsism, abstract thought, and non-Zen Buddhism to what seems a merging of self with nature, a move from abstract to concrete perception, and the mild satori and understanding of Zen thought.

462. Hunt, Timothy A. "On The Road: An Adventurous American Education." In Jack Kerouac, On The Road: Text and Criticism, pp. 465-484. Edited by Scott Donaldson. New York: Penguin Books, The Viking Critical Library, 1979.
Hunt finds that On The Road is a complex and subtle book which is steeped in American traditions and archetypes. It is deserving of continued reading and analysis as a result. He sees the book as being structurally coherent rather than disjointed (as past critics have tried to label it). It has great relevance to the process of "visioning and questioning" that is central in American literature.

463. Jacobson, Dan. "America's 'Angry Young Men': How Rebellious Are the San Francisco Rebels?" Commentary, December 1957, pp. 475-479.
Jacobson is largely critical of the Beat writers, especially Kenneth Rexroth, Allen Ginsberg and Kerouac. He does see some good in Ginsberg and Kerouac, however; the latter writes with simplicity and openness of mind, and is truthful about himself. Jacobson sees Dean Moriarty as a bore rather than the exemplary Beat hero.

464. Jones, Granville H. "Jack Kerouac and the American Conscience." In Lectures on Modern Novelists, pp. 25-39. Pittsburgh: Carnegie Institute of Technology,

Department of English, 1963. Rpt. in Jack Kerouac, On The Road: Text and Criticism (citation 438).

Jones' approach to Kerouac is as a serious figure in modern fiction. Kerouac's gift, according to Jones, is his ability to write autobiography which expresses the thoughts of a generation that responds to the American conscience.

464a. Jones, LeRoi. "Correspondence," Evergreen Review, No. 8 (1959): 253-256.

This letter to the editor by Jones is a comment and criticism on Kerouac's "The Essentials of Spontaneous Prose" (published in an earlier issue of Evergreen Review). Jones analyzes and dissects Kerouac's theories and actual performance as put forth in On The Road and other of his writings.

465. Jones, LeRoi, ed. The Moderns: An Anthology of New Writing in America. New York: Corinth Press, 1963.

Jones mentions Kerouac throughout the introduction to this book. He sees Kerouac's writing as having a basis in the Joycean mode and his spontaneous prose as an integral part of a very personal style.

465a. Kamstra, Jerry. "Jack's 'Road' Was the Beat Children's Beacon," San Francisco Sunday Examiner & Chronicle, 16 November 1969, This World sec., p. 51.

Kamstra believes that, although faded, the blueprint of the dream and the guidebook to an unmechanized and untraveled America, that is found in Kerouac's On The Road, is still going strong. He sees Kerouac, not as the man who started the Beat movement and all that followed/flowed from it, but rather as the person who "simply took notes and described it." His spontaneous writing style was hardly ever to fail him; and his best books contain energy and excitement, power and insight. To Kamstra, Kerouac is a visionary, a gifted artist, and a writer of prose that reads like poetry.

466. Kastel, Warren. "The Road to Nowhere," Rogue, August 1959, pp. 40-42, 50, 68-69.

. In this article, Kastel reviews On The Road and The Subterraneans. He feels that the novels have little to offer although On The Road is the better

written of the two: Kerouac writes in an obscure
pseudo-style--which is devoid of meaning--to a cap-
tive audience of immature youth rebelling against the
real world.

467. Kazin, Alfred. Contemporaries. Boston: Little,
Brown, 1962.
Kazin compares Kerouac's On The Road to Norman
Mailer's Deer Park, and although he feels Mailer is
the more gifted writer, he believes the two share
the themes of loneliness, emotionlessness, and emptiness.

468. Kazin, Alfred. "Psychoanalysis and Contemporary
Literary Culture," Psychoanalysis and the Psychoanalytic Review, 45 (1958): 41-51. Rpt. in Partisan Review, 26 (1959): 45-55.
The theme of Kazin's article is that the works of
some contemporary writers lack feeling, direction
and point, but are accompanied, conversely, by an
abundance of sexual activity and description of experience. Authors who are used as examples of
this are: Norman Mailer, Kerouac, Tennessee Williams, Henry Miller, and Allen Ginsberg. Kazin
sees Kerouac as writing about the search for experience rather than the experience itself.

469. Krim, Seymour. Introduction to Desolation Angels.
New York: Bantam, 1966. Rpt. as "The Kerouac
Legacy." In Shake it for the world, smartass, pp.
193-216. New York: Dial Press, 1970.
Krim writes a very strong case for Kerouac's
support as a writer, autobiographer, and social historian. He also sees it as the time when Kerouac
needs to change his writing; to reshape himself as
an artist and to "transform his expression into yet
another aspect of himself."

470. Krim, Seymour. "King of the Beats," Commonweal,
2 January 1959, pp. 359-360.
Krim sees Kerouac as pioneering and breaking
open the boundaries of writing, boundaries set by
both writers and society. Kerouac uses his form-
less art to bring to print details of a frantic modern
scene. Subjects usually not found in contemporary
writing are gloried in his books: promiscuity, pot-
smoking, kicks, excitement and fast cars.
See also citation 481.

471. Leer, Norman. "Three American Novels and Contemporary Society: A Search for Commitment," Wisconsin Studies in Contemporary Literature, 3, No. 3 (1962): 67-86.

     Leer examines post-War writing. He acknowledges a search for values and identity in a world where mass society has stripped away all frameworks and fixed backgrounds against which to rebel; a world of sameness which negates values and individuality. Kerouac, in The Dharma Bums, is seen as searching for a recovery of total involvement in a singular experience, one that lacks dullness and sameness and turns out to be a mystic endeavor.

472. Lomas, Herbert. "Benzedrine to Booze," London Magazine, New Series, 14, No. 5 (1974-1975): 73-86.

     Lomas describes Kerouac as a nihilist throughout this article. Comparisons to other literary figures finds Kerouac wanting and undeveloped. He also reviews KEROUAC by Ann Charters and finds it academic and without life.

473. Mahoney, Stephen. "The Prevalence of Zen," Nation, 1 November 1958, pp. 311-315.

     Mahoney examines Beat Zen, as exemplified in Kerouac's The Dharma Bums, and Square Zen, as lectured by Alan Watts, especially in Nature, Man, and Woman. He finds Kerouac's work lively, and Beat Zen as full of real feeling although it does not do well on the deliberative level.

     See also citations 419 and 509.

473a. "Mail On Last Year's Kerouac Issue," Two Hands News, No. 21 (1979), p. 7.

     As the above title states, this is correspondence in response to the article on Kerouac which appeared in issue no. 17 of Two Hands News (citation 499).

474. Merrill, Thomas F. Allen Ginsberg. New York: Twayne, 1969.

     This critical work on Allen Ginsberg alludes at times to his relationship with Kerouac and to Kerouac's influence on Ginsberg's work.

475. Miller, Chuck. "Kerouac Reappraised," New York Times Book Review, 8 April 1973, p. 34.

     This letter to the editors rejects an earlier review

of Kerouac's Visions of Cody by Aaron Latham (citation 273) and extolls Kerouac as a great American
novelist.

476. Miller, Henry. Preface to The Subterraneans. New
York: Avon, 1958. Rpt. in The Casebook on the
Beat (citation 590). Also reprinted in Italian (citation 379) and in German (citation 365).
Henry Miller has nothing but praise for Kerouac
as a writer. He likes his language, his philosophy,
and his characterizations.

477. Mosley, Edwin M. "Lost and Hollow, Beat and Angry--
The Significant Gestures of Two Generations," Ball
State Teachers College Forum, 1, No. 2 (1960-1961):
44-54.
Mosley describes On The Road as a picaresque
novel which makes no advances on the early undeveloped examples of the type.

477a. Mottram, Eric. Introduction to The Scripture of the
Golden Eternity. Second edition. New York: Corinth
Books, 1970.
Mottram sees Scripture as Kerouac's statement
of belief and confidence that he was one with the
universe of energy and form. It is Kerouac's sor-
rowful looking backward after he has seen the dis-
maying future. It is a confession, a sutra, a scripture of selfless contemplation.

477b. Nolan, Dick. "The City," San Francisco Examiner,
26 August 1959, sec. 2, p. 1.
Nolan, several years his senior, was born and
raised in Lowell, Massachusetts, as had been Kerouac. Also, the newspaper columnist reveres Kerouac because he writes fondly of their hometown.
Nolan's column on Kerouac is in response to the
poor critical reception of his novel, Maggie Cassidy.
He feels that Kerouac's innovative writing style com-
municates and that it is a kind of literary shorthand
which (was written in and) reads at a hurried or
compressed pace rather than at a leisurely one.
But he finds that this style promotes untidiness; it
must be read image for image rather than word for
word.
See also citation 671.

478.   Ohashi, Kenzaburo; Kanaseki, Hisao; Ohashi, Kichino-
        suke; and Suwa, Masaru. "Symposium: Beat Litera-
        ture." In American Literature--the 1950's, pp. 269-
        279. Edited by Kenzaburo Ohashi. Tokyo: Tokyo
        Chapter of the American Literature Society of Japan,
        1976. (In English.)
            In this symposium on Beat literature, Kichinosuke
        Ohashi, in his part, examines Kerouac's involvement
        with the Beat movement. To him, Kerouac was not
        a central figure in the movement; he was more a
        chronicler of the Beat generation than a part of it.

479.   Oliphant, Robert. "Public Voices and Wise Guys,"
        Virginia Quarterly Review, 37, No. 4 (1961): 522-
        537.
            In this article, a comparative literature essay on
        language, Oliphant discusses two kinds of narrators
        in the modern novel: the speaker with the "public
        voice" who pleads his case and tries to make signi-
        ficant statements about experience and tends to be
        identified with the author; and the voice of the "wise
        guy" which is not identified as the author's, stands
        at a distance from the speaker, and presents an
        entertainment which is to be neither accepted nor
        rejected. Kerouac is seen as one example of the
        "public voice."

480.   Øverland, Örm. "West and Back Again." In Jack Ker-
        ouac, On The Road: Text and Criticism, pp. 451-
        464. Edited by Scott Donaldson. New York: Pen-
        guin Books, The Viking Critical Library, 1979.
            Øverland finds On The Road as much a novel about
        returning as one about leaving. In part one, Sal
        Paradise, the restless narrator, progresses from
        dream (of the West as free, open and wild country,
        and the East as closed, tame and lacking of free-
        dom) to disillusionment (with the West, of dreams
        ever collapsing upon themselves, and the realization
        of the East as being a home to return to, a quiet
        place to recuperate from restlessness, and of having
        its own wilderness to tame). Other road trips are
        seen as a cure to the restlessness bug put in him
        by Dean Moriarty. Sal does not expect to find a
        new life, only new places; he follows not the dream
        but the road and Dean. At the end, Sal realizes
        that home is his best place; finally resigning himself
        to life rather than accepting it.

481. Owen, Donald H. "Communications: The Beat Generation," Commonweal, 30 January 1959, pp. 470-471.
Owen's letter is in response to Seymour Krim's
article on Kerouac (citation 470). He feels that Kerouac's content is more important than his methodol-
ogy, and that his content is nothing more than an
espousal of carpe diem attitudes mixed with diatribes
against and avoidance of society.

482. Pivano, Fernanda, and Luigi Castigliano, editors. On
The Road. [Milano, Italy]: Edizioni Scholastiche
Mondadori, 1974. (In English.)
Pivano wrote an introduction to this new English
language, Italian edition of On The Road. It is a
mini-biography of Kerouac concerned mostly with
that period before the first publication of the book
in 1957. She also discusses Kerouac's spontaneous
prose method, some important critical writings on
Kerouac, and the meaning of Beat as expounded by
both Kerouac and John Clellon Holmes. Castigliano
contributes "A Note on American Pronunciation."
It describes, for Italian readers, the difference between American English and British English (for a
better understanding of Kerouac).

483. Podhoretz, Norman. "The Know-Nothing Bohemians,"
Partisan Review, 25 (1958): 305-318. Rpt. in Do-
ings and Undoings: The Fifties and After in American Writing, pp. 143-158. New York: Farrar,
Straus, 1964. Also reprinted in The Beats (citation
575), A Casebook on the Beat (citation 590), and
Jack Kerouac, On The Road: Text and Criticism
(citation 438).
Podhoretz attacks the Beat generation through the
writing of Jack Kerouac. He says that the primitivism - affinity for sex and adulation of blacks -
and spontaneity in Kerouac are really a cover-up
for hostility toward intelligence and a poverty of
feeling. Kerouac's theory behind spontaneous bop
prosody is seen as an inability to express anything
in words, and his style is solipsistic and inward.
Ultimately, Podhoretz sees the Beat generation as
regressive and primitive, as embracing violence,
criminality and brutality as something which is to
be admired.
See also citation 432.

483a. Portugés, Paul. The Visionary Poetics of Allen Ginsberg. Santa Barbara, California: Ross-Erickson,
1978.
Kerouac is frequently referred to in this book on
Allen Ginsberg's poetic theories. Portugés shows
that Ginsberg developed his own thoughts on spontaneous writing based on Kerouac's urgings and theories,
his "The Essentials of Spontaneous Prose."

483b. Poteet, Maurice. "The Delussons and the Martins:
Some Family Resemblances," Moody Street Irregulars: A Jack Kerouac Newsletter, No. 5 (1979):
4-6.
Poteet unfolds some major similarities between
Kerouac's The Town and The City (1950) and Jacques
Ducharme's The Delusson Family (1939). These
correspondences, from a Franco-American viewpoint,
encompass family size and characterizations, specific
events present in both books, and the theme of home/
road.

483c. Poteet, Maurice. "The 'Little (Known) Literature' of
Kerouac's 'Little Canada,'" Moody Street Irregulars:
A Jack Kerouac Newsletter, No. 5 (1979): 4-6.
Poteet generally examines the possible influence
of the literature of "little Canada" (Lowell-Pawtucket-
ville, Massachusetts) on Kerouac's writing. He finds
thematic, structural, and formal aspects which are
common to both bodies of work.

484. Primeau, Ronald. "'The Endless Poem': Jack Kerouac's Midwest," Great Lakes Review, 2, No. 2
(1976): 19-26.
Primeau examines the descriptions of the Midwest
in On The Road: Kerouac's sensitivity to its geo-
graphy and people and his own place in it while
dashing, gawking, stopping in it with his photographic
memory eyes while riding across America. Kerouac's
expression is called Midwestern optimism, and mid-
America is seen in mythic proportions.

485. Pritchett, V. S. "The Beat Generation," New Statesman, 6 September 1958, pp. 292, 294, 296.
Pritchett talks about the Beat generation, Beat
writing, Norman Mailer's hipsters, and Kerouac's
On The Road. The Beat generation is purely American: they are digging their orgiastic experiences

and hoping for a better tomorrow. Beat writing is skilled, and it shows tenderness, energy and restlessness in a world with fluid values. Hipsters are of the night who have created a mode, ritual and secret language in jazz and in the helpless condition of the blacks. Kerouac is the moving spirit of the Beat generation and has reached literary respectability with On The Road: one can feel, smell and see the American continent and sense the dramatic loneliness in the wild traveling.

486. Rexroth, Kenneth. "Beat Generation? DEAD AS DAVY CROCKETT CAPS, SAYS REXROTH, PASSING THROUGH." In The Village Voice Reader, pp. 309-311. Edited by Daniel Wolf and Edwin Fancher. New York: Grove Press, 1963.

Rexroth, in this brief letter to the Village Voice, says that Kerouac is one of the finest prose writers around but that he is naive because he has been caught and branded in the growing commercialism known as the Beat generation.

486a. Rexroth, Kenneth. "San Francisco's Mature Bohemians," Nation, 23 February 1957, pp. 159-162.

In the first half of this article, Rexroth describes the regional literary renaissance taking place in San Francisco, its backgrounds, and the current scene. The second half takes up introducing the city's most important young writers, mostly poets. But in fiction, Rexroth praises Kerouac as a hybrid mixture of nearly half a dozen other important writers: a writer whose prose, at its best, can be called a "smashing indictment"; a writer who, behind all the Beat and frantic prose, is really "an outraged Puritan."

486b. Reynolds, Stanley. "Stanley Reynolds recalls a 'fifties hero: Jack, back on the road," The Guardian (England), 10 November 1979, p. 12.

On the tenth anniversary of Kerouac's death, Reynolds recalls him as a truly original writer. He hopes that the current interest in the man is based on something more substantive than nostalgia for the 1950's or that he was a friend of Neal Cassady (who drove the Merry Pranksters' bus).

487. Roberts, John G. "The Frisco Beat," Mainstream,

11, No. 7 (1958): 11-26.

Roberts speaks about the various Beat and un-Beat writers in the San Francisco bay area, but mostly about the Beats. He says that they basically lack the inertia to live up to their professed values which is betrayal to themselves. Kerouac is referred to in the article and he is thought to be underrated both as a sociological reporter and for his honesty. He is seen as failing to find the meaning of America for the despairing and lacks a world view which might give him more understanding about what he describes.

488. Ross, Basil. "California's Young Writers, Angry and Otherwise," Library Journal, 15 June 1958, pp. 1850-1854.

Basil Ross contrasts the "new authoritarian" literary group with the Beat generation while concentrating on introducing the various Beat writers and giving a synopsis of their work. Kerouac's On The Road and The Subterraneans are discussed briefly.

489. Schroeder, Joan. "Jack Kerouac: Energies of the Free Flowing Art of Jazz," Statesman, 12 February 1975, Take Two sec., pp. 2-3.

Schroeder, in this short article in the Statesman, the college newspaper of the State University of New York at Stony Brook, gives a short introduction to Kerouac's work by noting his energy, his characterizations, and his jazz rhythms.

490. Scott, James F. "Beat Literature and the American Teen Cult," American Quarterly, 14 (1962): 150-160.

Scott sees the rise of the Beat generation as originating from the American adult's surrendering of once powerful authority symbols for entertainment suited to an adolescent mentality: this attitude is rooted in a deep concern for the teen-ager's feelings. He says that the Beats represent this mystique and deify it; they show aggressive spontaneity of adolescence, are nay-saying to the world around them, and refuse to grow up mentally. At the most, they might shock people into re-examining the American dream. Kerouac's interpretation of Zen Buddhism is suggested as having an adolescent cast; its idealogy is nominally preserved, scaled down, washed out and distorted. His spontaneous writing - conceived as creativity through an absence of form - is seen as adolescent and in contempt of literary discipline.

491. Seelye, John D. "The American Tramp: A Version
of the Picaresque," American Quarterly, 15 (1963):
535-553.
Seelye suggests that Kerouac regards the tramp
as a ghost of the 19th-century frontiersman but not
as a heroic figure; he gives him token respect and
his life-style is sentimentalized. Kerouac's heroes
are not tramps -- although they can be descended
from them -- but they are akin to saintly wanderers,
restless bohemians, and conmen, racing down roads,
lost among crisscrossing railroad tracks, in the im-
mensity of America; they retrace the routes of the
pioneers. His new frontiersmen, Cody Pomeray and
Dean Moriarty, remind us that past promises have
not been fulfilled in the present; that the great experiment of the 19th century was not wholly success-
ful.
See also citations 417, 441, 515, and 609.

492. Sheed, Wilfrid. "Beat Down and Beatific," New York
Times Book Review, 2 January 1972, pp. 2, 21.
Rpt. in The Good Word and Other Words, pp. 116-
120. New York: Dutton, 1978.
In this short essay, Sheed says that the Beat generation was a genuine movement and that it was a
literary one. Kerouac is referred to throughout
the piece.

493. Sheed, Wilfrid. "The Beat Movement, Concluded,"
New York Times Book Review, 13 February 1972,
pp. 2, 32. Rpt. in The Good Word and Other Words,
pp. 121-126. New York: Dutton, 1978.
Sheed sees the Beat era as ending in 1960 with
few of the survivors willing or offering to trace
links to the hippies. He notes that the Beat life-
style predated Kerouac at Columbia by four years
with Thomas Merton and his group, starting about
1936. Their history is sketched out with references
to Kerouac throughout.

494. Spevack, Marvin. "Young Voices on the American
Literary Scene: The Beat Generation." In Spirit
of a Free Society: Essays in Honor of Senator
James William Fulbright on the Occasion of the
Tenth Anniversary of the German Fulbright Program,
pp. 313-330. By the United States Educational Com-
mission in the Federal Republic of Germany. Heid-
elberg: Quelle & Meyer, 1962.

Spevack first defines the Beat generation, then examines the work of its major writers: Ginsberg's Howl and Kerouac's On The Road. Kerouac's work is said to be a modern day picaresque novel exploring the oldest and simplest forms.

495. Spiller, Robert E. , et al. , editors. Literary History of the United States: History. 3rd edition, revised. New York: Macmillan, 1963.
The authors refer to Kerouac throughout the volume: his fiction is a celebration of life, and he brought a distinct American rhythm and a new kind of vision to it.

496. Stevenson, David L. "James Jones and Jack Kerouac: Novelists of Disjunction. " In The Creative Present: Notes On Contemporary American Fiction, pp. 193-212. Edited by Nona Balakian and Charles Simmons. Garden City, New York: Doubleday, 1963.
Stevenson sees Kerouac and Jones as naive blunderers into the initiated literary scene of the 20th-century novel. They write in styles that are as disconnected from language and syntax as their characters and ideas are from society.

497. Straumann, Heinrich. American Literature in the Twentieth Century. New York: Harper & Row, 1965.
This work includes a small section devoted to the Beat generation. Kerouac is examined as the movement's chief novelist, and The Subterraneans is reviewed and noted as proof of his originality as a writer.

497a. Sutherland, Donald. "Petronius And The Art Of The Novel, " Denver Quarterly, 13, No. 3 (1978): 7-16.
In reaction to a review of a new translation of Petronius' Satyricon which says that Petronius is similar to the Beat novelists like Kerouac, Sutherland discusses Petronius as a novelist and interjects comparisons to and contrasts with Kerouac throughout the piece.

498. Tallman, Warren. "Kerouac's Sound, " Tamarack Review, No. 11 (1959): 58-62, 64-74. Rpt. in Evergreen Review, 4, No. 11 (1960): 153-169. Also reprinted in The Casebook on the Beat (citation 590),

Jack Kerouac, On The Road: Text and Criticism (citation 438) and Open Letter, Third Series, No. 6 (1976-1977): 7-19.

Tallman offers that Kerouac, like the jazz musician and the hipster (who have created their own music -- bop -- and language -- hip talk -- and improvise on each, and who live outside of the time continuum in the NOW moment - when they can), has created his own sound/writing, a beat, bop prose, and has joined the ranks of his fellows to play variations on the moments, to get maximum spontaneity out of himself and onto the page and into his characters, his scenes, his narratives, into his holiness themes, into his life sound, the American grain, a true sound, the promised land of NOW, of truth of moment and, that, although he fails ultimately, has created new ground for fiction writers to stand upon and improvise from.

499. Two Hands News, No. 17 (1978): 1-4.

Two Hands News is a Chicago poetry bookstore's newsletter. Half of this issue is devoted to Kerouac. It is a combination of review of his life and works, criticism, update on current Kerouacia, extrapolation/synthesis of a small part of Big Sur, Beat history, Kerouac bibliography, and literary problem finder.

See also citation 473a.

500. Tytell, John. "The Beat Generation and the Continuing American Revolution," American Scholar, 42 (1973): 308-317.

Tytell reconstructs the political and social framework underlying the formation of the Beat movement and the aesthetics of their beliefs and their writing. The Beat writers -- William S. Burroughs, Allen Ginsberg, Kerouac, and Gary Snyder -- shared attitudes rather than common form (as much of their work was experimental), and their literature planted the seed of awareness of what is significant in life in the minds of the young. In his examination of Kerouac, Tytell sees On The Road as a characteristically American novel because it illustrates the search for escape from society and boredom and from the spiritual corruption of materialism. Much of the action is frantic energy, speed and intense feeling, and hysteria with wild, impulsive coast to coast marathons in automobiles. The Dharma Bums, on the other hand, goes in a different direction. The narrator is seen as starting on an inward search for new roots. Preparation is made for a change of values through Buddhism and the individual being isolated in nature and retreating toward meditation and contemplation.

501. Tytell, John. Naked Angels: the lives & literature of the Beat Generation. New York: McGraw-Hill, 1976. Several excerpts appear in Jack Kerouac, On The Road: Text and Criticism (citation 438).

Tytell's book is an examination of the life and works of Kerouac, Allen Ginsberg, and William Burroughs. First, he describes the Beat's social milieu and their rebellion. Next, he gives biographical information aimed at explaining their motivations. And thirdly, he ends with criticisms of their works. See also citations 827-837.

502. Vaidyanathan, T. G. "Jack Kerouac and Existentialist Anxiety," Osmania Journal of English Studies, No. 2 (1962): 61-66.

The author feels that Kerouac's work is a relief compared to other contemporary authors. His work affirms life: it tells of a quest, sometimes spiritual, to overcome the undermining anxiety of emptiness and meaninglessness in life; a quest that must be undertaken because of the loss of a spiritual center.

503. Van Den Haag, Ernest. "Kerouac Was Here," Social Problems, 6 (1958): 21-28. Excerpted as "Kerouac and the Beat: 'They've Nothing to Say And They Say It Badly,'" Village Voice, 5 November 1958, pp. 5, 12. Appeared in shortened form as "Conspicuous Consumption of Self," National Review, 11 April 1959, pp. 658-660.

The author states that being Beat is an affectation rooted in wishing for and assuming feelings that are not really felt because the self is valueless. The Beat tries to convince himself of his enthusiasm for what he would like to believe in by loudly convincing others of these assumed beliefs. The author sees this attitude, however, as arising out of the boredom of material prosperity and the increasing routinization in society. Kerouac's novels are seen as banal

and lacking characterization. He has nothing to say,
says it badly, but is sincere.

504. Vopat, Carole Gottlieb. "Jack Kerouac's On The Road:
A Re-Evaluation, " Midwest Quarterly, 14 (1973):
385-407. Rpt. in Jack Kerouac, On The Road:
Text and Criticism (citation 438).
Vopat sees Kerouac not as a great writer but as
a good one, one who has more depth and control than
has been conceded. In this scholarly study, On The
Road is seen more as a criticism of the Beat generation than a wild embracing of it. Kerouac's road
characters seem to be fleeing life rather than looking
for it; they are running from identity and responsibility instead of seeking self and roots.

505. Wakefield, Dan. "Jack Kerouac Comes Home, " Atlantic Monthly, July 1965, pp. 69-72.
Kerouac had forsaken the Beat scene before the
publication of On The Road, and he did not tell about
it until 1965 when Desolation Angels was published
(two-thirds of which was written before 1957, along
with 10 other novels). Because of this fact, Wakefield feels that Kerouac has had the last laugh on
his condescending critics who had spent much of
their venom on him. He feels that Desolation Angels is "the most thoroughly American book since
the autobiography of William Allen White, " and that
Kerouac needs to be reconsidered in light of its rev-
elations.

506. Walsh, Joy. "Jack Kerouac: An American Alien in
America, " Moody Street Irregulars: A Jack Kerouac
Newsletter, 1, No. 1 (1978): 8-10. Appeared earlier as "The King Of The Beats In Search Of His
Royal Roots. " In Berkeley Barb, 18-24 November
1977, p. 8. Rpt. in Palantir, No. 8 (1978): 31-33.
A longer version appears in Street Magazine, 2, No.
4 (1978): 45-52.·
Walsh's theme is that Kerouac did not feel any
ties to an American tradition because of his French-
Canadian descent. He was an alien without roots
and identity in America; but he loved the country
in a big way, the way an immigrant loves his new-
found homeland. Kerouac's feelings did not stop
him, however, from searching/pursuing an identity
in his heritage, the one he grew up with in Lowell.

507. Walsh, Joy. "Kerouac: A Reichian Interpretation,"
Moody Street Irregulars: A Jack Kerouac Newsletter,
1, No. 2 (1978): 3-5.
Walsh views Kerouac through a psychoanalytic eye.
His problem in coping with life seemed to be the result of a Catholic upbringing. His writer's eye gave
him the insight to see life but religion restricted him
in his ability to live it.

508. Waterman, Arthur E. "The Novels of Jack Kerouac:
An Attempted Rescue." In Flight and Search: Three
Essays on The Modern American Novel, pp. 23-41.
Atlanta, Georgia: Georgia State College School of
Arts and Sciences Research Paper Number 7, Febru-
ary 1965.
The author discusses the central theme of time
and its effect on the American experience in five of
Kerouac's works: On The Road, The Subterraneans,
The Dharma Bums, Maggie Cassidy, and Tristessa.

509. Watts, Alan W. Beat Zen, Square Zen, and Zen.
San Francisco: City Lights, 1959. Rpt. in This Is
IT and Other Essays on Zen and other Spiritual Experience, pp. 77-110. New York: Pantheon Books,
1960. Appeared earlier in shorter form in Chicago
Review, 12, No. 2 (1958): 3-11.
Watts' essay goes to length describing the philosophy and feeling of Zen, particularly Beat Zen and
square Zen: Beat Zen generally having an "anything
goes" attitude and square Zen being rather orthodox,
doctrinaire and disciplined. Kerouac's The Dharma
Bums is focused on as falling into the Beat Zen category.
See also citations 419 and 473.

510. Webb, Howard W., Jr. "A Hard Stare At Our Top
Writers," Chicago Tribune, 20 December 1964,
Books Today sec., pp. 1-2.
A thumbnail dossier and critique of Kerouac as a
writer extracted mainly from Webb's essay (citation
511). The author feels that the judgment of Kerouac's
work must, at present, be qualified.

511. Webb, Howard W. "The Singular Worlds of Jack Kerouac." In Contemporary American Novelists, pp.
120-133. Edited by H. T. Moore. Carbondale:
Southern Illinois University Press, 1964.

Drawing entirely from his works (and other Beat writers), Webb examines Kerouac's relationship with the Beat generation and its world, and with his gravitation toward life and youth experience in Lowell.

512. West, Paul. The Modern Novel, Volume 2: The United States and Other Countries. London: Hutchinson University Library, 1963.

In this comparative overview of contemporary writing, when Kerouac is brought up he usually follows the mention of Thomas Wolfe. West sees Kerouac as a convincing novelist but not without flaws.

513. Widmer, Kingsley. "The American Road: The Contemporary Novel," University of Kansas City Review, 26 (1960): 309-317.

Widmer examines the "road" as a lyric American image in the contemporary novel. It is embraced as a means to escape sterile society, to gain knowledge, and to experience sensation. The road, however, ends as it begins -- with society, the real world. Those who have traveled it usually give up their flight. The road exorcises them and they re-emerge into society. Widmer examines this concept in The Dharma Bums and On The Road, and compares Kerouac to J. D. Salinger.

514. Widmer, Kingsley. "The Beat in the Rise of the Populist Culture." In The Fifties: Fiction, Poetry, Drama, pp. 155-173. Edited by Warren French. Deland, Florida: Everett Edwards, 1970.

Widmer gives some background to the formation of the Beat movement, its successors, and its effects on society and literature; he sees it more as a cultural movement rather than a literary one. Kerouac is seen as being guilty of adolescent romanticism in his works. They are juvenile, delinquent, childish and paranoid; they are vague both intellectually and socially and rarely display insight or profundity. The basis of Kerouac's work is the pursuit of lost dreams and a return to childhood innocence which is not handled well; these themes become fragmented and dip into sentimentality. Widmer does admit that Kerouac describes the contemporary American scene well. He also talks about William Burroughs, Beat poetry and Allen Ginsberg.

515. Widmer, Kingsley. "The Hobo Style. " In The Liter-
      ary Rebel, pp. 91-107. Carbondale: Southern Illi-
      nois University Press, 1965.
          In this article, Widmer focuses on the hobo as an
      image of rebellion in American fiction. He sees
      Kerouac basically as a childish and adolescent writer,
      yet with some insights, perceptions and awareness
      in the American scene. (Similar to citation 514.)
      See also citations 417, 441, 491, and 609.

516. Wolfe, Bernard. "Angry At What?" Nation, 1 Novem-
      ber 1958, pp. 316, 318-322.
          Wolfe examines the work of four writers -- three
      being Angry Young Men (from England) and the fourth
      being Kerouac -- to determine just what they are
      angry at. He concludes, through the relationships
      in the works, both heterosexual and homosexual,
      that they are angry at women rather than at society
      (with its conformity and respectability); they are
      angry with their personal matters rather than with
      matters concerning the community.

517. Woods, Crawford. "Reconsideration: Jack Kerouac, "
      New Republic, 2 December 1972, pp. 26-30.
          Woods' reconsideration takes the form of finding
      more topics to criticize Kerouac on than those to
      praise him. He remembers Kerouac is at his best
      when he deals with maudlin day-to-day affairs. "The
      Essentials of Spontaneous Prose" is seen as being
      academic -- one thing Kerouac warred against -- and
      a strict, slick computer formula used to write the
      same book a dozen times -- the escape of a lazy
      writer; but good enough and of sufficient originality
      to be given 1950's period honors.

B. GENERAL, NON-LITERARY WORKS ABOUT KEROUAC'S
        PERSONAL LIFE, INCLUDING BIOGRAPHIES,
            PLUS ARTICLES ON THE BEATS,
          AND OTHER RELATED MATERIAL

(For additional articles related to this section,
see also Section G, Part II.)

518. Adkins, Carl. "Jack Kerouac: Off the Road for Good. "

In Story, the Yearbook of Discovery/1971, pp. 27-
35. Edited by Whit and Hallie Burnett. New York:
Four Winds Press, 1971.
   The author reminisces on his friendship and his
adventures with Jack Kerouac in St. Petersburg,
Florida. He tells of Kerouac's ability to overwhelm
people and to stir them into frenzies. Adkins sees
him as a very emotional person sliding from laughter
to tears effortlessly: a man who felt deeply and who
acted that way because of his innocence.

519. Albelli, Alfred. "Beat Bard Denies He's the Daddy-
   O, " New York Daily News, 14 December 1961, p. 4.
   Kerouac denies paternity of a daughter, Janet
Michele, borne by his second wife, Joan Haverty
Kerouac, after she sues him for child support.

520. Allen, Steve. From unpublished autobiography entitled
   "Garage Sale, " pp. 568-574.
   In this excerpt on Kerouac from his autobiography,
Steve Allen remembers the events surrounding his
recording with Kerouac, an all-night drinking and
talking fest by and with Kerouac at Allen's home in
New York, and the last time he saw Kerouac.

521. Allsop, Kenneth. "Beaten, " Spectator, 13 March 1959,
   p. 350.
   This short piece describes a meeting between Kerouac and Kenneth Rexroth. The article mentions a
rift between the two caused by Kerouac's drunken appearance at Rexroth's home.

522. Amis, Kingsley. "The Delights of Literary Lecturing, "
   Harper's, October 1959, pp. 181-182.
   Amis discusses the problem of lecturing by describing a boring literary lecture which he gave in
Philadelphia, and then a zany performance by Kerouac
which he, Amis, co-hosted. Kerouac seems a mad
egotistical upstaging child, being argumentative without cause. However, as Amis sees it, Kerouac knows
how to appeal to a college audience.
   Compare with citations 586c, 595, and 602. Contrast with citations 523, 532, and 534.

523. Amram, David. Vibrations: The Adventures and Musical Times of David Amram. New York: Macmillan, 1968.

This book contains remembrances by Amram of
the beginnings of jazz poetry readings in New York
City and with Kerouac being an integral part of the
movement: especially a passage where Kerouac shows
up drunk to a lecture he is supposed to give at
Brooklyn College. Amram also traces the filming
of Pull My Daisy by Alfred Leslie to which Kerouac
improvised the narration (and Amram scored the music).

See also citations (related to Kerouac's Brooklyn
College lecture) 532 and 534.

524. Anastas, Peter. "Reflections of a Kerouac lover; Of
the time the author of 'On the Road' came to Gloucester," Gloucester Daily Times (Massachusetts),
5 October 1974, North Shore '74 sec., pp. 3-4.
The author tells of his interest in Kerouac and
about Kerouac's visit - along with two of his brothers-
in-law--to poet Charles Olson's home in Gloucester in 1968. Anastas knew Olson who told him
the story.

See also citation 531a.

525. Aronowitz, Alfred G. "The Beat Generation," New
York Post, 9, 10, 11, 16, 19 March 1959.
Aronowitz wrote a long documentary series on the
Beats for the Post. The above dates are those
specifically relating to Kerouac. Included are separate interviews with Kerouac and Neal Cassady.
The origins and the meaning of the Beat generation
are defined plus its effects on the succeeding gener-
ation(s) are explored. Also discussed is Zen Buddhism in Beat philosophy.

526. Aronowitz, Alfred G. "The Beat Generation - Beaten?"
New York Post, 27 December 1957, pp. 5, 10.
Aronowitz talks about the circumstances of Kerouac's reading at the Village Vanguard in 1957. He
also relates following Kerouac to another club after
his reading to listen to Stan Getz and to talk with
other Beat poets.

See also citations 584, 596, and 601.

527. Aronowitz, Alfred G. "Kerouac Doesn't Live Here Any
More," New York Post, 23 June 1960, p. 2.
Kerouac is blamed/scapegoat for the emergence
of the beatniks on MacDougal Street in New York

City. They are trying impossibly to relive the Beat
generation years, 1946-1949, in 1960. They are
trying to be characters out of Kerouac's books.

528. Balaban, Dan. "Witless Madcaps." In The Village
Voice Reader, pp. 31-32. Edited by Daniel Wolf
and Edwin Fancher. New York: Grove Press, 1963.
Appeared originally in Village Voice, 13 February
1957, p. 3.
Balaban records the flippant conversations of Kerouac, Allen Ginsberg, and Gregory Corso who are
back in New York City from San Francisco but on
their way out to Tangiers. He juxtaposes this with
the fact that they are having success at being Beats
and getting their work published.

529. Basinski, Michael. "Ti Jean In Lowell," Moody Street
Irregulars: A Jack Kerouac Newsletter," 1, No. 1
(1978): 13-15.
Basinski explores Kerouac's French-Canadian
Catholic upbringing as essential to explaining his
writing and his attitudes. The parochial education,
working class community, ethnicity, and extended
family all contribute to an understanding of Kerouac.

529a. "The 'Beat' Letters," Ludd's Mill (England), No. 14
(n. d.): 16-17.
Here is a collection of letters in response to Pete
Faulkner's Kerouac article in Ludd's Mill no. 12
(citation 549a).

530. "Beat Mystics," Time, 3 February 1958, p. 56.
This short piece from Time's religion section is
segments of an interview among Mike Wallace, Kerouac, and Philip Lamantia in which the Beats describe the movement as mystical. Kerouac explains
that love will cause a mystical religious revival in
modern Western society.

530a. Benedetto, Rosanne. "The Kerouac Symposium: An
Afterword," Soundings/East (formerly Gone Soft),
Vol. 2, No. 2 (1979): 91-96.
Benedetto, a student of Jay McHale's class on
Kerouac and the Beats at Salem State College during
which time she wrote this paper, contrasts Allen
Ginsberg and Gregory Corso and sees their divergent
lives and points of view as manifestations of Jack
Kerouac's own contradictory personality.

531.   Berriault, Gina.   "Neal's Ashes," Rolling Stone, 12
       October 1972, pp. 32, 34, 36.
           Neal Cassady is recollected by his second wife,
       Carolyn Cassady.   She says his real life was very
       different and opposed to the one Kerouac depicted in
       writing.   Neal went through much grief, especially
       as he grew older and more burned out.   Carolyn
       also describes Kerouac's stay with them on the West
       coast.   She tells how Neal shared her and his other
       women with Kerouac.

531a. Boer, Charles.   Charles Olson in Connecticut.   Chicago:
       Swallow Press, 1975.
           This book has a very brief account of a meeting
       between Charles Olson and Kerouac.
           See also citation 524.

531b. Boles, Robert.   "Kerouac - Beat is rythm (sic), not
       an act," The Register (Yarmouth Port, Massachu-
       setts), 29 July 1976, The Register Summary Maga-
       zine sec., p. 11.
           Robert Boles became a good friend of Kerouac's
       (when he lived in Hyannis).   In this place Boles
       writes about some of the things that happened to
       Kerouac when he lived in the city as well as his
       thoughts, dreams, and frustrations as a man and
       as a writer.

532.   Boroff, David.   Campus U.S.A.:   Portrait of American
       Colleges in Action.   New York: Harper, 1961.
           Boroff briefly recounts a lecture Kerouac gave to
       a group of students at Brooklyn College in New York
       City.
           See also citations 523 and 534.

533.   Breslin, James E.   "The Beat Generation: A View
       From the Left," Village Voice, 16 April 1958, p. 3.
           Breslin reports on a meeting of the Young Social-
       ist League in Greenwich Village.   One speaker crit-
       icizes Kerouac as being one American who honors
       and continues a certain tradition of mindlessness.
       Breslin, however, sees good in Kerouac: his works
       breathe an air fresher than that of the literary aca-
       demicians.

534.   Breslin, James.   "The Day Kerouac Almost, But Not
       Quite, Took Flatbush," Village Voice, 5 March 1958,
       p. 3.

Article about a Kerouac lecture to Brooklyn College students in New York City.
See also citations 523 and 532.

534a. Brouillette, Paul. "An Evening With Jack Kerouac," Moody Street Irregulars: A Jack Kerouac Newsletter, No. 2 (1978): 10-11.
Brouillette describes the happenings at the opening night of a month-long exhibit on Kerouac at the Lowell (Massachusetts) Museum. Much of the evening was filled with readings of Kerouac's work and listening to a tape of Kerouac's Pull My Daisy narration.
See also citation 699.

535. Brustein, Robert. "The Cult of Unthink," Horizon: A Magazine of the Arts, 1, No. 1 (1958): 38-45, 134-135.
Brustein's dislike of Beat art is clear throughout this article. He sees the Beats' sullen, herdist and anti-social behavior as exemplifying a "Cult of Unthink." Kerouac is lambasted for his lack of sensitivity and aliveness - in that although he describes the beauties of nature and people (in On The Road), his characters are unthinking, undeveloped, and unchanging.

536. Burroughs, William. "My Life In Orgone Boxes," Oui, October 1977, pp. 58-59.
Burroughs states that Kerouac's account of Burroughs' Texas adventures in On The Road is a good story but pure fiction. Kerouac never went to Texas and probably exaggerated stories of Burroughs' farm life from Neal Cassady, who did visit.
See also citation 653.

536a. Case, Brian, and Tony Parsons. "Sideswipe," New Musical Express (England), 8 January 1977, pp. 22-23.
In this two-part article, Case gives an overview of the rise and fall of the Beat movement. He refers to Kerouac throughout. Parsons' piece is a biographical sketch of Kerouac which also notes his involvement with Neal Cassady and his chaotic life-style.

537. Cassady, Carolyn. "Coming Down." In The Beat Book, pp. 4-22. Edited by Arthur Winfield Knight and Glee Knight. California, Pennsylvania: 1974.
Carolyn Cassady's continuing accounts/autobiography

of her life with Kerouac and Neal Cassady. This piece contains ten letters and postcards from Kerouac.

538. Cassady, Carolyn. "from The Third Word." In The Beat Journey, pp. 64-90. Edited by Arthur Winfield Knight and Kit Knight. California, Pennsylvania: 1978.

Carolyn talks about the last several times she saw Kerouac - and friends - on the West Coast. This was the summer Kerouac lived at Big Sur (1960), and later wrote about.

539. Cassady, Carolyn. Heart Beat: My Life with Jack & Neal. Berkeley: Creative Arts Book Company, 1976. The second edition (1978) included an introduction by John Clellon Holmes (citation 562a).

Carolyn Cassady's reminiscences of life with Neal Cassady and Kerouac in the early 1950's in San Francisco and the West Coast.

See also citations 752-754, and 838-840.

540. Charters, Ann. "Allen Ginsberg and Jack Kerouac," Columbia Library Columns, 20, No. 1 (1970): 10-17.

Charters talks about Kerouac's and Allen Ginsberg's college days at Columbia, alluding to their early literary interests and their disappointment with university life. Kerouac began Columbia as a football star, but after an injury, became disenchanted with his career and, thereby, with the school. He later returned to spend time at and around Columbia when Ginsberg was a student.

541. Charters, Ann. KEROUAC: A Biography. San Francisco: Straight Arrow, 1973. Excerpted as "Jack & Neal & Luanne & Carolyn: In Which Jack Hits the Road," Rolling Stone, 29 March 1973, pp. 30-32, 34.

This biography is the first to be published on Kerouac. Charters explains that he was one of her secret heroes and that she just naturally fell into writing about his life.

See also (other biographies) citations 552, 568, 576, and 599. See also citations 598 and 755-783.

542. Charters, Ann. Scenes Along the Road: Photographs

of the Desolation Angels/1944-1960.   New York:
Portents/Gotham Book Mart, 1970.
   This work contains pictures of the Beats, Kerouac
included.   Most are photos which had not appeared
elsewhere.
   See also citations 784-785.

542a.   Cherkovski, Neeli.   Ferlinghetti, A Biography.   Garden
   City, New York: Doubleday, 1979.
      This biography of Lawrence Ferlinghetti refers to
   Kerouac (in various contexts) throughout.   Ferlinghetti's early reluctance to publish Kerouac's work
   is (one subject) mentioned.

542b.   Christy, Jim.   "About The Night And What It Does To
   You, " Soft Need, No. 9 (1976):   99-105.
      In this short autobiographical/explanatory piece,
   Christy recalls the circumstances of his life around
   the time he first discovered Jack Kerouac and what
   this "outsider of modern Western culture" has ultimately meant to him.

543.   Christy, Jim.   "The Last Beatnik, " Globe and Mail
   (Toronto), 23 March 1978, Fanfare sec. , p. 3.
      This article is a sketch of John Montgomery, a
   West Coast friend of Kerouac's, who appears in
   several of Kerouac's books either as "Henry Morley"
   or "Alex Fairbrother. "   Christy sees Montgomery
   as basically unchanged from the Beat days except
   for being older.   There are references to Kerouac
   throughout the piece.

544.   Ciardi, John.   "Epitaph for the Dead Beats, " Saturday
   Review, 6 February 1960, pp. 11-13, 42.   Rpt. in
   The Casebook on the Beat (citation 590).
      Ciardi feels that the Beat rebellion is basically
   an adolescent one.   Its orthodoxy is rigid; its intel-
   lectualism posing; its writers non-literary; its belief in Zen undisciplined.   Kerouac is referred to
   throughout but isn't regarded highly as a writer.
   Ciardi, however, sees rebellions as being noble and
   the Beat movement as no exception to this.

545.   Cook, Bruce.   The Beat Generation.   New York:
   Charles Scribner's Sons, 1971.
      Cook talks about Kerouac's style: it was the pro-
   genitor of the personal journalistic style of the 1960's.

He spends much time tracing the history and publication of Kerouac's novels: On The Road was respon-
sible for the general public becoming aware of the
Beat generation, and also for giving Kerouac instant
notoriety; Big Sur is examined for the causes of Kerouac's nervous breakdown in California. Finally,
Cook interviewed Kerouac in his hometown of Lowell,
Massachusetts, in a bar.
See also citations 786-797.

546. Cravens, Gwyneth. "Hitching Nowhere: The aging
young on the endless road," Harper's, September
1972, pp. 66-70.
Cravens talks about the dream that the road to
somewhere - which Kerouac created and populated
with beatific characters, which then created the beatniks, the hippies and the drug culture - is really a
hitchhiked-out, strung-out high scene road to nowhere,
fantasized more from a desk and a book than lived
at from the insides of a car going down Route 66 or
a thumb out to the wind.

547. DiPrima, Diane. Memoirs of a Beatnik. New York:
Traveller's Companion, 1969.
DiPrima describes an orgy in which she, Kerouac,
Allen Ginsberg, and two young men took part.

547a. Dretzka, Gary, interviewer. "Kerouac's road retraced
by his biographer," Los Angeles Herald Examiner,
4 September 1979, pp. A1, A9.
Dretzka questions Dennis McNally, author of the
biography, Desolate Angel: Jack Kerouac, the Beat
Generation and America, about Kerouac's life and
writing.

547b. Dunn, William. "A 'beat' era love story: She recalls
marriage to author Kerouac," Detroit News, 19 August 1979, pp. 1A, 18A-19A.
In this article, Frankie Edith Parker recalls her
life with and marriage to Jack Kerouac. She was
Kerouac's first wife. Parker also quotes from letters Kerouac wrote to her little more than a month
before his death. In one, he talks about being beaten
up in a St. Petersburg (Florida) bar. She feels that
Kerouac's death was as a result of internal bleeding
(caused by injuries from the fight) rather than the
hemorrhaging of a hernia or alcoholic dissipation (as
has been believed up until now).

548. Edmiston, Susan, and Linda D. Cirino. Literary New York: A History and Guide. Boston: Houghton Mifflin, 1976.

In the sections devoted to the Beat generation, the authors talk about its development and history in the East Village of New York City. Kerouac is referred to often and many of the places where he lived are listed and mapped.

548a. Eldridge, Bob. "Carolyn, Neal & Jack; A Three-Faced Love," Honey (England), June 1979, pp. 74-76, 79, 81.

This piece is a recounting of the relationship between Kerouac and Neal and Carolyn Cassady with quotes from Carolyn's book Heart Beat.

549. Falacci, Frank. "Lowell Girl Wed To Jack Kerouac," Boston Sunday Herald, 20 November 1966, p. 16.

Without knowing much of anything, admittedly, about Kerouac, Falacci interviewed him on a rather non-descript wedding day.

549a. Faulkner, Pete. "Old angel midnight; Jack Kerouac & his circle," Ludd's Mill (England), No. 12 (n. d.): 3-6, 10-20.

Faulkner's article is a short biography of Kerouac with comments on his life and his works. The author also includes mini-biographies of Allen Ginsberg, William Burroughs, Neal Cassady, Gary Snyder, and Michael McClure.

See also citation 529a.

549b. Fitch, Robert Elliot. Odyssey of the Self-Centered Self, or Rake's Progress in Religion. New York: Harcourt, Brace & World, Inc., 1961.

This book on self, culture, Christian philosophy, and progress toward religious thought, refers to Kerouac throughout and to his characters from On The Road and The Dharma Bums. Fitch is generally critical of Kerouac and his philosophic characterizations.

550. Freilicher, Lila. "Random House to Publish Biography of Kerouac," Publishers Weekly, 29 May 1972, p. 25.

This announcement of a biography-in-progress on Kerouac by Aaron Latham includes some of Latham's views of Kerouac and the Beat generation.

See also citations 560 and 576.

551.   Gifford, Barry.   Kerouac's Town: On the Second An-
        niversary of His Death.   Santa Barbara: Capra,
        1973.   Expanded and revised edition, Kerouac's Town.
        Berkeley: Creative Arts Book Co., 1977.
            In Part 1 of the revised edition, Gifford recalls
        a trip to Lowell, Massachusetts, with Marshall Clem-
        ents, on the second anniversary of Kerouac's death.
        Part 2 is an account of Gifford visiting Stella, Ker-
        ouac's third wife, in St. Petersburg, Florida.

552.   Gifford, Barry, and Lawrence Lee.   Jack's Book: An
        Oral Biography of Jack Kerouac.   New York: St.
        Martin's, 1978.
            A compilation of interview statements from people
        who knew Kerouac and put together in a way to re-
        veal the man, his work, and the myth.
            See also (other biographies) citations 541, 568,
        576, and 599.   See also citations 798-810.

553.   Ginsberg, Allen, and Neal Cassady.   As Ever: The
        Collected Correspondence of Allen Ginsberg and Neal
        Cassady.   Edited by Barry Gifford.   Berkeley:
        Creative Arts Books Co., 1977.
            This book of correspondence between Allen Gins-
        berg and Neal Cassady through the 1940's, the 1950's
        and the 1960's is indexed quite thoroughly so that all
        the references to Kerouac - which are many - can
        be picked out easily.
            See also citations 811-812.

554.   Goldman, Ivan.   "Visit in Summer of 1947 - Jack
        Kerouac's Denver Friends Formed Theme for Novel,"
        Denver Post, 29 December 1974, p. 34.   (This cita-
        tion and the following three by Goldman are listed
        chronologically by date rather than alphabetically by
        title.)
            Introductory article to a series by Goldman on the
        reminiscences of people in Denver who remember and
        were part of Kerouac's circle of friends there during
        the summer of 1947.

555.   Goldman, Ivan.   "Cassady 'A Bum,' Says Kerouac
        Figure - Bob Burford's Summer of '47: A Different
        Story," Denver Post, 30 December 1974, p. 12.
            Robert F. Burford - Ray Rawlins in On The Road -
        recalls Neal Cassady as being a coward and a per-
        petual juvenile delinquent, and he relates a story

about insulting a meek Cassady in a Denver bar.
Kerouac and Allen Ginsberg impressed him as both
being very serious about and very sure of their writing.

556. Goldman, Ivan. "Babe on 'On The Road' - 'Doll of the
West' Recalls How It Was With Kerouac, Friends,"
Denver Post, 31 December 1974, p. 21.
  Beverly Burford De Berard - Babe Rawlins, sister
of Ray Rawlins, in On The Road - remembers Kerouac and Cassady during that summer - their drinking
and partying, and also when she lived in California
near them. Kerouac's romantic attachment to Denver
and the West is noted. More about Cassady's un-
trustworthiness and antics are mentioned.

557. Goldman, Ivan. "Architect Ed White Jr. - Kerouac's
Friend Helped Spark Style of 'On The Road,'" Denver
Post, 1 January 1975, p. 49.
  Justin Brierly - also characterized in On The
Road - is noted as the person who put Kerouac and
Neal Cassady in touch with each other. He recalls
his own friendship with Kerouac and sees Cassady as
basically untrustworthy and trying to live up to his
"Dean Moriarty" image. Ed White - Tim Gray in
On The Road - remembers Cassady's last visit to
Denver in 1967. White is mentioned as being given
credit by Kerouac for the idea of "sketching" which
Kerouac put to use in developing his writing style.
The question of Kerouac's homosexuality is discussed,
his trip to Denver with his mother, and his prolific
correspondence with White.

558. Grieg, Michael. "The Old Beat Gang Is Breaking Up,"
San Francisco Examiner, 28 September 1958, Highlight sec., p. 18.
  This article reports, basically, that the Beats -
Kerouac, Allen Ginsberg, and company - are no longer in San Francisco; success has moved them into
the world they had earlier rebelled against.

559. Gutman, Walter Knowlton. The Gutman Letter. New
York: Something Else Press, 1969.
  Gutman recalls his part in the production of Pull
My Daisy and his relationship with and remembrances
of Kerouac.

559a. Hamill, Pete. "For Jack Kerouac," New York Post,
10 April 1974, p. 43.
   In this memorial piece, Hamill talks about being
in San Francisco one day and knowing that it had
once been Kerouac's town. City Lights Bookstore
is part of the tourist route although it still sells the
authors which made it famous. He nostalgically recalls his first reading of Kerouac, buying new copies
of his old books, and the awful treatment and effects
of the critics on Kerouac.

560. Harrison, Pat. "Who Really Gave Birth to the Beats?"
New York Magazine, 7 June 1976, pp. 12-13.
   This is a reply to and attack against Aaron Latham's depiction of the character of David Kammerer
from his biographical piece on Kerouac and the Beats
which appeared in an earlier issue of New York Magazine (citation 576).
   See also citation 550.

560a. Harrison, William. "Memory Babe," Moody Street
Irregulars: A Jack Kerouac Newsletter, No. 4
(1979): 11.
   Harrison describes Gerald Nicosia's upcoming biography of Kerouac, "Memory Babe," as a piece of
good research. Rather than a book written about
Kerouac, the work transforms him into a first-hand
experience and places him into recognizable cultural
contexts.
   See also citations 581c and 599.

561. Harte, Barbara, and Carolyn Riley. Contemporary
Authors, Volumes 5-8. Detroit: Gale Research
Co., 1963.
   This piece gives an overview of Kerouac; introduces him through a short biography; and gives a
listing of works, personal outlooks, and reviews by
his literary critics.

561a. Hill, Richard. "Jack Kerouac: Sad In The Sixties,"
Knight, September 1970, pp. 24-25, 85-87.
   Hill met Kerouac several months before he died.
(Jack McClintock was another. See citation 579.)
He tells of their first meeting; one of many. Hill
describes: Kerouac's various moods - sometimes
he would show his youthful enthusiasm and curiosity
when he wasn't a cranky old man; his physical health

and condition; topics of conversation - politics, writing, and old friends; and his life-style.

562. Hill, Richard. "Jack Kerouac & the strange gray myth of the west," Los Angeles Free Press, 7 August 1970, p. 36.
    Hill writes about Jack Kerouac's love/hate relationship with the West. While he records some personal reminiscences about Kerouac and other Beat literary figures, Hill takes the position that the West wore Kerouac down heavily.

562a. Holmes, John Clellon. Introduction to Heart Beat. By Carolyn Cassady. Second edition. Berkeley: Creative Arts Book Company, 1978.
    In this brief introduction, Holmes describes Kerouac, Neal and Carolyn Cassady, and Allen Ginsberg, and their relationship and mutual dependencies.

563. Holmes, John Clellon. "Three Letters: J. C. H. to J. K. (1948-1952)." In The Beat Diary, pp. 116-125. Edited by Arthur Winfield Knight and Kit Knight. California, Pennsylvania: 1977.
    The first letter: John Clellon Holmes' reactions to reading Kerouac's journals. The second: Holmes' advice to Kerouac on writing after hearing of difficulties with On The Road. The third: Holmes urges Kerouac to write a book that will put together the "Hip Generation."

564. Houston, Darrell. "A Man Named Cassady," Seattle Post-Intelligencer, 6 April 1969, Northwest Today sec., pp. 12-14.
    An article about Neal Cassady with references to Kerouac and On The Road throughout. One main theme in the piece is that although Cassady was not a writer per se, he affected the writing of the people he came in contact with, most notably: Kerouac, Allen Ginsberg, and William Burroughs.

565. Huebel, Harry Russell. "The 'Holy Goof': Neal Cassady and the Post-War American Counter Culture," Illinois Quarterly, 35, No. 4 (1973): 52-61.
    Huebel examines the life, personality, behavior and beliefs of Neal Cassady as recorded by those writers who knew him, including Kerouac. The author sees Cassady as an authentic hero and as completely representative of the counter culture.

566. Hyams, Joe. "Good-by To The Beatniks!" Boston
Sunday Herald, 28 September 1958, This Week magazine sec., pp. 4-5, 33-34. Also, San Francisco
Chronicle, 28 September 1958, This Week magazine
sec., pp. 4-5, 33-34.
        Hyams defines the Beats and the beatniks through
their language, hangouts, literature and life-style.
He conveys the feeling that the Beat generation is
dying because of the inroads of outsiders into the
movement and the success of its leaders. Kerouac
is a topic for discussion several times.

567. Isaacs, Stan. "Playing 'Baseball' With Jack Kerouac,"
Newsday (Garden City, New York), 17 February 1961,
p. 16-C.
        Isaacs describes playing a baseball card game with
Kerouac, which the latter had invented.

567a. "Jack Kerouac Reads, Etc., at Lowell," Harvard Crim-
son, 25 March 1964, p. 1.
        This short illustrated piece reports on a reading
that Kerouac gave at Harvard University. It tells of
his choice of the greatest poets and prose writers of
the 20th century. He is described as being drunk,
but coherent.
        See also citation 681.

567b. Jahoda, Gloria. "Strangers in a Strange Land." In
River of the Golden Ibis, pp. 370-382. New York:
Holt, Rinehart and Winston, 1973.
        This piece gives a brief biography of Kerouac,
but concentrates on his last years in Florida; on his
behavior, attitudes, and disillusionment; on his home
in St. Petersburg, the neighborhood, and those who
saw and visited him; and on his death and afterwards.

568. Jarvis, Charles E. Visions of Kerouac. Lowell, Massachusetts: Ithaca Press, 1974.
        Jarvis, a native of Lowell, gives a good deal of
pre-Beat background information on Kerouac which
is helpful to piecing together the Duluoz legend. A
poem by Jarvis, entitled, "Jack Kerouac Never Left
Lowell," is reprinted here from the Lowell Sun (citation 690).
        See also (other biographies) citations 541, 552,
576, and 599. See also citations 818-821.

569. Jarvis, Paul C. "Who Conceived Jack Kerouac -
      Family or America?" In Visions of Kerouac, Second
      edition, pp. 217-228. By Charles E. Jarvis. Lo-
      well, Massachusetts: Ithaca Press, 1974.
          Paul Jarvis speculates that Kerouac's devotion/
      rejection of middle working-class America is based
      on his relationship to his parents and his guilt about
      his brother's death, and his responsibility for his
      mother's well-being.

569a. Kerouac, Joan. "My Ex-Husband, Jack Kerouac, Is
      An Ingrate," Confidential, August 1961, pp. 18-19,
      53-54.
          Joan Kerouac, in this exposé, tells about her life
      with Kerouac from the time they met, through their
      marriage, and finally their separation. Jack Kerouac
      is presented as being weakwilled and undecisive,
      greatly attached to his mother, unconcerned and un-
      caring as a father, and having little work ambitions
      other than writing.

569b. "Kerouac Issue," Soundings/East (formerly Gone Soft),
      Vol. 2, No. 2 (1979): 1-96.
          This magazine is a transcription of a symposium
      on Jack Kerouac held at Salem State College (Massa-
      chusetts) in April 1973. Professor Jay McHale of
      the college's English Department brought together a
      variety of people to participate in the symposium.
      His intent was to "enlarge the scope of his course
      on Jack Kerouac and the Beat Writers by inviting
      people who had figured in the Beat movement, au-
      thors who had written biographies and scholarly works
      on Kerouac, and others who had known Kerouac in
      Lowell, Massachusetts." The symposium partici-
      pants were: Gregory Corso, Allen Ginsberg, Peter
      Orlovsky, McHale, Charles Jarvis, Aaron Latham,
      John Clellon Holmes, Stanely Twardowicz, Scotty
      Beaulieu, and Bruce Cook.
          For additional references, see Index.

570. Knight, Arthur Winfield, and Glee Knight, editors.
      The Beat Book, Volume 4: the unspeakable visions
      of the individual. California, Pennsylvania: 1974.
          This book contains letters to and from, poems by,
      and pictures of Jack Kerouac as well as many ref-
      erences to him. Also, many of Kerouac's contem-

poraries who were of or connected/sympathetic to the
Beat movement are contributors. Most material is
previously unpublished.
See also citation 822.

571. Knight, Arthur Winfield, and Kit Knight, editors. The
Beat Diary, Volume 5: the unspeakable visions of
the individual. California, Pennsylvania, 1977.
This book is very similar to the previous one
(citation 570). It contains several letters from Kerouac to John Clellon Holmes where he talks about
his and Holmes' writing and about his life which
seems crazy, dark and full of death.
See also citation 823.

572. Knight, Arthur Winfield, and Kit Knight, editors. The
Beat Journey, Volume 8: the unspeakable visions of
the individual. California, Pennsylvania: 1978.
This book is very similar to the previous two
works (citations 570 and 571). It contains letters
between Kerouac and John Clellon Holmes about their
traveling. Also, there is a letter from Kerouac to
Allen Ginsberg which discusses On The Road and
other writing projects including Kerouac's discovery
of sketching.
See also citation 824.

573. Kramer, Jane. Allen Ginsberg in America. New
York: Random House, 1969.
Kerouac is referred to throughout this biography
of Allen Ginsberg.

574. Kramer, Peter. "Kerouac Remembered Mama," Books,
July 1965, p. 2.
This interview with Kerouac's mother, Gabrielle,
describes his devotion to her and her needs.

575. Krim, Seymour, ed. The Beats. Greenwich, Connecticut: Gold Medal Books, 1960.
Krim edited a source book of Beat poetry, prose
and philosophy, and its consequent criticism. It
contains three excerpts from Visions of Cody. (This
work is listed primarily as a reference source for
reprints of articles cited elsewhere in this bibliography.)

576. Latham, Aaron. "The Columbia Murder That Gave
Birth to the Beats," New York Magazine, 19 April

1976, pp. 41-53.

Sterling Lord, Jack Kerouac's literary agent, gave Aaron Latham the rights to compile an "authorized" biography of Kerouac - which is yet unpublished. The episode printed here from that work involves the murder of Dave Kammerer by Lucien Carr: Kammerer being the self-imposing lover of Carr; Carr being a member of the Beat circle.

See also (other biographies) citations 541, 552, 568, and 599. See also citations 550, 560, and 604a-604h.

577.   Leonard, William. "In Chicago, We're Mostly Unbeat," Chicago Tribune, 9 November 1958, Magazine sec., pp. 8-9.

In this article, Leonard fairly claims that the Beats are not welcome in Chicago and are always gently prodded to move elsewhere. Kerouac is touted as a poseur, the fashionable leader of a group without any real direction.

577a. Leslie, Alfred. "'Daisy': 10 Years Later," Village Voice, 28 November 1968, p. 54.

At the beginning of this article, Leslie calls up the visage of Walter Gutman who helped finance the cost of the production of Pull My Daisy. He then refutes and makes comments on the belief - "errors of fact and conclusion" - that the film is cinéma vérité, spontaneous, or improvisational.

578.   Lipton, Lawrence. The Holy Barbarians. New York: Julian Messner, 1959.

Lipton describes Kerouac's prose style as a prose-poetic, one which is not wholly fitted to its idiom. He sees The Subterraneans as the novel in which Kerouac most closely touches the language of his time, "the authentic voice of the people." In The Dharma Bums, Lipton feels the scope of the ideas is too narrow and non-representative of the Beat movement, and that Kerouac had misrepresented the Beat movement, and that Kerouac has misrepresented the philosophy of Zen Buddhism.

579.   McClintock, Jack. "This is How the Ride Ends: Not with a bang, with a damn hernia," Esquire, March 1970, pp. 138-139, 188-189.

McClintock recounts the evenings he spent with Kerouac in St. Petersburg before his death. He felt Kerouac come alive during these visits, recalling his youth, discussing literature, and remembering old friends.

Compare to other McClintock piece, citation 640.

580. McGrady, Mike. "Jack Kerouac: Beat, Even in Northport," Newsday (Garden City, New York), 19 April 1973, p. 11. Appeared in edited form as "The 'other side' of Jack Kerouac," Chicago Sun-Times, 13 May 1973, Showcase sec., p. 14. Rpt. in Italian (citation 377).

This memorial piece includes personal reminiscences about Kerouac while he lived in Northport, New York.

581. McGrady, Mike. "Kerouac: The Northport Years," Newsday (Garden City, New York), 25 October 1969, pp. 3W-4W, 29W.

McGrady recounts how he met Kerouac and Kerouac's seemingly sad life in Northport, but his reluctance to leave it for Florida. McGrady is sympathetic and brings out Kerouac's facility with words and story-telling.

581a. McHarry, Charles. "On the Town: A Case for Kerouac," New York Daily News, 11 January 1961, p. 56.

Local personality news columnist, McHarry briefly describes the case of Joan Haverty suing Kerouac for child support. Kerouac is written as being the "darling of the unwashed."

581b. McNally, Dennis. Desolate Angel: Jack Kerouac, the Beats and America. New York: Random House, 1979.

McNally's biography of Kerouac traces him and the Beats against the historical and cultural framework (of America) in which they all lived.

See also (other biographies) citations 541, 552, 568, 576, and 599.

581c. McNally, Dennis. "The Echo of the Beat Generation in America," Newsday (Garden City, N.Y.), 2 December 1979, Ideas sec., p. 5.

In this article, which he refers to as "essentially a condensed, cleaned up version of all those interviews" (he did for the promotional tour of his Kerouac

biography, Desolate Angel), Dennis McNally places
Kerouac into the framework of American life from
the late 1950's up to the approaching 1980's.   He
sees Kerouac's On The Road (and his other work)
as containing a dream of (a past) America, an "image
of freedom," that each generation of young people
have taken to heart (since it was published in 1957):
no book seems to have been as influential in trans-
cending generations (of readers) nor continues to be
as totally relevant and timely.   Without the Beats,
perhaps America would not have been able to throw
off the yoke of spiritual, material, and social con-
formity.

581d. Mante. "Off Jack!" Reader (Chicago), 1 June 1979, p. 2.
      This letter to the editor is in response to an ar-
      ticle on Gerald Nicosia and his upcoming biography
      on Kerouac (citations 560a and 599).   The author
      feels that another biography is not needed as every-
      thing about Kerouac is in his books: anyone who
      picks one up will find the man there.

582.   Mitchner, Stuart.   "Those Phony Beatniks," Chicago
      Tribune, 8 November 1959, Magazine sec., pp. 47-
      49.
      Mitchner has contempt for the Beat generation,
      yet he loves what Kerouac is doing, likes his likes,
      and shares the vision of American tradition with
      him.   The author, rather, thinks the Beat movement
      has become faddist and has gone far afield in thinking
      and acting from its true origins and beliefs.

583.   Montgomery, John.   Jack Kerouac: A Memoir.   Fres-
      no, California: Giligia Press, 1970.
      John Montgomery, a friend of Kerouac's, having
      appeared in several of his books, in this work, con-
      jures up memories and views of Kerouac and his
      writing.

584.   Montgomery, John.   "Kerouac vs. the Professor,"
      Nation, 1 February 1958, inside front cover.
      In this letter to the editor, Montgomery defends
      Kerouac against an attack by an academician.
      See also citations 526, 596, and 601.

585.   Montgomery, John.   Kerouac West Coast: a Bohemian
      Pilot, Detailed Navigational Instructions.   Palo Alto,

California: Fels & Firn, 1976. Extracts appeared in Palantir, No. 8 (1978): 1-4; Street Magazine, 2, No. 4 (1978): 23-29; and The Limberlost Review, No. 2 (1977): 4-19.

This work is much the same as Montgomery's other work (citation 583), but expanded with more memory detail and wide-angle views of Kerouac and friends.

See also citation 825.

586. Moore, Harry T. "Enter Beatniks: The Bohème of 1960." In Garrets and Pretenders: A History of Bohemianism in America, pp. 376-395. Edited by Albert Parry. New York: Dover, 1960.

Moore, who, in this article, relies heavily on the observations of many others, does not have any praise for the Beats. He finds them more somber than the Bohemians who they seem descended from, but also not fitting the definition of Norman Mailer's hipsters. The author uses borrowed terms to call them disaffiliated, disengaged and anti-intellectual. Although he concedes a few good points to Kerouac, Moore does not see any value in his work or other Beat fiction in the future - except for sociological purposes. He continues in the same vein about Beat poetry and philosophy, and conversely, on the absence of the allied arts in the Beat community, especially music and painting.

586a. Morissette, Father Armand "Spike." "A Catholic's View of Kerouac," Moody Street Irregulars: A Jack Kerouac Newsletter, No. 5 (1979): 7-8.

Father Spike recalls his first meeting with Kerouac (in church) and his discussion on being a writer. He talks generally of Lowell's effect on Kerouac and Kerouac's effect on Lowell, his religiosity, his brother Gerard, and his birth, marriage (to Stella), death, and burial.

586b. Mungo, Raymond. Total Loss Farm: A Year in the Life. New York: E. P. Dutton, 1970.

In this combination travel book/descriptive diary, Mungo passes through Lowell, Massachusetts, on his way elsewhere, with friends, looking for other friends. He invokes Kerouac and wonders about his childhood in the mill town and his current (1968-1969) reasons for living there and not being able to really get/stay away from it.

586c. Newfield, Jack. "The Beat Generation And The Un-
Generation." In A Prophetic Minority, pp. 35-48.
New York: New American Library, 1966.
Newfield juxtaposes what he calls the "un-genera-
tion" - that generation reaching adulthood in the
1950's; a generation without positive distinguishing
characteristics to set it apart - against the Beat
generation - fully developed in the later 1950's: a
non-political, anti-social, subculture which gave
steam to the New Left of the 1960's. He also recalls and reacts to the Hunter College debate on "Is
There a Beat Generation?" which involved Kerouac,
Kingsley Amis, James Wechsler, and Ashley Montague. Newfield sees Kerouac as a less creative and
gifted writer than either Allen Ginsberg or William
Burroughs.
See also (for other Hunter College debate reports)
citations 522, 595, and 602.

586d. Nicosia, Gerald. "Kerouac's daughter: The beat goes
on," Chicago Sun-Times, 21 October 1979, Living
sec., pp. 5, 9.
In this article by Nicosia, Jan Kerouac talks about
her father, the several times she met him or spoke
with him on the telephone, and her views of him as
a writer, a human being, and a father.

586e. Norris, Hoke. "The Big Table Has Scant Menu,"
Chicago Sun-Times, 5 April 1959, sec. 3, p. 4.
Norris calls Big Table magazine and its contro-
versial first number (from the entire contents of the
suppressed Winter 1959 issue of the Chicago Review)
as an historical literary footnote. He finds the works
in the issue dull and lacking in literary distinction.
Kerouac's "Old Angel Midnight" is referred to as
being sophomoric.

587. "October Pier Reading, New York City," Moody Street
Irregulars: A Jack Kerouac Newsletter, No. 3
(1979): 12.
This brief piece describes the fourth of an annual
meeting held in New York City to honor Kerouac.
The meeting is a series of open air memorial readings.

588. O'Neil, Paul. "The Only Rebellion Around," Life,
30 November 1959, pp. 114-116, 119-120, 123-124,
126, 129-130. Rpt. in The Casebook on the Beat

(citation 590).

This article by O'Neil mainly tries to discredit the Beat generation through disparaging language and acute hyperbole. Kerouac is seen as Columbia University's former disillusioned, small-town football star who dropped out, bummed around the country, and wrote down anything that came into his head and called it literature. O'Neil treats the other major Beat figures and the entire movement similarly, including mixing and equating Beats and beatniks.

589. "On the Road Revisited," AMERICA: The Datsun Student Travel Guide 1974, pp. 4-6.

This article is a light history of cross-country traveling and mentions Kerouac's travels as the type for the 1960's.

590. Parkinson, Thomas, ed. A Casebook on the Beat. New York: Crowell, 1961.

Parkinson edited a source book of Beat prose and poetry, and its consequent commentary and criticism. It contains five pieces by Kerouac. (Listed primarily as a reference source for reprints of articles cited elsewhere in this bibliography.)

590a. Plummer, William. "Jack Kerouac: The Beat Goes On," New York Times Magazine, 30 December 1979, pp. 18-23, 39-41, 44.

Plummer looks at the current interest in Kerouac and his relationship to his times, his literary importance and influence on the novel, and his meteoric, mythic, yet tradition-based life, from birth to death.

591. Rigney, Francis J., and L. Douglas Smith. The Real Bohemia: A Sociological and Psychological Study of the "Beats." New York: Basic Books, 1961.

The authors, in this study, examine the Beats from both the sociological and psychological points of view. Kerouac is referred to throughout the work.

591a. Ross, Andrew M. "Crisis: The Personal Versus the Social," Moody Street Irregulars: A Jack Kerouac Newsletter, No. 4 (1979): 4-6.

Ross believes that Kerouac's life was one long tragedy - culminating in a series of personal disasters - because he was unable to feel comfortable with either himself or society. He could not find a balance between fulfilling his dreams and functioning in society and communicating with people; between achieving inner peace and happiness while remaining an individual. Ross goes on to support his claims through an analysis of Big Sur.

592. Saijo, Albert. "A Recollection." In Trip Trap: Haiku along the Road from San Francisco to New York 1959, pp. 1-13. By Jack Kerouac, Albert Saijo, and Lew Welch. Bolinas, California: Grey Fox Press, 1973.
Saijo recalls his trip cross-country with Kerouac and Lew Welch in 1959. He describes Kerouac's behavior, his house in Northport, and his mother. He also talks about Welch and his Willys jeep.

593. Saroyan, Aram. Genesis Angels: The Saga of Lew Welch and the Beat Generation. New York: William Morrow & Co., 1979.
Although primarily about poet Lew Welch, almost one-third of this work deals with Kerouac's life. See also citation 826.

594. Schaap, Dick. "The pre-hippie hippie pulls off the road," Chicago Sun-Times, 4 February 1968, Book Week sec., p. 2.
In this sketch, Schaap touts Kerouac's denunciation about being a beatnik and his conservative politics.

595. Schleifer, Marc D. "THE BEAT DEBATED - IS IT OR IS IT NOT?" In The Village Voice Reader, pp. 238-240. Edited by Daniel Wolf and Edwin Fancher. New York: Grove Press, 1963. Appeared originally in Village Voice, 19 November 1958, pp. 1, 3.
Kerouac, in this excerpted coverage of a debate he and several other people participated in, is edited down to defining and defending the Beat generation in one hundred words or less. See also citations 522, 586c, and 602.

595a. Shepard, Sam. Rolling Thunder Logbook. New York: Penguin, 1978.
Shepard, in this travelogue of Bob Dylan's Fall 1975 concert tour of New England, has sections dealing with the Lowell, Massachusetts, stay. He mentions visiting Nick's Lounge - owned by Kerouac's brother-in-law (although at a different time than Sloman's visit: citation 595b), the filming of Dylan and Allen Ginsberg at Kerouac's grave, and other Lowell/Kerouac images.

595b. Sloman, Larry. On the Road With Bob Dylan; Rolling
      With the Thunder. New York: Bantam, 1978.
          Sloman followed Bob Dylan (and company) - as a
      reporter for Rolling Stone - during his Fall 1975
      concert tour of New England. He reports about Dyl-
      an's concert and stay in Lowell, Massachusetts, which
      included the filming of Dylan and Allen Ginsberg at
      Kerouac's grave. Later, accompanied by a friend,
      Sloman visits the bar owned by Nicky Sampas, Ker-
      ouac's brother-in-law, and Nicky tells them about
      Kerouac's last years in Lowell, his drinking, and
      other adventures.
          See also citation 595a.

596. Smith, Howard. "Jack Kerouac: OFF THE ROAD,
      INTO THE VANGUARD, AND OUT. " In The Village
      Voice Reader, pp. 236-238. Edited by Daniel Wolf
      and Edwin Fancher. New York: Grove Press, 1963.
      Appeared originally in Village Voice, 25 December
      1959, pp. 1-2.
          This short piece is a description of a reading by
      Kerouac in New York City at the Village Vanguard
      to an enthusiastic audience.
          See also citations 526, 584, and 601.

597. Sobol, Louis. "Kerouac Protests Legend, " New York
      Journal-American, 8 December 1960, p. 25.
          Kerouac resents and replies to the legend built up
      about him being the "King of the Beats" or a beatnik
      at all. He wants to be seen only as a serious writer.

598. "Straight Arrow Rushing Biography of Jack Kerouac, "
      Publishers Weekly, 8 January 1973, p. 55.
          Advance notice of Ann Charters' biography of Ker-
      ouac but mentions another biography-in-progress by
      Aaron Latham, also to be published soon.
          See also citation 541.

598a. Stuhlmann, Gunther, editor. The Diary of Anaïs Nin:
      1955-1966. New York: Harcourt Brace Jovanovich,
      c1976, 1977.
          In her diary, Nin refers to Kerouac more than
      several times. She recounts a meeting between the
      two of them: Kerouac is drunk when he arrives and
      insists on listening to one of his own recordings in-
      stead of speaking himself.

598b. Tallmer, Jerry. Introduction to Pull My Daisy. New
York: Grove Press, 1959.
   Tallmer says that Pull My Daisy is a "pure" film
that shows people (he knows) doing the things they
do. It is spontaneous in that the camera moves or
flicks around the room (around the group of people)
like an eye does. He also goes into the background
of the shooting of the movie and Kerouac's narration
of it.

599. Tesser, Neil. "Searching for Kerouac," Reader (Chicago), 6 April 1979, sec. 1, p. 4.
   An article/interview with Gerald Nicosia and his
biography-in-progress on Kerouac.
   See also (other biographies) citations 541, 552,
568, and 576. See also citations 560a and 581d.

599a. "Time erases silence on marriage to writer," Milwaukee Sentinel, 21 August 1979, pt. 1, p. 3.
   This piece says that Frankie Parker has begun to
talk about her marriage with Kerouac. It also gives
a capsulation of their relationship.
   See also citation 547a.

600. Vickers, Larry. "Jack Kerouac: End of the Road,"
Father Joe's Handy Homilies, 1, No. 2 (1970): 1,
4-5.
   This memorial piece about Kerouac concentrates
on his final, lonely years. The author was a student
in Florida and his remembrances bring out Kerouac's
heavy drinking and boasting attitudes.

601. Wakefield, Dan. "Night Clubs," Nation, 4 January
1958, pp. 19-20.
   This article is a review of a reading by Kerouac
at the Village Vanguard in New York City in 1958.
   See also citations 526, 584, and 596.

602. Wechsler, James A. "The Age of Unthink." In Reflections of an Angry Middle-Aged Editor, pp. 3-18.
New York: Random House, 1960.
   Wechsler's remembrances on a symposium held
at Hunter College in 1958 with himself, Kingsley
Amis, Kerouac, and Ashley Montagu in attendance
as speakers. Kerouac's physical condition is recalled, his reading of a poem to Harpo Marx, and
his antagonistic attitude toward Wechsler.
   See also citations 522, 586c, and 595.

603. Wechter, Jayson. "Jack Kerouac, The Quest for Experience," Statesman, 12 February 1975, Take Two sec., pp. 2-3.

   Wechter, in this article for the Statesman, the student newspaper of the State University of New York at Stony Brook, gives a general overview of the concepts to be found in Kerouac's writing - the hopes and fears, dreams and observations of a man whose life was reflected in his work and who allowed his work the spontaneity found in his life.

603a. Weinberg, Jeffrey H. "Between the Glories," Moody Street Irregulars: A Jack Kerouac Newsletter, No. 4 (1979): 3.

   Weinberg recalls reading about Kerouac's high school football days in old issues of the Lowell Sun (on microfilm in the city library's basement). He says Kerouac's old friends lost touch with him after he left Lowell and dropped from football; they couldn't understand his changed behavior or his drinking when he visited town. Weinberg talked with Vinny Bergerac, one old buddy, who remembered a young Kerouac, before he left Lowell, still with dreams of football.

604. Woolfson, Peter. "The French-Canadian Heritage of Jack Kerouac As Seen In His Autobiographical Works," Revue De Louisiane/Louisiana Review, 5, No. 1 (1976): 35-43.

   Woolfson describes a number of strong value orientations in Kerouac's writing which are seen as being present as a result of his French-Canadian origins.

   The following eight articles from the New York Times document the events surrounding and the outcome of Lucien Carr's slaying of David Kammerer. The articles have been placed in chronological order. Those mentioning Kerouac have been asterisked. For a literary retelling of the incident, see citation 576.

*604a. Adams, Frank S. "Columbia Student Kills Friend And Sinks Body in Hudson River," 17 August 1944, pp. 1, 13.

   This article details the circumstances of the homicide. Kerouac is briefly mentioned at the end of the piece.   He was taken into custody and booked as a material witness although his connection to the case is not discussed.

604b. "Kammerer's Parents Prominent, " 17 August 1944, p. 13.
This short piece gives background information on David Kammerer and his parents.

*604c. "Student Is Silent On Slaying Friend, " 18 August 1944, p. 14.
Kerouac is mentioned as being held on a $5,000 bond for helping Carr bury Kammerer's eyeglasses. He asks for a reduced bond but the court denies the request.

*604d. "Student Is Indicted In 2d-Degree Murder, " 25 August 1944, p. 15.
Kerouac is escorted by the police to the municipal building where they witness his marriage to Edith Parker.   He is then taken back to the Bronx prison.

*604e. "Witness in Slaying Case Freed, " 31 August 1944, p. 19.
Kerouac is freed from jail on a reduced, $2,500 bond.

604f. "Guilty Plea Made By Carr In Slaying, " 16 September 1944, p. 15.
Carr pleads first-degree manslaughter.   The defense declares that he was emotionally unstable at the time of the homicide (because of Kammerer's homosexual advances).   Carr could be sentenced from 10-20 years.

604g. "Student Slayer Sent To The Reformatory, " 7 October 1944, p. 15.
This piece tells of Carr's sentencing to a reformatory rather than to prison.

604h. "Young Slayer Goes to Elmira, " 10 October 1944, p. 38.
Carr goes to the reformatory.

C.   MASTER'S THESES AND DOCTORAL
DISSERTATIONS

605.   Ball, Vernon Francis.   "Of Glory Obscur'd: Beatific
Vision in the Narratives of Jack Kerouac," Disserta-
tion Abstracts International, 38 (1977), 258A (Ball
State University).
This dissertation studies thirteen of Kerouac's
novels as individual steps in the quest of the hero,
Jack Duluoz, toward self-discovery and the beatific
vision.

606.   Bingham, Irwin D.   "Jack Kerouac: The Odyssey of
Existential Man."   Master's thesis, University of
Oklahoma, 1966.
Bingham sees Kououac as essentially existential,
as looking up from the bottom of his personality and
seeing nothingness - a vast void which must be dealt
with, and death.   With this in mind, he then examines
Kerouac as a myth-maker, a wanderer, a mystic,
and an artist.

607.   Cane, Suzanne.   "The Duluoz Legend: The Zen Influence on Jack Kerouac."   Master's thesis, Brooklyn
College, 1965.
This master's thesis discusses in detail the influences of Zen Buddhism on Kerouac's Duluoz legend.   The author feels that the Zen influence may
be periphery - as in On The Road - or it may be
pervasive - as in The Dharma Bums, which is spoken
of as "almost a literary photograph of the Zen community in action."

608.   Cunningham, Teresa.   "Jack Kerouac's Spontaneous
Prose, An Analysis and Evaluation of Three Novels."
Master's thesis, University of Delaware, 1972.

609.   Feied, Frederick J.   "The Hobo in the Works of Jack
London, John Dos Passos and Jack Kerouac."   Master's thesis, Columbia University, 1961.
In this thesis, Feied avoids a sociological approach
to the hobo.   He sees Kerouac's treatment as more
symbolic than economic: the characters in his books
took to the road as a form of protest against society
and as a means of searching for the values and beliefs that they gravitated toward.
See also citations 417, 441, 491, and 515.

609a. Gargan, William. "Jack Kerouac: the Individual and the Open Road." Master's thesis, Columbia University, 1973.

Using three of Kerouac's works - The Town And The City, On The Road, and The Dharma Bums - Gargan examines the theme of the "individual who seeks the promise of the American dream, but who constantly finds a disparity between the ideal and the reality."

610. Gebhardt, Eike. "Strategic Anomie and Contingent Valuation: Three Writers of Non-Political Dissent," Dissertation Abstracts International, 34 (1974), 7190A (Yale University).

This dissertation investigates the psychological ramifications of "non-political dissent" in the works of Kerouac, William Burroughs and Lawrence Ferlinghetti.

611. Hudson, Lee. "Beat Generation Poetics And The Oral Tradition of Literature," Dissertation Abstracts International, 34 (1973), 2800A (University of Texas at Austin).

Hudson's theme is the examination of the claim that the Beat writers represent a return to an oral tradition of literature. Allen Ginsberg's "Howl" is considered as a prime example. Kerouac is not mentioned in the abstract.

612. Huebel, Harry Russell, Jr. "The Beat Generation and the Bohemian-Left Tradition in America." Dissertation Abstracts International, 31 (1971), 4087A (Washington State University).

This history dissertation stresses the political ramifications of the Beat writers. The author draws a distinction between the Beats and the bohemian left because the Beats "failed" to believe in political mobilization.

613. Hunt, Timothy Arthur. "Off the Road: the Literary Maturation of Jack Kerouac." Dissertation Abstracts International, 36 (1975), 2821A (Cornell University). Appeared in shortened and revised form as "The Composition of On The Road." In Jack Kerouac, On The Road: Text and Criticism (citation 438).

This literary dissertation compares/contrasts the five original versions of On The Road which led to the published work. This novel is then compared extensively to Visions of Cody, a novel in which Hunt feels Kerouac defined and made coherent the concerns of On The Road.

614. Jagger, William Grant, Jr. "The War of the Gods: Orgy and Community in Kerouac's Beat America." Dissertation Abstracts International, 31 (1970), 3057A (Emory University).
 This dissertation is both social and religious in scope and explores the Beat's wish "to overcome the anomic" modern world and to find a mystical community. Kerouac's works are the main focus of this study.

615. Johnson, Russell H. "Jack Kerouac, An American Romantic." Master's thesis, Wagner College, 1971.

616. Jones, Granville H. "Walt Whitman, Thomas Wolfe and Jack Kerouac: Common Origins and Common Aims." Master's thesis, Columbia University, 1969.
 This master's thesis hypothesizes that the common bond between Whitman, Wolfe and Kerouac is their interest and acute awareness in the democratic environment of America. The author ascribes each figure as a representative of his times in his devotion to democratic ideals.

616a. Kastin, David. "A Study of Religion in Four Novels by Jack Kerouac: On the Road, Dharma Bums, Visions of Gerard, and Big Sur." Master's thesis, Brooklyn College, 1972.
 Kastin believes that the one serious element of Kerouac's writing, the religious, has been treated with shallowness and superficiality. The goal of this thesis is to sort out the various streams of religious thought which merge in Kerouac's work, such as the synthesis of Christ and Buddha.

617. Krupat, Arnold. "The Saintly Hero: A Study of On The Road and Henderson the Rain King." Master's thesis, Columbia University, 1964.

618. Krupat, Arnold. "The Saintly Hero: A Study of the Hero in Some Contemporary American Novels." Dissertation Abstracts International, 28 (1967), 2251-A (Columbia University). Excerpted as "Dean Moriarty

as Saintly Hero. " In Jack Kerouac, On The Road: Text and Criticism (citation 438).

Some of Kerouac's works are studied in this dissertation on the evolution of the saintly hero in contemporary American fiction. The saintly hero is characterized primarily by his religious temperament and his actions which are both fantastic and grotesque.

619. Lemire, Bernice M. "Jack Kerouac: Early Influences. " Master's thesis, Boston College, 1963.

This thesis deals not with literary influences on Kerouac, but with those of his family, friends and school teachers.

620. Rao, Vimala C. "Oriental Influence On The Writings Of Jack Kerouac, Allen Ginsberg, and Gary Snyder. " Dissertation Abstracts International, 35 (1975), 6677A-6678A (University of Wisconsin - Milwaukee).

The oriental influence in Kerouac's writing is seen in his embracing of Buddhism in order to synthesize a personal faith - he called himself a Catholic Buddhist - and to seek a philosophy that would show him the happiness in life - the beatific vision.

621. Roundy, Peter Edward. "Recurring Motifs In Three Novels By Jack Kerouac. " Masters Abstracts, 15 (1977), 39 (Florida Atlantic University).

Roundy examines the journey motif and its various permutations of "road" imagery, where much of the action takes place, in three of Kerouac's books: On The Road (America's highways), The Subterraneans (city streets and alleyways), and The Dharma Bums (mountain trails).

622. Schwartz, Marilyn Merritt. "From Beat To Beatific: Religious Ideas In The Writings Of Kerouac, Ginsberg, and Corso. " Dissertation Abstracts International, 37 (1977), 5833-A (University of California, Davis).

Schwartz first studies the development of the Beats from a post-War disorientation to their beatific/ religious vision. Then she examines their influence in the San Francisco Bay area's literary scene. Individually, she shows how Kerouac - because of his shattered hopes in America - uses his experiences in his works to restructure society into one that has potential.

623. Skau, Michael Walter. "Jack Kerouac." In "Themes
     And Movements In The Literature Of The Beats,"
     pp. 17-70. Dissertation Abstracts International, 34
     (1974), 5995A (University of Illinois at Urbana-
     Champaign).
         This dissertation is a detailed literary survey of
     the works of Kerouac, William Burroughs, Lawrence
     Ferlinghetti, Gregory Corso and Allen Ginsberg.

623a. Sterne, Elaine Mary. "The Conservative Response
     Amidst Decades of Change: Jack Kerouac and William
     Saroyan," Dissertation Abstracts International, 37
     (1977), 7755-A (Saint Louis University).
         This study compares the works of Kerouac and
     William Saroyan in terms of their "manifest conser-
     vatism" and "political tendencies" rather than simply
     an analysis of their styles. Factors which can be
     used as indicators of the degree of conservatism -
     such as anti-intellectualism, rugged individualism,
     patriotism, and continuity - are analyzed. These
     are related to the social values prevalent at the time
     when both these authors lived.

624. Williams, Bruce Keith. "The Shrouded Traveler On
     The Road: Death And The Work Of Jack Kerouac."
     Dissertation Abstracts International, 38 (1977), 2132-A
     (Claremont Graduate School).
         Williams, in his dissertation, examines the the-
     matic unity of death that is present in Kerouac's
     works. Kerouac was neither fearful nor attracted
     to death, but rather acknowledged its presence re-
     peatedly and developed responses to try to deal with
     it. Kerouac is seen as a major influence and helped
     to revive the traditions of American Romanticism.

         D. INTERVIEWS WITH KEROUAC AND
             THOSE WHO KNEW HIM

(For additional articles related to this section, see also
Section G, Part II.)

625. Altman, Peter. "His Generation Was Backed Against
     the Wall," Books, May 1965, p. 7.
         This article is about John Clellon Holmes - one
     of the Beat writers. He defines the Beat generation

and talks about his writing. His style is compared/
paralleled to Kerouac's throughout the piece.

625a.   Ardinger, Richard; Ardinger, Rosemary Powers; and
        Morency, Judy, interviewers. "An Interview With
        Carolyn Cassady," Palantir, No. 10 (1978): 17-24.
        Rpt. from The Limberlost Review, No. 3 (1977):
        42-51.
            In this interview, Carolyn Cassady responds to
        questions about her relationship to both Kerouac and
        Neal Cassady, their effect on each other, some of
        Kerouac's ideas and attitudes, Ann Charters' biog-
        raphy of Kerouac, her own writing - Heart Beat
        and "The Third Word," others' writings on the Beats
        and Kerouac, and her future.

625b.   Baizer, Eric; Divad, Reywas; and Peabody, Richard,
        Jr., interviewers. "An Interview With Allen Gins-
        berg," Gargoyle, No. 10 (1978): 2-5.
            Ginsberg talks about Kerouac's importance as a
        prose writer, his influences and theories of writing,
        and how critics and publishing companies treated
        him. He also speaks on Kerouac's extant materials
        and Ann Charters' biography as well as Charles
        Jarvis'.

626.   Bellamy, Joe David. "Jack Kerouac's Last Years:
        An Interview with Robert Boles," Falcon, No. 1
        (1970): 5-9.
            Boles remembers Kerouac not only as being a
        great drinker, but also as a kind, open and honest
        man; a spontaneous individual who could not control
        the happenings he created; a person difficult to tol-
        erate unless you knew him.

627.   Berrigan, Ted. "The Art of Fiction LXI: Jack Ker-
        ouac," Paris Review, 11, No. 43 (1968): 60-105.
        Rpt. in Writers at Work, The Paris Review Inter-
        views, Fourth Series, pp. 360-395. Edited by
        George Plimpton. New York: Penguin, 1977. Also
        reprinted in Jack Kerouac, On The Road: Text and
        Criticism (citation 438).
            Berrigan interviews Kerouac in his Lowell, Massa-
        chusetts, home. Kerouac talks about his prose style,
        writing poetry - especially haikus, and spontaneous
        prose. He also speaks on the writing of the other
        Beats, influences on his own writing, and the early
        days of Beat-dom.
            See also citation 633.

627a. Bockris, Victor. "William Burroughs," High Times:
The Magazine of High Society, No. 42 (1979): 42-
45, 47, 49.
   At one point in this interview Burroughs responds
to questions about Kerouac's influence on him, Kerouac's role as a writer, and the last time he saw
Kerouac.

628. Brouillette, Paul. "Interview with Joseph Chaput,"
Moody Street Irregulars: A Jack Kerouac Newsletter,
No. 3 (1979): 8-9.
   In this interview, Chaput, a friend of Kerouac's
during his last four years, responds to diverse ques-
tions about Kerouac from Brouillette.
   See also citation 655a.

628a. Byers, William. "I Call On Jack Kerouac," Last
Word, Spring 1960, pp. 4-5, 32-33.
   This general and brief interview, published in the
Northport (New York) High School magazine, is preceded by a description of the things which happened
before the interviewer and Kerouac finally settled
down to their formal question and answer session.

629. Clark, Roy Peter. "Kerouac: Another Generation
Picks Up the Beat," St. Petersburg Times, 29 October 1978, p. 1-G.
   Clark brings together more last impressions of
Kerouac by two local St. Petersburg writers - Jack
McClintock and Richard Hill - who interviewed and
visited him regularly, and who were some of the
last ones to see him alive. He notes the sounds of
America in Kerouac's work, the recent renewed interest in him, and that, in the end, Kerouac abandoned his past and fittingly settled down to a life of
lonely respectability with his wife and mother and
booze in St. Petersburg, a town where so many come
to die.

629a. Clark, Thomas, interviewer. "Allen Ginsberg; An In-
terview: The Art of Poetry VIII," Paris Review,
No. 37 (1966): 12-55. Rpt. in Writers at Work:
The Paris Review Interviews, Third Series, pp. 279-
320. Edited by George Plimpton. New York: Vi-
king Press, 1967. Also rpt. in The Radical Vision:
Essays for the Seventies, pp. 129-165. Edited by
Leo Hamalian and Frederick R. Karl. New York:
Thomas Y. Crowell Co., 1970.

Kerouac is referred to at the beginning and end of this craft interview with Allen Ginsberg. He recalls Kerouac's encouragement to William Burroughs to write, Kerouac's discovery that the subject of his writing was what people actually said to each other, Kerouac's long prose line, and Kerouac being the best poet in the U.S. because he was the most free and spontaneous and a master of the haiku.

630. Clarke, Gerald. "Checking in with Allen Ginsberg: Notes in passing on life-in-progress," Esquire, April 1973, pp. 92-95, 168, 170.
    In this interview, Ginsberg speaks on Kerouac as a lover, on his portrait as Carlo Marx in On The Road, and on his last attempt to see Kerouac before he died.

631. Colbert, Alison. "A Talk with Allen Ginsberg," Partisan Review, 38 (1971): 289-309.
    Over the course of this interview, Ginsberg refers to Kerouac several times: first, in reference to Kerouac's seeing/hearing/writing new rhythms in poetry as a result of his listening to bop music; second, about Kerouac as the great unacknowledged poet; and third, about Kerouac's Buddhist studies and writing.

632. Duncan, Val. "Life With The Beat Bard: Some Nights He Writes," Chicago Daily News, 12 December 1964, Panorama sec., p. 6.
    This is a description of an interview stressing Kerouac's personal idiosyncrasies and his writing habits.

632a. Duncan, Val. "What Is the Beat Generation, Part Two," Newsday (Garden City, New York), 4 August 1959, p. 15c.
    In this second part of a five-part series on the Beats, Duncan intertwines dialogue from a Kerouac interview with descriptions in his books (which are called the "documentation of a disaffiliate").

633. Ehrlich, Rosanne, Ron Kostar, and Zack Rogow, interviewers. "An Interview With Ted Berrigan," City 6, Fall 1977, pp. 78-92.
    During the course of this interview, Berrigan recalls the circumstances of his interview with Kerouac for the Paris Review (citation 627).

634. "Excerpts From An Interview With Jack Kerouac (1964)," Street Magazine, 1, No. 4 (1975): n. pag.

   In this interview, Kerouac speaks on whatever subject or aside the interviewers direct at him. The most sustained topic is Kerouac's travels through France in 1957.

   For a complete transcript of this interview see citations 647, 648 and 649.

635. Ginsberg, Allen. "Craft Interview With Allen Ginsberg," New York Quarterly, No. 6 (1971): 12-40.

   Ginsberg talks about the craft of writing poetry. He recalls the influence of Kerouac's work and theories of writing on his own work. Ginsberg feels that Kerouac has much craft in his work but people just cannot/do not want to see it.

636. Ginsberg, Allen, and Allen Young. Gay Sunshine Interview. Bolinas, California: Grey Fox Press, 1974.

   Appeared earlier in various forms: first, as "Ginsberg," Gay Sunshine, January-February 1973, pp. 1, 4-10; and second, as "The Life and Loves of Allen Ginsberg," The Real Paper, 28 March 1973, pp. 8-12, 14.

   At the beginning of this interview, Ginsberg talks about Kerouac's writing and personality, and about his sexual relationship with Kerouac.

637. Goodman, Richard, Jr. "An Evening With William Burroughs," Michigan Quarterly Review, 13, No. 1 (1974): 18-24.

   In this interview, when asked about Kerouac, Burroughs talks about the last times he saw him.

638. "He Scorns 'Beatniks,'" Detroit News, 24 August 1958, p. A-2.

   In this interview, Kerouac denounces juvenile delinquency, explains how he coined the term "Beat," and talks about rock and roll and baseball.

638a. Holmes, John Clellon. Personal interview conducted (in Old Saybrook, Connecticut) for the Oral History Research Office of Columbia University by William Gargan. 28 March 1976.

   Kerouac and his work are referred to throughout Holmes' memoir of the Beat movement and his involvement in it.

639.   "'I Simply Plan a Completely Written Lifetime,'" <u>Chic-</u>
       <u>ago Daily News</u>, 24 August 1963, Panorama sec.,
       p. 8.   Rpt. as "'Visions' in the Kerouac Tale." In
       <u>San Francisco Chronicle</u>, 8 September 1963, This
       <u>World</u> magazine sec., p. 28.
           In this interview, Kerouac introduces and answers
       questions about <u>Visions of Gerard</u>.

639a. Kostakis, Peter, and Art Lange, interviewers.   "Inter-
       view With Paul Carroll," <u>Brilliant Corners: a maga-</u>
       <u>zine of the arts</u>, No. 6 (1977):   41-58.
           In this interview, Paul Carroll talks about the
       birth, life, and death of <u>Big Table</u>.   Kerouac is re-
       ferred to throughout, especially his naming of the
       magazine.

640.   McClintock, Jack.   "Jack Kerouac Is On The Road No
       More," <u>St. Petersburg Times</u>, 12 October 1969,
       Floridian sec., pp. 4, 6-10.   An edited version ap-
       pears as "Jack Kerouac Is Alive and Not-So-Well in
       St. Petersburg," <u>Miami Herald</u>, 12 October 1969,
       Tropic Magazine sec., pp. 8-10.
           This interview with Kerouac shows the Beat writer
       lonely and drunk.   (It appeared only 10 days before
       his death.)

641.   McDonald, Gregory.   "Off The Road...the Celtic twi-
       light of Jack Kerouac," <u>Boston Sunday Globe</u>, 11
       August 1968, Globe sec., pp. 8, 11-12, 14, 16, 18.
           This interview finds Kerouac drunk and lonely in
       Hyannis with his wife and mother.   Kerouac speaks
       about his love of America and his disillusionment
       with the way it is treating him.

642.   McKenzie, James.   "An Interview With Allen Ginsberg."
       In The Beat Journey, pp. 2-45.   Edited by Arthur
       Winfield Knight and Kit Knight.   California, Pennsyl-
       vania: 1978.
           During the course of this interview, Ginsberg
       speaks about Kerouac's characterizations of himself,
       Neal Cassady and the other Beats.   He reviews
       Charters' biography of Kerouac and notes the errors
       dealing with <u>On The Road</u> which included troubles
       with the paraphrasing of Kerouac's letters because
       permission was not granted to reprint them.   Ker-
       ouac's influence by Neal Cassady is mentioned and
       his subsequent writing of <u>Visions of Cody</u>.   Plus
       other references to Kerouac throughout.

643. McKenzie, James, and Robert King. "'I'm Poor Simple Human Bones' - An Interview with Gregory Corso." In The Beat Diary, pp. 4-24. Edited by Arthur Winfield Knight and Kit Knight. California, Pennsylvania: 1977.
    During the course of this interview, Corso talks about Kerouac's fiction, personal life, and alleged homosexuality.

644. Meltzer, David, ed. The San Francisco Poets. New York: Ballantine, 1971.
    This work consists of interviews with six San Francisco poets plus examples of their work. In their interviews, Lawrence Ferlinghetti recalls an attempt by Henry Miller to meet Kerouac; Kenneth Rexroth briefly remembers a jazz-poetry reading with Kerouac present; and Michael McClure tells of a vision he had of Kerouac after his death.

645. "On the Road Back: How the Beat Generation Got That Way, According to Its Seer," San Francisco Examiner, 5 October 1958, Highlight sec., p. 18.
    In this short interview, Kerouac answers questions about the Beat generation and about the importance of San Francisco to its growth.

646. Robinson, Mark. Ginsberg's Improvised Poetics. Buffalo, New York: Anonym Press, 1971.
    In this interview formated book, Ginsberg, at one point, discusses Kerouac's development of and theory of spontaneous writing and how it affected his own writing.

647. Scesny, Diana, ed. "Jack Kerouac At Northport," Athanor, 1, No. 1 (1971): 1-17.

648. Scesny, Diana, ed. "Jack Kerouac At Northport, Part 2," Athanor, 1, No. 2 (1971): 1-15.

649. Scesny, Diana, ed. "Jack Kerouac At Northport, Part 3," Athanor, 1, No. 3 (1972): 1-24.
    The previous three articles (citations 647, 648 and 649) are the various parts of a loosely organized, highly informal and unstructured, and generally drunken interview with Kerouac while he was living in Northport, New York. In part 1, Kerouac discusses painting and writing; in part 2, his family history

and writing; and in part 3, Kerouac discusses his traveling in Europe, Northport, the Beats, writers, religion, belief and God.

For an excerpt of this interview, see citation 634.

650. Sinclair, Iain. "Ginsberg: the 'kodak mantra diaries'; Allen Ginsberg's London Summer, " Second Aeon, No. 14 (n. d.): 86-93.

In this interview, Ginsberg speaks somewhat on the subject of drugs and its relation to awareness. The Beats used drugs but their breakthrough in thought came naturally rather than being induced. Ginsberg says that Kerouac took drugs but achieved greater visions through his Buddhist meditations.

651. Tallmer, Jerry. "Jack Kerouac: Back to the Village - but Still on the Road. " In The Village Voice Reader, pp. 32-34. Edited by Daniel Wolf and Edwin Fancher. New York: Grove Press, 1963. Appeared originally in Village Voice, 18 September 1957, pp. 1, 4.

Kerouac is back in New York after being abroad and is being interviewed by Tallmer. He talks about a television interview, his sudden recognition, and his disillusionment with it all.

652. Tytell, John. "An Interview with Carl Solomon. " In The Beat Book, pp. 163-171. Edited by Arthur Winfield Knight and Glee Knight. California, Pennsylvania: 1974.

Carl Solomon used to work for his uncle, A. A. Wyn, the publisher of Ace Books. During the course of the interview, Solomon mentions the house's abortive plan to publish Kerouac's On The Road.

653. Tytell, John. "An Interview with Herbert Huncke, " the unspeakable visions of the individual, 3, Nos. 1 & 2 (1973): 3-15. Edited by Arthur Winfield Knight and Glee Knight. California, Pennsylvania: 1973.

In this interview, Huncke talks about his impressions of the Beat scene and the Beats: Ginsberg, Burroughs, Cassady and Kerouac. Kerouac is treated only briefly. Huncke, however, corroborates Burroughs' story of Kerouac not visiting Burroughs' Texas ranch (citation 536).

654. Tytell, John. "An Interview with John Clellon Holmes."
In The Beat Book, pp. 37-52. Edited by Arthur
Winfield Knight and Glee Knight. California, Pennsylvania: 1974.
    In this interview, Holmes talks about Kerouac's
life and works as well as some of the other Beats
and the Beat movement.

655. Wallace, Mike. "Mike Wallace Asks Jack Kerouac -
What Is the Beat Generation?" New York Post, 21
January 1958, p. 16. Rpt. in the Lowell Sun (citation 669).
    In this interview, Kerouac flippantly presents the
mysticism and religion of the Beat generation.

655a. Walsh, Joy. "Chaput," Moody Street Irregulars: A
Jack Kerouac Newsletter, No. 5 (1979): 2.
    Walsh brings out some discrepancies that turned
up in an interview with Joseph Chaput, a Lowell
friend of Kerouac's in the mid-1960's, by Paul
Brouillette (citation 628) (which appeared in an earlier issue of Moody Street Irregulars).

656. Wechter, Jayson. "Jack in Northport; a View from
Main Street," Statesman, 12 February 1975, Take
Two sec., pp. 3-4.
    In this interview with Stanley Twardowicz for the
Statesman, the student newspaper of the State Univer-
sity of New York at Stony Brook, he recalls his
friendship with Kerouac and his impressions of the
Beat writer.

E. ARTICLES AND RELATED PIECES ON
KEROUAC'S COMMERCIAL RECORDINGS

(See also citation 520.)

657. Aronowitz, Alfred G. "Jack Kerouac: 'It's Not at
All Dirty,'" New York Post, 26 March 1959, p. 8.
    Kerouac says that a record of him reading his
prose and poetry, with Steve Allen playing piano in
the background, is not dirty but sweet. The president of Dot Records decided to withdraw the recording
from circulation because he "wouldn't want [his]
children to hear it."

657a. Blackburn, Paul. "Writing for the ear," Big Table, No. 4 (1960): 127-132.

In this review of five albums of poetry, Kerouac's "Poetry for the Beat Generation" and "Blues & Haikus" are described by Blackburn as being "pleasant and lively" and "interesting, but short of being anyone's artistic triumph."

658. Hendricks, Alfred D. "The Kerouac and Allen Record: They Weren't Beat - They Won," New York Post, 3 June 1959, p. 75.

"Poetry for the Beat Generation," a combined effort at jazz-poetry by Kerouac and Steve Allen - on piano - is reissued on a different label after being recalled by its original producer.

658a. Millstein, Gilbert. Liner notes to Blues and Haikus, by Jack Kerouac, featuring Al Cohn and Zoot Sims. 1 phonodisc, 33-1/3 rpm. Hanover HML 5006, n. d.

Millstein talks about the recording session with Kerouac reading his poetry to the accompaniment of Zoot Sims and Al Cohn. He also quotes Kerouac on the musicians, whom he asked to perform, and his feeling for them as well as an explanation of the American haiku.

658b. Millstein, Gilbert. Liner notes to Poetry For the Beat Generation, by Jack Kerouac and Steve Allen. 1 phonodisc, 33-1/3 rpm. Dot 3154, n. d.

These liner notes give an introduction to Kerouac and tell about the first meeting between him and Steve Allen - set-up spontaneously by Millstein - at the Village Vanguard and their subsequent recording session as well as Kerouac's account of it. After the album was removed from circulation by Dot and reissued on another record label, Millstein again wrote the liner notes (citation 659).

659. Millstein, Gilbert. Liner notes to Poetry For the Beat Generation, by Jack Kerouac and Steve Allen. 1 phonodisc, 33-1/3 rpm. Hanover HML5000, n. d. Rpt. in abbreviated form, along with two poems from the album, in The Jazz Word, pp. 74-76. By Dom Cerulli, Burt Korall and Mort Nasatir. London: Dennis Dobson, 1962.

In the liner notes to this album, Millstein comments on the concept of the record and Kerouac's poetry.

See also citation 658b.

660. Randle, Bill. Liner notes to Readings by Jack Kerouac on the Beat Generation. 1 phonodisc, 33-1/3
   rpm. Verve MGV-15005, n. d.
   Randle presents a brief sketch of Kerouac's life
   and work, and of the Beat generation.

661. Richards, Patrick. "Poetry For The Beat Generation
   by Jack Kerouac & Steve Allen, " Sidewalk, 1, No. 1
   (n. d.): 79, 81.
   Brief favorable review of the Kerouac and Allen
   record. Five other poetry recordings are also reviewed.

   F. PARODIES OF KEROUAC'S WORKS

661a. "The Dramamine Bums, " National Lampoon, April
   1975, pp. 29-32.
   In this parody of Kerouac writing letters home to
   his mother while on the road he is depicted as completely square, obtuse, and gullible.

662. "Kerouac: The Suburbterraneans. " In Esquire's World
   of Humor, pp. 40-41. Commentary by David Newman. New York: Esquire, Inc. , 1964.
   This anonymous piece is a satire of both Kerouac's
   writing style and his subject matter, the Beats.

663. Pinkus, Philip. "More on 'Kerouac's Sound': The
   First Book of Beat, " Tamarack Review, No. 12
   (1959): 72-73.
   A Genesis-type/Biblical-feel poem-parody of the
   birth/creation of the Beat generation.

664. Ross, Stan. "The Dislocated Hipsters, " The Realist,
   No. 1 (1958): 32.
   In this parodying interview of a Kerouac-type char-
   acter, Jack Krackerjack is talking about his "Hip
   Generation" novel called On The Beat.

665. Scott, Martin. "Hickory, Dickory, Kerouac, " Playboy,
   March 1958, p. 65.
   This piece is a satire of On The Road.

666. Updike, John. "On the Sidewalk: (After Reading, At

Long Last, 'On the Road', by Jack Kerouac), " New Yorker, 21 February 1959, p. 32. Rpt. in Twentieth Century Parody, American and British, pp. 114-116. Edited by Burling Lowrey. Introduction by Nathaniel Benchley. New York: Harcourt, Brace, 1960.

Updike parodies Kerouac. The characters, Lee and Gogi, race across the block where they live - but no further than the bordering street - on tricycle and scooter, respectively, to whatever adventures await them, both physical and philosophical.

667. Zilber, Jacob. "More on 'Kerouac's Sound': The Love Song of J. Alfred Beatnik, " Tamarack Review, No. 12 (1959): 73-75.

A poem that parodies the beatniks and ultimately Kerouac (without mentioning his name).

G. ARTICLES ON KEROUAC AND RELATED PIECES FROM THE LOWELL SUN
(Citations are arranged in this section chronologically by date rather than alphabetically by author or title.)

668. Sampas, Charles G. "Sampascoopies, " 9 September 1957, p. 5.

Sampas recalls the advice he gave to Kerouac to leave his hometown to write his "Lowell Novel, " and the subsequent publication of The Town And The City and then, On The Road. He feels proud of Kerouac's success and his own small part as a literary patron.

669. Wallace, Mike. "Interview With: Jack Kerouac - Lowell Author Gives His Version of Beat Generation, " 3 March 1958, p. 15. Rpt. from the New York Post (citation 655).

670. Pertinax. "The Beat and the Angry, " 24 June 1958, p. 5.

This short piece tells of the mixed reception of Kerouac's On The Road in Britain.

670a. Crosby, John. "Hecht Asks Confoundest Questions, " 7 November 1958, p. 25.

A short piece about an interview of Kerouac by Ben Hecht and the interviewer's techniques.

671. Nolan, Dick. "Kerouac Booster: Dick Nolan Applauds Jack's Book," 12 October 1959, p. 4.

    In this article, reprinted from his San Francisco Examiner column (citation 477b), Dick Nolan, a former Lowell inhabitant, gives his support for Kerouac's Maggie Cassidy. He admits that he may not understand what Kerouac is doing with his shorthand, compressed writing method, but that this does not stop him from appreciating what Kerouac does with words. He also likes Kerouac's fond remembrances of his hometown.

672. Pertinax. "Sometimes, It's Sour Grapes," 24 November 1959, p. 5.

    This article defends the Lowellites who have become big names on the outside - especially Jack Kerouac. It says the soreheads and those jealous of Kerouac should gripe at home in private.

673. Pertinax. "Kerouac in Lowell," 19 September 1962, p. 7.

    This article relates Kerouac's return to Lowell on the eve of the publication reviews of Big Sur. It describes his trip there and his drinking and talking throughout the day.

674. Pertinax. "Conversations With Kerouac," 20 September 1962, p. 7.

    This article continues the previous one, giving flashes of Kerouac's moods and views while pub-crawling one Sunday in his hometown of Lowell.

675. Pertinax. "Kerouac Leaves Lowell," 25 September 1962, p. 5.

    Kerouac remained in Lowell for a week. The article recalls his last day in town, his admirerers, and a week's worth of impressions of him.

676. Pertinax. "On The Road With Marty and Jack," 2 October 1962, p. 5.

    When Kerouac left Lowell he was driven to New York City by Marty Gouveia. This article recounts Gouveia's experiences traveling with Kerouac.

677. Pertinax. "Kerouac, Joyce, Proust," 24 October 1962, p. 7.

    This is the first of two parts of a letter from

Kerouac commenting on the recent columns in the Lowell Sun on his visit, and other matters.

678. Pertinax. "Kerouac Remembers Them All," 25 October 1962, p. 7.
     This is the second of two parts of a letter from Kerouac commenting on the recent columns in the Lowell Sun on his visit, and other matters.

679. Pertinax. "This Daisy Is A Dilly," 4 June 1963, p. 5.
     This article is about Pull My Daisy and its reception in critical circles.

680. Pertinax. "Visions of Gerard," 10 September 1963, p. 5.
     This piece is a recounting of Visions of Gerard through paraphrase and quotes from the book.

681. Pertinax. "'No Apprentice To Suffering,'" 30 March 1964, p. 7.
     This article recounts Kerouac's one-night appearance in Lowell after speaking at Harvard University. See also citation 567a.

682. Pertinax. "'A Real American Dream,'" 23 June 1965, p. 7.
     This article affirms that Kerouac was off the road with his mother and through with the Beat generation long before the publication of his recent book, Desolation Angels, which ends on this note.

683. "Jack Kerouac, Lowell novelist, dies at 47," 21 October 1969, p. 1.
     Unsigned obituary on Kerouac.

684. Charney, Marc. "Jack Kerouac remembered by Beat, Hip generations," 23 October 1969, p. 3. Edited and unsigned version appeared in the Evening Independent (St. Petersburg) (citation 716).
     This article is about Allen Ginsberg's eulogy for Kerouac given at Yale the day after his death.

685. Sampas, Charles G. "Sampas Scoopies," 23 October 1969, p. 45.
     Charles Sampas remembers Kerouac through two letters written to him from the writer. One letter answers a question about a football game Kerouac did not play in for Columbia. The other re-introduces

Kerouac to Sampas and tells him about his about-to-be-published book, The Town And The City.

686. "Poets join in tribute to Kerouac," 24 October 1969, p. 1.

This article recounts some of the people who attended Kerouac's wake and funeral mass, and the eulogy by Father Armand Morissette.

687. "Jack Kerouac eulogized as exponent of Beatitudes," 26 October 1969, p. B6.

This article lists some of the people who appeared at Kerouac's funeral. It also prints Father Armand Morissette's eulogy for Kerouac.

687a. Sampas, Charles G. "Jack Kerouac: He wrote the great Lowell novel," 26 October 1969, Sunday magazine sec., p. 4.

In this dedication piece, written less than a week after his death, Sampas says that Kerouac wrote the "Great Lowell Novel," The Town And The City, and that no one, past or future, will capture the life and living of Lowell as Kerouac did.

688. Theodoros, Patricia M. "The mourning of novelist Jack Kerouac," 28 October 1969, p. 28.

This piece eulogizes Kerouac and talks about his depiction of Lowell and its people.

689. Sampas, Charles G. "Sampas Scoopies," 31 October 1969, p. 33.

In this column, Sampas includes a letter from one of Kerouac's classmates, a poem written on his death from a Canadian fan - David McFadden, and quotes from an article on Kerouac in the National Review.

690. Pertinax. "Tribute to Jack Kerouac," 21 October 1970, p. 15.

This column contains a poem by Charles E. Jarvis, one of Kerouac's biographers, about the Beat writer. Jarvis describes it as a spiritual biography. (The poem - entitled, "Jack Kerouac Never Left Lowell" - is reprinted in Jarvis's book, Visions of Kerouac (citation 568).

691. Pertinax. "Kerouac fans... rolltops...," 2 March 1972, p. 7.

This column contains a letter from an Irish Kerouac fan who requests some of Kerouac's works which he can't get, and also pen-pals interested in the Beat writer.

692. Pertinax. "'Long along the road,'" 13 September 1972, p. 15.
      This article talks about the anonymous visitors to Kerouac's grave and to Lowell. It also prints a poem written by Rex Kaser to Kerouac and left at the cemetery office.

693. Pertinax. "A Kerouac symposium," 9 April 1973, p. 7.
      This article recounts the people, discussions and events at the Jack Kerouac Symposium held at Salem State College on April 5, 1973.

694. Pertinax. "Kerouac symposium, continued," 10 April 1973, p. 7.
      A continuation of the preceding article recounting the people, discussions and events at the Jack Kerouac Symposium held at Salem State College on April 5, 1973.

695. Pertinax. "Kerouac symposium quotes," 11 April 1973, p. 13.
      A continuation of the previous two articles on the Kerouac Symposium at Salem State College.

696. Pertinax. "Note from a boyhood pal," 17 April 1973, p. 9.
      This column concludes the series on the Kerouac Symposium at Salem State College. It contains a letter from one of Kerouac's long-time boyhood pals who tries to set the record straight on some aspects of Kerouac's personality.

697. Pertinax. "Words for Gabrielle," 5 December 1973, p. 13.
      This article talks about Kerouac's mother, known as Mémêre, being immortalized in her son's works. It also contains the eulogy for her spoken by Father Armand Morissette.

698. Calio, James. "5 years later the Kerouac legend continues to grow," 10 November 1974, pp. 2-3.

This article recounts Kerouac five years after his death. The author marvels at those people affected by him and who search out his old haunts in Lowell and abroad. He also recalls Kerouac in Lowell and a letter from the author to Charles Sampas.

698a. Sampas, Mary. "A tribute to genius of Jack Kerouac," 8 March 1978, p. 21.
      Mary Sampas outlines the tribute to Kerouac which the Lowell Museum held in April 1978.

699. Weber, Bill. "The two sides of Jack Kerouac," 6 April 1978, p. 20.
     This article describes the opening and some of the contents of a special Kerouac exhibit at the Lowell Museum, plus it briefly recounts Kerouac's life, works and personality.
     See also citation 534a.

699a. Thomas, Bob. "Kerouac and the Beats: Dark side of the '50s," 19 September 1978, p. 31.
      Thomas talks about the film version of Carolyn Cassady's book, Heart Beat.

H.   LITERARY STUDIES IN OTHER MEDIA

700. Ginsberg, Allen, and Harold Hayes. Focus on Allen Ginsberg. 1 cassette tape, 1-7/8 ips. Center for Cassette Studies, No. 38673, n. d.
     In this conversation with Harold Hayes, Ginsberg recalls the early days of the Beat movement, including his involvement with such figures as William Burroughs and Kerouac, and he relates his work both to his philosophy and the events of his life.

701. Podhoretz, Norman, Marya Mannes and John Ciardi. The "Beat Generation". 1 cassette tape, 1-7/8 ips. Center for Cassette Studies, No. 6229, n. d.
     Three establishment critics take a close look at the phenomenon of the Beat generation - a movement led by Kerouac and Allen Ginsberg which challenged the system and proposed a life-style that both intrigued and threatened it.

702. Wilson, Graham C. The Literary Rebel: An assess-
ment of the Beats and the Angry Young Men. 1 cas-
sette tape, 1-7/8 ips. Center for Cassette Studies,
No. 12012, n. d.
   Beginning with the "hipsters" after World War II,
Dr. Wilson examines the parallel phenomena of the
Beat writers in San Francisco and the Angry Young
Men in England as represented in the work of Allen
Ginsberg, Kerouac, John Osborne, Kingsley Amis,
John Braine, Kenneth Tynan and others.

703. Wilson, Graham C. Perennial Frontiersman: Ameri-
can literary heroes from Natty Bumppo to Robert
Jordan. 1 cassette tape, 1-7/8 ips. Center for
Cassette Studies, No. 12009, n. d.
   Dr. Wilson looks at the earliest prototype of "the
American hero" - Daniel Boone, and contends that -
in various aspects and in various guises - this hero's
traits persist in the literature all the way from James
Fenimore Cooper to Ernest Hemingway and Norman
Mailer.

I. ARTICLES ON KEROUAC'S DEATH, WAKE AND FUNERAL,
   INCLUDING EULOGIES AND OBITUARIES

(For additional articles related to this section, see also Section G, Part II and Section C, Part III.)

704. Amram, David. "In Memory of Jack Kerouac, " Evergreen Review, 14, No. 74 (1970): 40-41, 76-77.
   Amram deals essentially with the same material
as in his book (citation 523). However, he goes on
to say that Kerouac "was ahead of his time spiritual-
ly" and the result of this is that his work "is constantly being rediscovered. "

705. Aronowitz, Alfred. "Jack Kerouac: Beyond the Road, "
New York Post, 22 October 1969, p. 100.
   Aronowitz wrote a eulogy on Kerouac after his
death. In it he says that On The Road was a book
that did much to change young America and its life-
style; but the revolution that Kerouac started against
American literary form left him alone and forgotten.

705a. Aronowitz, Alfred G. "Kerouac Gone," New York Post, 21 October 1969, p. 6.
  Obituary.

706. Bangs, Lester. "Elegy for A Desolation Angel," Rolling Stone, 29 November 1969, p. 36.
  This obituary traces Kerouac's life and the origins of the Beat generation. It reviews his main works and describes, through Kerouac's writing, the archetypal Beat, Neal Cassady. At the end of the piece, Kerouac is accused of selling out and giving up the dreams the Beats had created.

706a. Burns, Jim. "Kerouac and the Beats," Tribune (London), 28 November 1969, p. 7.
  Obituary.

707. Clendinen, Dudley. "Jack Kerouac At Road's End," St. Petersburg Times, 22 October 1969, pp. 1-A, 2-A. Alternately titled in later edition, "Jack Kerouac Dies Here At 47."
  Obituary.

708. Cloves, Jeff. "Madman Bum and Angel Beat," Peace News (England), 7 November 1969, p. 8.
  In this eulogy, Cloves juxtaposes Kerouac's critics against the millions who have bought his books - fairly or unfairly reviewed.

709. Cook, Bruce. "An Immense Talent, Jack Kerouac Tried to 'Redeem Life from Darkness,'" National Observer, 27 October 1969, p. 16.
  Obituary.

710. Coyne, J. "Jack Kerouac, RIP," National Review, 4 November 1969, p. 1104.
  Obituary.

711. Crocket, Douglas. "Traditional Rites For Jack Kerouac, 47," Boston Globe, 25 October 1969, p. 25.
  This obituary lists some of Kerouac's friends in attendance at his funeral. A priest who knew him since childhood reminisces the past.

712. Ehrmann, Eric, and Stephen Davis. "There is really nothing inside," Rolling Stone, 29 November 1969, p. 34.

A detailed description of Kerouac's funeral and the
reaction and comments of the literary figures who
attended.

713. "End of the Road, " Time, 31 October 1969, p. 10.
Time's obituary is surprisingly uncomplimentary.

714. Finley, Larry. "End of the road for Jack Kerouac, "
Chicago Daily News, 22 October 1969, p. 11.
Obituary.

715. Ginsberg, Allen. "Dear Playboy, " Playboy, May 1973,
p. 14.
Letters to Playboy responding to John Clellon
Holmes' piece, "Gone in October" (citation 720),
which described Kerouac's funeral. Among the letters is one by Allen Ginsberg reflecting on the funeral, and on death and the body's metamorphosis.

716. Ginsberg, Allen. "Ginsberg Eulogizes Kerouac At
Yale, " Evening Independent (St. Petersburg), 23 Octo-
ber 1969, p. 16-A. A longer version appears in the
Lowell Sun (citation 684).
Description of Ginsberg's eulogy given at Yale.

717. Gornick, Vivian. "Jack Kerouac: 'The Night And
What It Does to You, '" Village Voice, 30 October
1969, pp. 1, 27, 30.
Gornick attended and reported on Kerouac's funeral
and burial in Lowell. She tries to come to grips
with feelings of what Kerouac means to her, to those
who loved and admired him, and to America.
See also citation 728.

717a. Grieg, Michael. "The Beat Epoch's Jack Kerouac
Dies, " San Francisco Chronicle, 22 October 1969,
p. 5.
Obituary.

718. Halpert, Stephen. "So Long, Dean Moriarty, " Fusion,
No. 24 (26 December 1969), p. 34.
In a very earthly style, Halpert eulogizes Kerouac
as being misrepresented and generally ignored by
society; or, the rock generation's lament to the death
of an unsung hero, the unknown Beat.

719. "He hit the road, Jack, " Boston Globe, 25 October

1969, p. 6.
Obituary loosely discussing the causes of Kerouac's drinking problem.

720. Holmes, John Clellon. "Gone In October," Playboy, February 1973, pp. 96-98, 140, 158-160, 162-166.
John Clellon Holmes, Kerouac's friend of twenty-odd years, ruminates over his friend's death. This event has affected him deeply as it has other close associates: Allen Ginsberg, Peter Orlovsky and Gregory Corso. Holmes, and company, attend the wake, funeral and burial of Kerouac in Lowell, Massachusetts.
See also citation 715.

721. "Jack Kerouac, 'beat' writer, dies at 47," Chicago Sun-Times, 22 October 1969, p. 80.
Associated Press obituary.

722. "Jack Kerouac Dead at 47; 'Beat' Writer: 3d wife at Bedside in Florida," Chicago Tribune, 22 October 1969, sec. 2, p. 12. Appeared also in New York Daily News, 22 October 1969, p. 104; and was reprinted in Jack Kerouac, p. 88 (citation 348).
United Press International obituary.

723. "Kerouac, honored prophet," Chicago Daily News, 25-26 October 1969, p. 10.
Editorial note on Kerouac's death.

724. "Kerouac Not Jack, But Jean," Evening Independent (St. Petersburg), 25 October 1969, p. 3-A.
This article describes Kerouac's will, in which he left everything to his mother.

725. Krim, Seymour. "Kerouac Dies for Me in Spain, with Wreath by Aronowitz." In You & me, pp. 105-114. New York: Holt, Rinehart and Winston, 1974. Published originally in altered form as "On a Groovy Obit." In Village Voice, 20 November 1969, pp. 4, 68.
Krim's memorial piece on Kerouac's death glorifies Kerouac. Krim also takes the opportunity to reject and elaborate on Al Aronowitz's shallow memorial to Kerouac (citation 705) which appeared prior to Krim's piece.

726. Lankford, John. "Beat's First Author Dies," Evening
Independent (St. Petersburg), 21 October 1969, p.
1-A.
    Obituary.

726a. Lee, Timothy. "The Road Ends for Jack Kerouac,
47," New York Post, 21 October 1969, p. 2.
    Obituary.

727. Lelyveld, Joseph. "Jack Kerouac, Novelist, Dead;
Father of the Beat Generation," New York Times,
22 October 1969, p. 47. Rpt. in edited and a-
bridged version in Chicago Today, 26 October 1969,
Now! sec., p. 14.
    A long, detailed obituary written in a somewhat
sympathetic tone.

728. "Letters to the Editor: Kerouac's Will; Satori in
Lowell," Village Voice, 6 November 1969, p. 4.
    Letters to the Village Voice in praise of Vivian
Gornick's coverage of Kerouac's funeral (citation
717). One writer says, however, that Kerouac is
not as important to the "hip" generation as thought.

729. Lipton, Lawrence. "Jack Kerouac, a memoir," Los
Angeles Free Press, 31 October 1969, pt. 2, p. 33.
    Quoting heavily from Kerouac's last published
article, Lipton wants to pinpoint his self-torture and
his shattered life. Also, Lipton does not want to
call Kerouac a writer; instead he says he is a
"wordman" of "leading influence" on Beat "word-
craft."

730. "Lowell's Jack Kerouac Hippie Literary Pioneer,"
Boston Globe, 21 October 1969, p. 43.
    Obituary.

731. McClintock, Jack. "What Can I Say, Jack?" St.
Petersburg Times, 22 October 1969, p. 1-D.
    Short automatic writing on Kerouac's death. Mc-
Clintock was one of the few who regularly visited
Kerouac in St. Petersburg.

732. McDonald, Gregory. "Rap-up: 'I knew Jack Kerouac,'"
Boston Globe, 26 October 1969, p. 54-A.
    McDonald writes this memorial based mainly on
his interview with Kerouac in Hyannis (citation 641).

733. Murphy, Jeremiah V. "Jack Kerouac's Days on the
Road Are Ended," Boston Globe, 22 October 1969,
p. 3.
Obituary.

734. "Obituary: Mr. Jack Kerouac, Novelist of the beat
generation," Times (London), 22 October 1969, p.
12.
Obituary.

735. "Polarity Finder," Christian Science Monitor, 24 October 1969, p. 18.
Editorial note on Kerouac's death.

736. "Stricken at 47: 'Beat' writer Kerouac dies," Chicago
Daily News, 21 October 1969, pp. 1, 6.
Associated Press obituary.

737. Weil, Martin. "'Beat' Spokesman Jack Kerouac Dies,"
Washington Post, 22 October 1969, p. C-7.
Obituary.

737a. Werbin, Stuart. "The Death, the Wake, and the Fun-
eral of Jack Kerouac," Cambridge Phoenix, 30 Octo-
ber 1969, pp. 8-9.
"Metropolitan Boston's Weekly Journal of News,
Opinion and the Arts'" reporter was in attendance at
Kerouac's wake and describes it here.

738. Werry, Richard R. "Kerouac forgotten by tribe he
spawned," Detroit News, 22 October 1969, p. A-3.
Obituary.

J.   KEROUAC BIBLIOGRAPHY AND RELATED WORKS

739. Akeroyd, Joanne Vinson. Where Are Their Papers?
A Union List Locating the Papers of Forty-two Contemporary American Poets and Writers. Bibliography Series, no. 9. Storrs, Connecticut: University of Connecticut Library, 1976.
This work lists 12 libraries, archives and special
collections where some of Kerouac's papers are lo-
cated. Some other Beat writers with listings are:
Gregory Corso, Lawrence Ferlinghetti, Allen Ginsberg and Gary Snyder.

739a. Ardinger, Richard K., compiler. An Annotated Bibliography of Works by John Clellon Holmes. Pocatel-
lo, Idaho: Idaho State University Press, 1979.
This work is very similar in format to Ann Charters' bibliography of Kerouac's works (citations 741
and 742). Kerouac is referred to throughout; and
Holmes comments on many of his works, including
several listed in this bibliography: Go (citation 844b)
and "Gone in October" (citation 720).

740. The Beat Generation & Other Avante-garde Writers.
Catalog Three. Santa Barbara, California: Anacapa
Books, n. d.
This catalog, from a California bookseller, serves
not only as a bibliography of the major works of the
Beat generation writers - in their various editions -
but also as an indicator of the current market value
and collectability of these works.

741. Charters, Ann, compiler. A Bibliography Of Works By
Jack Kerouac (Jean Louis Lebris De Kerouac), 1939-
1967. New York: Phoenix Book Shop, 1967.
This is a compilation of almost all of Kerouac's
work appearing in book, magazine, ephemeral and
recorded formats, both in English and in foreign
languages.

742. Charters, Ann, compiler. A Bibliography Of Works By
Jack Kerouac (Jean Louis Lebris De Kerouac), 1939-
1975. Revised edition. New York: Phoenix Book-
shop, 1975.
This is a revision of the preceding work (citation
741). It includes several illustrations; one is of
Kerouac.

742a. Jack Kerouac. Catalogue Five: Walter Reuben Collection of Jack Kerouac. Introduction by William S.
Burroughs. Santa Barbara, California: Bradford
Morrow, Bookseller, n. d.
This annotated catalog of Kerouac materials includes many of the items listed in Ann Charters'
bibliography (citations 741 and 742), manuscript and
archival materials, foreign editions of Kerouac's
works, critical and secondary works, plus other related items. Profusely illustrated.

743. "Jack Kerouac 1922-1969." In First Printings of Amer-
Authors; Contributions Toward Descriptive Checklists,

Volume 1, pp. 217-219.   Series editor, Matthew J.
Bruccoli.   Detroit: Gale Research, 1977.
   A listing of the first printings of Kerouac's works
without bibliographical descriptions; some title page
illustrations.

744.   Leiker, Louise.   "Kerouac Being Kept 'Alive;' Maga-
       zine Dedicated to Late 'Beat King, '" Buffalo Courier-
       Express, 21 January 1979, pp. E1-E2.
          Article about Moody Street Irregulars: A Jack
       Kerouac Newsletter (citation 750), with background
       information on the editors, Michael Basinski and
       Joy Walsh, and Kerouac.

745.   LePellec, Yves.   "Jack Kerouac and the American
       critics: a selected bibliography, " Caliban, 9 (1973):
       77-92.
          In his annotated bibliography, LePellec selects a
       small number of American books and articles on
       Kerouac to describe in detail.   The problem with
       Kerouac criticism, LePellec notes, is its violent
       rejection of him during his time because of opposing
       political and social stances and then its sparseness
       after the social uproar subsided in the 1960's.

746.   Libman, Valentina A.   Russian Studies of American
       Literature.   Chapel Hill: University of North Caro-
       lina, 1969.
          Libman's work is a bibliography of works in Rus-
       sian on American writers, Kerouac and the Beats
       included.   Some of the listings in her work are in-
       corporated into the Russian language review section
       of this present work: citations 399-406.

747.   Masheck, Joseph, ed. Beat Art: Drawings by Gregory
       Corso, Jack Kerouac, Peter Orlovsky, Philip Whalen,
       and Others from the Rare Book and Manuscript Li-
       brary of Columbia University.   New York: Butler
       Library, Columbia University, 1977.
          In the introduction to this catalog of a Beat art
       exhibit held at Columbia University's Butler Library,
       March 2-May 19, 1977, Masheck finds correlations
       between Beat art, Abstract Expressionist painting in
       the 1950's, automatic writing, Kerouac's spontaneous
       prose method and On The Road, and the surrealist
       manifesto.   Kerouac and On The Road are mentioned
       throughout the piece.   Nine drawings by Kerouac are

described and critiqued as well as two by Robert
LaVigne of Kerouac.

747a. Maynard, Joe, and Barry Miles, compilers. William
S. Burroughs: A Bibliography, 1953-73. Charlottes-
ville: University Press of Virginia, 1978.
This work lists all the relevant bibliographic in-
formation on Burroughs' and Claude Pélieu's work,
Jack Kerouac (citation 348).

748. Montgomery, John. "Continuation Of: Draft Index To
Book Of Dreams," Moody Street Irregulars: A Jack
Kerouac Newsletter, 1, No. 2 (1978): 7-9.
This is a name, topic and happenings index to
Kerouac's Book of Dreams.
See also citation 749.

749. Montgomery, John. "Draft Index to Book of Dreams:
A Name Index With Kerouac Topic Index," Moody
Street Irregulars: A Jack Kerouac Newsletter, 1,
No. 1 (1978): 12.
This is a name, topic and happenings index to
Kerouac's Book of Dreams.
See also citation 748.

750. Moody Street Irregulars: A Jack Kerouac Newsletter.
Vol. 1, No. 1, 1978- . Clarence Center, New
York.
A quarterly newsletter which includes "announce-
ments, queries, articles, controversy, and notes of
special interest to Kerouac scholars and those, for
love of Jack, who are involved in the mind-bending
experience of Kerouac" (from vol. 1, no. 1).

750a. O'Shea, Michael. "Kerouac newsletter debuts," Spec-
trum, 3 March 1978, p. 4.
This article, which appeared in the student newspaper of the State University of New York at Buffalo
(SUNYAB), introduces Moody Street Irregulars, a
newsletter on Jack Kerouac, and describes its purposes. It also gives a short background to Kerouac
and the Beat generation.

750b. Peace, Warren. Peace Record Guide Volume 3. Kal-
amazoo, Michigan: Peace Press, 1979.
This primarily rock record guide is dedicated to
Kerouac. It lists prices for his three albums plus

puts values on other Kerouac related recordings, including The Subterraneans soundtrack and John Clellon Holmes recordings of Kerouac listed in Ann Charters' bibliography (citations 741 and 742). Also compiled is a directory of collectors and dealers, including those interested in Kerouac (materials).

750c. "The Property of a Lady." In Printed Books & Autograph Letters, n. pag. New York: Sotheby Parke Bernet Inc., 1979.

This auction catalog describes, quotes from, and illustrates more than 14 Kerouac items - letters, postcards, drawings, autograph haikus, and other associated pieces - dated 1959 to 1967. (These items belonged to Lois Sorrells Beckwith, a poet and intimate friend of Kerouac. The lot was auctioned off for $16,000 in May 1979.)

K.   REVIEWS OF SECONDARY WORKS

1.   BEAULIEU, Victor-Lévy.   Jack Kerouac: a chicken-essay.   (citation 423)

751.   Guzlowski, J. Zbigniew.   "Jack Kerouac: A chicken-essay," Modern Fiction Studies, 23 (1977-1978): 662-664.

2.   CASSADY, Carolyn.   Heart Beat: My Life with Jack & Neal.   (citation 539)

751a. Burns, Jim.   "The Heart Still Beats," Poetry Information (London), No. 17 (1977): 42-46.

752.   Kirsch, Robert.   "Heartthrob of Beat Movement," Los Angeles Times, 16 November 1976, pt. 4, pp. 5-6.

753.   McMurtry, Larry.   "A Still Silenced Voice," Washington Post, 16 August 1976, p. B12.

754.   Wilson, Nina K.   "Heart Beat," Library Journal, 15 September 1976, p. 1848.

3. CHARTERS, Ann. KEROUAC: A Biography. (citation 541)

755. "American drama...and American dream," Times Literary Supplement, 13 September 1974, p. 971.

756. Bowering, George. "Tragic Jack," Open Letter, Second Series, No. 7 (1974): 84-86.

756a. Burns, Jim. "A trip along Kerouac's eventful road," Tribune (London), 26 July 1974, p. 7.

757. Cook, Bruce. "Kerouac and 'Bird': No Courtly Muses, But Art That Suits a Makeshift Land," National Observer, 31 March 1973, p. 23.

758. Coyne, J. R., Jr. "Living a Legend," National Review, 3 August 1973, p. 853.

759. Cross, Leslie. "The 'Beat King' Returns," Milwaukee Journal, 28 January 1973, pt. 5, p. 4.

760. Deck, John. "At the very least, an inspired kind of typing," New York Times Book Review, 15 April 1973, p. 23.

761. Edelstein, Eleanor. "Lonely Off the Road," Sunday Star and the Washington Daily News, 1 April 1973, p. G-2.

762. Gelfant, Blanche H. "Jack Kerouac," Contemporary Literature, 15 (1974): 415-422.

763. Hill, Richard. "End of the Road," St. Petersburg Times, 1 July 1973, p. 3-G.

764. Homberger, Eric. "Beating it," New Review (London), 1, No. 3 (1974): 85-86.

765. Horowitz, Michael. "Those were the daze," Spectator, 10 August 1974, p. 181.

766. Johnston, Albert H. "KEROUAC," Publishers Weekly, 22 January 1973, p. 64.

766a. Kamstra, Jerry. "A Biographical Monument To a Scene Chronicler," San Francisco Chronicle, 1 April 1973, This World Magazine sec., p. 35.

767. "KEROUAC," Choice, July-August 1973, p. 773.

768. "KEROUAC," Kirkus Reviews, 1 February 1973, p. 156.

769. "KEROUAC," New Yorker, 12 May 1973, pp. 147-148.

770. Kirsch, Robert. "Kerouac and the Wanderjahr That Lasted a Lifetime," Los Angeles Times, 25 March 1973, Calendar sec., p. 48.

771. Krim, Seymour. "In the '50s, One of the Most Creative Americans Alive," Newsday (Garden City, New York), 18 March 1973, Ideas sec., pp. 20, 24.

772. LaSalle, Peter. "Sad Jack Kerouac without the myths: A man of heart who worked and suffered," Chicago Daily News, 24 March 1973, Panorama sec., p. 4.

773. Lomas, Herbert. "Benzedrine to Booze," London Magazine, New Series, 14, No. 5 (1974-1975): 73-86.

774. MacManus, Patricia. "Kerouac's Lonely Road," Progressive, June 1973, pp. 55-57.

775. Murray, G. E. "Rambling boy of the 1950's," Chicago Sun-Times, 25 March 1973, Showcase sec., p. 19.

776. Noble, Donald R. "Kerouac: A Biography," Southern Humanities Review, 9 (1975): 333-334.

777. Oberbeck, S. K. "Beat Boswell," Newsweek, 2 April 1973, pp. 91-92.

778. Salzman, Jack. "End of the Road," Washington Post, 8 April 1973, Book World sec., p. 3.

779. Sheppard, R. Z. "Sweet Jack Gone," Time, 22 January 1973, p. 71.

780. Theroux, Paul. "Back to Mom," New Statesman, 31 May 1974, pp. 772-774.
    See also citation 454a.

781. Warner, Jon M. "KEROUAC," Library Journal, 1 April 1973, p. 1166.

782. Weber, Brom. "Kerouac: A Biography," American Literature, 45 (1973): 479-480.

783. Yaryan, Bill. "Kerouac Revisited: The Beat Goes On," Coast, June 1973, pp. 28-30.

4. CHARTERS, Ann. Scenes Along the Road. (citation 542)

784. Brodey, Jim. "Scenes Along the Road," Crawdaddy, 16 May 1971, sec. 1, pp. 14-16.

785. Wilson, Mark. "Scenes Along the Road," Rolling Stone, 7 January 1971, p. 60.

5. COOK, Bruce. The Beat Generation. (citation 545) (See also foreign language review, citation 414.)

786. "The Beat Generation," Choice, January 1972, p. 1451.

787. "The Beat Generation," New Republic, 22 January 1972, p. 28.

788. Carroll, Paul. "Sense and nonsense from the Beat scene," Chicago Daily News, 18-19 September 1971, Panorama sec., p. 10.

789. Coyne, J. R., Jr. "Coopting Kerouac," National Review, 5 November 1971, pp. 1246-1247.

790. Dunham, Terry. "Are We Sons of the Beat Generation?" Atlanta Journal, 21 January 1973, p. 6-C.

791. Knoll, Gerald M. "The Beat Generation," America, 13 November 1971, p. 408.

792. Lask, Thomas. "Milestones Along the Road," New York Times, 26 August 1971, p. 35.

793. Latham, Aaron. "Kerouac, Ginsberg & Co.," Chicago Tribune, 17 October 1971, Book World sec., pp. 18, 21. See also Washington Post, 17 October 1971, Book World sec., pp. 18, 21.

794. Leary, Lewis. "The Beat Generation," American Literature, 44 (1972): 336-337.

795. Parkinson, Thomas. "Back in 1958 a certain group of writers...," New York Times Book Review, 29 August 1971, pp. 3, 24.

796. Sheppard, R. Z. "The Longest Footnote," Time, 6 September 1971, p. C11.

797. Tytell, John. "The Beat Generation," Commonweal, 17 December 1971, pp. 285-286.

6. GIFFORD, Barry, and Lawrence Lee. Jack's Book. (citation 552)

798. Brunette, Peter. "Memories of a Wild and Woolly Genius," The Chronicle of Higher Education, 27 November 1978, The Chronicle Review sec., p. r13.

798a. Burns, Jim. "Kerouac's influence," Tribune (London), 17 August 1979, p. 6.

799. Calleri, Michael. "Book on Kerouac - There's No Reason To Buy It," Moody Street Irregulars: A Jack Kerouac Newsletter, No. 3 (1979): 11. Printed originally in the Buffalo Courier-Express, 15 October 1978.

800. Christy, Jim. "Book on Kerouac - There's No Reason To Buy It," Moody Street Irregulars: A Jack Kerouac Newsletter, No. 3 (1979): 11. Printed originally in longer form as "Kerouac didn't crawl into a hole and drink himself to death - he chose to move around." In Globe and Mail (Toronto), 23 September 1978, p. 25.

801. Cook, Bruce. "Doomed to Success," Saturday Review, August 1978, p. 50.

801a. Davies, Russell. "The Dharma Bums," New Statesman, 23 March 1979, pp. 399-400.

802. Gornick, Vivian. "Hit the Road, Jack," Washington Post, 22 October 1978, Book World sec., p. E5.

802a. Harris, Lin Rosechild. "Jack's Book," Village Voice, 16 October 1978, p. 134.

803. Hogan, William. "'Jack's Book,'" San Francisco Chronicle, 16 October 1978, p. 39.

804. "Jack's Book," Booklist, 15 July 1978, p. 1713.

804a. "Jack's Book," Critic, No. 253 (January 1979): 7.

805. "Jack's Book," Kirkus Reviews, 15 June 1978, pp. 673-674.

806. "Jack's Book," Publishers Weekly, 3 July 1978, p. 57.

807. Kostelanetz, Richard. "Saint Jack," New York Times Book Review, 31 December 1978, p. 16.

808. Krim, [Seymour]. "The Beatification of 'Saint' Jack," Chicago Tribune, 20 August 1978, Book World sec., p. 1.

808a. Pergam, Jeannette M. "Jack's Book," Best Sellers, January 1979, p. 315.

808b. Sage, Lorna. "Beat generation gap," Observer (London), 8 April 1979, p. 38.

809. Stuttaford, Genevieve. "Barry Gifford," Publishers Weekly, 10 July 1978, p. 10-11.

810. White, William. "Jack's Book," Library Journal, July 1978, p. 1410.

7. GINSBERG, Allen, and Neal Cassady. As Ever. (citation 553)

811. "As Ever," Choice, May 1978, p. 397.

811a. Burns, Jim. "As Ever," Comstock Lode (England), No. 3 (1978): n. pag.

812. Curley, Arthur. "As Ever," Library Journal, 15 March 1978, p. 664.

812a. McNally, Dennis. "As Ever," Western American Literature, 13 (1978): 204-205.

8. HIPKISS, Robert A. Jack Kerouac: Prophet of the New Romanticism. (citation 456)

813. Guzlowski, J. Zbigniew. "Jack Kerouac: Prophet of the New Romanticism," Modern Fiction Studies, 23 (1977-1978): 662-664.

814. "Jack Kerouac: Prophet of the New Romanticism," Publishers Weekly, 1 November 1976, p. 69.

815. Justus, James H. "Jack Kerouac: Prophet of the New Romanticism," American Literature, 49 (1977): 288-289.

816. Martine, James J. "Jack Kerouac: Prophet of the New Romanticism," Library Journal, 15 October 1976, p. 2177.

817. Sipper, Ralph. "Jack Kerouac: '60s Pied Piper," Los Angeles Times, 8 June 1977, pt. 4, p. 8.

9. JARVIS, Charles E. Visions of Kerouac. (citation 568)

818. Burns, Jim. "Jivin' With Jack," Poetry Information (London), No. 14 (1975-1976): 53-54.

819. Green, James E. "Review Essay," Journal of Popular Culture, 8, No. 4 (1975): 912-913.

820. Hogan, Edward J. "Visions of Kerouac: The Life of Jack Kerouac," San Francisco Review of Books, October 1976, p. 14.

821. Nolan, Dick. "Visions of Kerouac," San Francisco Examiner, 13 March 1975, p. 35.

10. KNIGHT, Arthur Winfield, and Glee Knight, editors. The Beat Book. (citation 570)

822. Burns, Jim. "The Beat Book," Poetry Information (London), Nos. 12/13 (1975): 31-32.

11. KNIGHT, Arthur Winfield, and Kit Knight, editors. The Beat Diary. (citation 571)

823. Burns, Jim. "The Heart Still Beats," Poetry Information (London), No. 17 (1977): 42-46.

12. KNIGHT, Arthur Winfield, and Kit Knight, editors. The Beat Journey. (citation 572)

823a. Burns, Jim. "The Beat Journey," Comstock Lode (England), No. 5 (1979): no. pag.

823b. Burns, Jim. "On the Beat," Palantir, No. 10 (1978): 30-33.

824. Gifford, Barry. "The Beat Journey," San Francisco Review of Books, 4, No. 5 (1979): 20.

13. KRIM, Seymour, ed. The Beats. (citation 575)

824a. Aronowitz, Alfred G. "The Beats," Village Voice, 18 May 1960, pp. 7, 10.

14. MCNALLY, Dennis. Desolate Angel. (citation 581b)

824b. "Desolate Angel," Kirkus Reviews, 15 June 1979, pp. 727-728.

824c. "Desolate Angel," Publishers Weekly, 18 June 1979, p. 86.

824d. Dretzka, Gary. "Kerouac, Desolate Angel," Los Angeles Herald Examiner, 26 August 1979, sec. F, pp. 5-6.

824e. Gold, Herbert. "A Nostalgic Manifesto," New York Times Book Review, 12 August 1979, p. 3.

824f. Herman, Jan. "Could this have been Kerouac?" Chicago Sun-Times, 19 August 1979, Book Week sec., p. 12.

824g. Krim, Seymour. "A Most Riveting Look at Jack Kerouac," San Francisco Sunday Examiner & Chronicle, 2 September 1979, This World sec., p. 44.

824h. Leppanen, Garry V. "Kerouac, Ferlinghetti Biographies - And the Beats Go On," Worcester Sunday Telegram, 16 September 1979, p. 16E.

824i. Manning, Margaret. "Jack Kerouac's road to nowhere," Boston Sunday Globe, 5 August 1979, p. 52.

824j. Milazzo, Lee. "The unrelenting life of 'Beat' Jack

Kerouac," <u>Dallas Morning News</u>, 5 August 1979, p. 4G.

824k. Prado, Holly. "Kerouac: upbeat look at the beat," <u>Los Angeles Times</u>, 14 October 1979, Book Review sec., p. 18.

824l. Sigal, Clancy. "Pursuing a Dream of Kerouac," <u>Chicago Tribune</u>, 12 August 1979, Book World sec., p. 1.

824m. Starr, Kevin. "Walking the Beat," <u>San Francisco Examiner</u>, 16 August 1979, p. 27.

824n. Thiemeyer, Jay. "Candid Study Reveals Misfortune of Beats," <u>Atlanta Journal and Constitution</u>, 2 September 1979, p. 4-E.

15. MONTGOMERY, John. <u>Kerouac West Coast</u>. (citation 585)

825. Burns, Jim. "Kerouac West Coast," <u>Palantir</u>, No. 8 (1978): 72.

825a. Nowicki, R. E. "Strictly San Francisco," <u>San Francisco Review of Books</u>, May 1977, p. 4.

16. SAROYAN, Aram. <u>Genesis Angels</u>. (citation 593)

825b. Funsten, Kenneth. "Genesis Angels," <u>Library Journal</u>, 15 May 1979, pp. 1142-1143.

826. Latham, Aaron. "America Is the Favorite Word," <u>New York Times Book Review</u>, 29 April 1979, pp. 14, 54.
    In this review, Latham criticizes Saroyan's language and repetition of words. He sees the work as thin as Saroyan's own poetry and short on biographical data on Lew Welch. Kerouac's life story covers almost 1/3 of the book, and Latham finds Saroyan perpetuating "serious errors" about Kerouac: such as <u>On The Road</u> being written on a long roll of teletype paper; and <u>On The Road</u> being heavily edited to its published form. Both of these are refuted by Latham as he says he has seen the original manuscript of the work. (Latham had been the author

appointed by the Sterling Lord Agency - Kerouac's literary agent - to write an "authorized" biography of Kerouac and thereby having access to all the extant literary property in their possession.)

17. TYTELL, John. Naked Angels. (citation 501)

827. Burns, Jim. "The Heart Still Beats," Poetry Information (London), No. 17 (1977): 42-46.

828. Guzlowski, J. Zbigniew. "Naked Angels: The Lives and Literature of the Beat Generation," Modern Fiction Studies, 23 (1977-1978): 662-664.

829. La Hood, Marvin J. "Naked Angels," World Literature Today (formerly Books Abroad), 51 (1977): 101.

830. "Naked Angels," Choice, July/August 1976, p. 668.

831. "Naked Angels," Kirkus Reviews, 1 November 1975, pp. 1280-1281.

832. "Naked Angels," New Yorker, 5 April 1976, p. 137.

833. "Naked Angels," Publishers Weekly, 1 December 1975, p. 63.

834. Ott, William A. "Naked Angels," Library Journal, 15 April 1976, p. 1021.

835. Parkinson, Thomas. "Naked Angels," American Literature, 48 (1976): 428-430.

835a. Peters, Robert. "Naked Angels: Ginsberg, Kerouac, and Burroughs." In The Great American Poetry Bake-Off, pp. 148-151. Metuchen, New Jersey: Scarecrow Press, 1979. Appeared originally in Gay Sunshine, No. 29/30 (1976): 30-31.

836. Schjeldahl, Peter. "Claiming the Beats for American Literature," New York Times Book Review, 9 May 1976, p. 4.

837. Wallenstein, Barry. "The Beats," Contemporary Literature, 18 (1977): 542-551.

L. MOTION PICTURE ADAPTATION OF
A SECONDARY WORK

1. Heart Beat (citation 539)

838. "A Flood of Film Biography," Time, 1 January 1979,
pp. 84-85.

838a. Holder, Wayne. "Heart Beat Goes to Hollywood,"
Moody Street Irregulars: A Jack Kerouac Newsletter,
No. 5 (1979): 9-11.
Holder, who takes a wait-and-see attitude about
the final outcome of the movie version of Carolyn
Cassady's book, Heart Beat, has some behind-the-
scenes anecdotes on the film. He also expresses
strong feelings about films in general, the people involved with Heart Beat, Hollywood, and his interest
in the Beats.

839. "The spooky, spaced-out waif of Carrie...," Time,
25 September 1978, p. 88.

840. Turan, Kenneth. "Cassady and Kerouac, the Heart of
Beat; Hollywood's Celluloid Encounter With Shock
Troops of the '50s," Washington Post, 5 November
1978, pp. L1, L6-L8. Appeared in slightly different
form as "Three On The Road." In New West, 20
November 1978, pp. 43-49.

PART III:

CREATIVE WORKS INFLUENCED BY KEROUAC

A. MUSICAL SETTINGS

841. Alexander, Willie. "Kerouac," Willie Alexander and
the Boom Boom Band. 1 phonodisc, 33-1/3 rpm.
MCA MCA-2323, 1978.

841a. Amram, David. "Pull My Daisy," No More Walls.
1 phonodisc, 33-1/3 rpm. Flying Fish GRO-752,
1976. Originally part of a two-record set issued
with the same title (as above) by RCA, Red Seal
VCS-7089(2), [1971].
   In the liner notes Amram says, "Pull My Daisy
was written in 1959 for the underground film of the
same name. It was a silent film, with Jack Kerouac's narration and my music. Jack, Allen Ginsberg,
and Neal Cassidy (sic) wrote the lyrics to the song.
In the music I tried to show the poetic side of the
jazz experience and to capture some of the magic
of Jack's spirit. The song is recorded here for the
first time." Lynn Sheffield is the vocalist.

841b. Amram, David. "Pull My Daisy," Summer Nights,
Winter Rain. 1 phonodisc, 33-1/3 rpm. RCA
KLP1-0169, 1976.
   In a recorded live performance, David Amram
(and band) sings and performs the song "Pull My
Daisy." At the end of it, he spontaneously sings,
in a fast, scat-like manner, a short, musical biog-
raphy of Kerouac.

842. Fowler, Rex. "The Persecution & Restoration of Dean
Moriarty (On the Road)," Aztec Two-Step. 1 phonodisc, 33-1/3 rpm. Elektra EKS-75031, 1972.

842a. Previn, André. The Four Dimensions of Andre Previn: Composer, Arranger, Conductor, Pianist. 1
phonodisc, 33-1/3 rpm. MGM E-4186, n.d.
   This album contains four songs from the soundtrack to the movie version of Kerouac's The Subterraneans: "Why Are We Afraid?", "Should I,"
"Things Are Looking Down," and "Like Blue."

842b. Previn, André, and David Rose. Like Blue. 1 phono-
disc, 33-1/3 rpm. MGM E3811, n. d.
This album contains two songs from the soundtrack
to the movie version of Kerouac's The Subterraneans:
"Like Blue" and "The Blue Subterranean (Why Are
We Afraid?)."

842c. Previn, André; Mulligan, Gerry; McRae, Carmen; and
others. The Subterraneans. 1 phonodisc, 33-1/3
rpm. MGM E3812 ST, n. d. Reissued (as an exact
duplicate) in Japan by Polydor K. K., MM 2097.
This is the "original sound track album" for the
movie version of Kerouac's The Subterraneans. The
liner notes briefly describe the musicians, the com-
positional backgrounds, and the personnel on each cut.

843. Waits, Tom. "Medley: Jack & Neal," Foreign Affairs.
1 phonodisc, 33-1/3 rpm. Asylum 7E-1117, 1977.

843a. Weir, Bob. "Cassidy," Ace. 1 phonodisc, 33-1/3
rpm. Warner Bros. Records BS2627, 1972.

B. FICTION AND NON-FICTION

844. Breger, Udo. "Five Pieces On The Subject Of Kerouac," Moody Street Irregulars: A Jack Kerouac Newsletter, 1, No. 2 (1978): 6-7.
Breger writes about his impressions of and how
Kerouac changed his life. He also speaks on Kerouac's writing and of contacting his friends which
helped him experience Kerouac more fully.

844a. Hamblett, John. "The Neon Dream of Tom Waits,"
New Musical Express (England), 12 May 1979, pp.
19-21, 57, 61.
This article/interview about Tom Waits and his
performance in London includes a fictional account
of Kerouac flying to London to see Waits perform.
Waits also recalls a dream he had about Kerouac.

844b. Holmes, John Clellon. Go. New York: Scribner, 1952.
Rpt.: Mamaroneck, N.Y.: Paul A. Appel, 1978.
Holmes' book was the first novel published to depict the Beat generation. Scenes used by Holmes
were also used by Kerouac in his work. Kerouac is
called Gene Pasternak in Go.

845. Welch, Lew. "We Started For New York." In Trip Trap: Haiku along the Road from San Francisco to New York 1959, pp. 15-20. By Jack Kerouac, Albert Saijo, and Lew Welch. Bolinas, California: Grey Fox Press, 1973.

From an abandoned novel: Lew Welch describes part of his trip from San Francisco to New York in 1959 with Jack Kerouac and Albert Saijo.

845a. Wilding, Michael. "Bye Bye, Jack. See You Soon." In The West Midland Underground, pp. 181-194. Queensland, Australia: University of Queensland Press, 1975.

Deals with his emotions about Kerouac's death and the outcome of a memorial "wake" he planned.

C. POETRY AND DRAMA

(See also citations 568, 689-690 and 692.)

846. Barry, Peter. "for jack kerouac," Palantir, No. 7 (1977): 23.

846a. Berrigan, Ted. "'Telegram' to Jack Kerouac." In In The Early Morning Rain, no pag. Cover and drawings by George Scneeman. London: Cape Goliard Press, 1970.

846b. Cloves, Jeff. "Neal Cassady and The Romance Kid." [1979?] Broadside.

847. Cobble, Sue. Untitled poem ["Jack Kerouac what have you done?"], Truck, No. 6 (1971): verso of cover.

848. Conkle, D. Steven. "Mémère." 1975. Broadside.

849. Corso, Gregory. "Elegiac Feelings American (for the dear memory of John Kerouac)." In Elegiac Feelings American, pp. 3-12. New York: New Directions, 1970. Appeared in altered form as "Spontaneous Requiem." In Ramparts, 8, No. 9 (1970): 22-25.

This poem is a memorial to Kerouac by Corso. He fuses it with a lament to the America Kerouac loved and saw and wanted, and the America of today,

getting bitter and barren.
See also citation 451b.

849a. Dearn, Keith N. "jack," Ludd's Mill (England), No.
12 (n. d.): 1.

850. Duberman, Martin. Visions of Kerouac, A Play.
Boston: Little, Brown, 1977.
This is a biographical drama about Kerouac. The
author states that he has aimed for truth of mood
rather than truth of fact, and that the play is a med-
itation on Kerouac's life.
See also reviews of this work, Section D, Part
III.

851. Finch, Peter, ed. For Jack Kerouac: Poems On His
Death. Cardiff: Second Aeon Publications, 1970.
In the middle of this book of poems - dedicated
to Kerouac on the occasion of his death - is a brief
essay on the forms of his nonconformity as evidenced
in his first major works.

851a. Ginsberg, Allen. "Memory Gardens," Evergreen Review, No. 80 (1970): 27-29.

851b. Harriman, Eddie. "Somehow Cruelly Mean," Ludd's
Mill (England), No. 15 (n. d.): 15.

852. Joans, Ted. "The Wild Spirit of Kicks," Village
Voice, 30 October 1969, p. 30.

852a. Knight, Arthur Winfield. "Jack Kerouac," Soft Need,
No. 9 (1976): 98.

853. Lauer, Mirko. "Pity for the great eye hidden in the
heights," Second Aeon, No. 13 (n. d.): 47. Translated from the Spanish by David Tipton.

853a. McCaul, Barton. "Honky-Tonk Renaissance Man,"
Moody Street Irregulars: A Jack Kerouac Newsletter,
No. 4 (1979): 8.

853b. Nakagami, Tetsuo. "Poem of the Night Jack Kerouac
Called Me," Moody Street Irregulars: A Jack Kerouac Newsletter, No. 5 (1979): 6. Translated from
the Japanese by Frank Stewart.

854. Propper, Dan. "For Kerouac In Heaven," Moody Street
     Irregulars: A Jack Kerouac Newsletter, No. 3
     (1979): 7. Appeared originally in Harrison Street
     Review, No. 3 (1972).
         Propper eulogized Kerouac in this poem written
     on the day of his death.

855. Sjöström, Jonas. "Jack Kerouac," Eureka 12 (Sweden),
     [1976], pp. 24-25. (In English.)

855a. Slater, Dave. "Jean-Louis," Ludd's Mill (England),
     No. 15 (n.d.): 14.

856. Taylor, Kent. "3-18-68 (for jack kerouac)." In Cleve-
     land Dreams, pp. 13-14. Cardiff: Second Aeon
     Publications, n.d.

857. Tremblay, Bill. "Witness, Jack Kerouac's Funeral,"
     Massachusetts Review, 11 (1970): 442-448.
         A long poem about Tremblay's participation in
     Kerouac's funeral: his impressions of the ceremony
     and the people attending; plus his own feelings toward
     Kerouac in his death.

857a. Welch, Lew. "I Sometimes Talk To Kerouac When I
     Drive." In The Yes! Press Anthology, p. 20. Santa
     Barbara, California: Christopher's Books, 1972.

D. REVIEWS OF A DRAMATIC WORK

1. DUBERMAN, Martin. Visions of Kerouac, A Play (ci-
    tation 850)

858. Aros, Andrew. "Visions of Kerouac," Library Jour-
     nal, 1 November 1977, pp. 2274-2275. (Book re-
     view.)

859. Christon, Lawrence. "Catching Up With Kerouac's
     Beats," Los Angeles Times, 4 September 1977,
     Calendar sec., pp. 53-54, 56-57. (Stage review.)

860. Crossette, Barbara. "Kerouac Translated From Page
     to Stage," New York Times, 3 December 1976, p.
     C4. (Stage review.)

861. Gussow, Mel. "'Kerouac' by Duberman Limns One
     Side of the Beat Generation," New York Times, 7
     December 1976, p. 56. (Stage review.)

862. Sullivan, Dan. "'Kerouac' at the Odyssey," Los An-
     geles Times, 14 September 1977, pt. 4, pp. 1, 11.
     (Stage review.)

APPENDIXES

A. A CHRONOLOGICAL LISTING OF JACK KEROUAC'S MAJOR PUBLISHED WORKS AND ARTICLES

The Town And The City. New York: Harcourt, Brace, 1950.

On The Road. New York: Viking Press, 1957.

The Subterraneans. New York: Grove Press, 1958.

The Dharma Bums. New York: Viking Press, 1958.

"Essentials of Spontaneous Prose," Evergreen Review, 2, No. 5 (1958).

The Subterraneans. New York: Avon Publications, 1959. Preface by Henry Miller.

Doctor Sax; Faust Part Three. New York: Grove Press, 1959.

Maggie Cassidy. New York: Avon Book Division, Hearst Corp., 1959.

Mexico City Blues. New York: Grove Press, 1959.

Visions of Cody. New York: New Directions, 1959. Excerpts from the novel.

"The Origins of the Beat Generation," Playboy, June 1959, pp. 31-32, 42, 79.

"Old Angel Midnight," Big Table, 1, No. 1 (1959): 7-42.

Tristessa. New York: Avon Book Division, Hearst Corp., 1960.

The Scripture Of The Golden Eternity. New York: Totem Press, 1960.

Lonesome Traveler. New York: McGraw-Hill, 1960. Drawings by Larry Rivers.

Book Of Dreams. San Francisco: City Lights Books, 1961.

Pull My Daisy. New York: Grove Press, 1961. Text ad-
libbed by Jack Kerouac for the film by Robert Frank and
Alfred Leslie. Introduction by Jerry Tallmer.

Big Sur. New York: Farrar, Straus and Cudahy, 1962.

Visions of Gerard. New York: Farrar, Straus, 1963.
Drawings by James Spanfeller.

"Old Angel Midnight, Part Two," Evergreen Review, 7, No.
33 (1964): 68-71, 91.

Desolation Angels. New York: Coward-McCann, 1965.
Introduction by Seymour Krim.

Satori In Paris. New York: Grove Press, 1966.

Vanity Of Duluoz: An Adventurous Education, 1935-46. New
York: Coward-McCann, 1968.

The Scripture Of The Golden Eternity. Second edition. New
York: Corinth Books, 1970. Introduction by Eric Mottram.

Pic. New York: Grove Press, 1971.

Scattered Poems. San Francisco: City Lights Books, 1971.

Visions of Cody. New York: McGraw-Hill, 1972. Introduction by Allen Ginsberg.

Two Early Stories. New York: Aloe Editions, 1973. Con-
tains two short stories which appeared in The Horace
Mann Quarterly in 1939 and 1940: "The Brothers" and
"Une Veille de Noel."

Old Angel Midnight. London: Booklegger/Albion, 1973.

Trip Trap: Haiku Along The Road From San Francisco To
New York 1959. By Jack Kerouac, Albert Saijo, and
Lew Welch. Bolinas, California: Grey Fox Press,
1973. Contains haiku by Kerouac.

Heaven & Other Poems. Bolinas, California: Grey Fox
Press, 1977.

B. BIOGRAPHICAL CHRONOLOGY

1922   Jean Louis Lebris de Kerouac born on 12 March in
        Lowell, Massachusetts, to Leo Alcide Kerouac and
        Gabrielle Ange Levesque Kerouac (a. k. a. Mémêre).
        They reside at 9 Lupine Road.

1925   The family moves to 35 Burnaby St. and then to 34
        Beaulieu St.

1926   On 8 July brother Gerard dies, at the age of nine,
        of rheumatic fever.

1927   Move to 320 Hildreth Street for two years.

1929   Another move to 240 Hildreth Street.

1930   Now to 66 West Street for three years.

1933-   Address unknown -- perhaps 16 Phebe.
1934

1935   35 Sarah Avenue for four years.

1939   Graduates from Lowell High School.   The family
        moves to 736 Moody St.

1939-   Spends year at Horace Mann Prep School in the
1940   Bronx, New York City.

1940-   Attends Columbia University on an athletic scholar-
1941   ship.   Breaks leg in freshman football game (October
        1940) and subsequently drops out of school (September
        1941).

1941   Leo and Mémêre reside at 74 Gershom Avenue.

1942   In the spring signs on with the Merchant Marine and
        ships out on the S. S. Dorchester for Greenland.   Re-
        turns in October.   Re-enrolls at Columbia but quits
        again after the first football game.   His parents
        move to 125 Crawford Street.

1943   In February enlists in the Navy and by June is dis-
        charged honorably with an indifferent character
        (based on psychiatric grounds). Signs on again with
        the Merchant Marine in June and ships out on the
        S.S. George Weems for Liverpool. Returns in Octo-
        ber.

        By June Leo and Mémêre move from Lowell and re-
        settle in Ozone Park, New York City.

1944   Meets Lucien Carr, Allen Ginsberg, and William
        Burroughs in June. Marries Edie Parker on 22
        August and by October separates from her. (This
        marriage is annulled in 1945.)

        On 14 August Lucien Carr stabs and kills David
        Kammerer.

1946   In May meets Neal Cassady.

        During May Leo Kerouac dies of Banti's disease,
        cancer of the stomach, at the age of 57.

1946-   Writes The Town And The City.
1949

1947   Hitchhikes to Denver in July and meets Cassady and
        others; then catches a bus to San Francisco to meet
        with Henry Cru. In October leaves Cru and catches
        a bus to Los Angeles; meets and lives with Bea
        Franco and works the fields near Bakersfield. Lat-
        er, leaves and catches a bus to Pittsburgh, then
        hitches to New York City.

1948   Meets John Clellon Holmes on 3 July.

1949   On 19 January drives with Cassady and others to
        New Orleans to visit Burroughs, then to San Fran-
        cisco. By mid-February returns by bus to New
        York. In March gets a letter from Robert Giroux
        that Harcourt Brace will publish The Town And The
        City. Moves with Mémêre to Westwood, Colorado,
        in May.

        Mémêre leaves by July and returns to a new apart-
        ment in New York (Richmond Hill: 94-21 134th
        Street).

Gets a letter from Cassady in July urging a trip to San Francisco: leaves for there on a bus. By August, after being evicted with Neal by Carolyn Cassady, the two catch several driveaway cars; first to Denver, then to Chicago. Take bus to Grosse Pointe, Michigan, to visit Edie Parker, then another driveaway to New York.

1949- Early drafts of ideas for On The Road.
1950

1950 The Town And The City is published in March.

During March visits Lowell on a publicity tour for the book. In June takes a bus to Denver and meets Cassady; they drive with Frank Sheperd to Mexico City to visit Burroughs and his wife, Joan. Deserted there by Cassady; stays until early fall and then returns to New York. Marries Joan Haverty on 17 November.

1951 Writes On The Road in three weeks during April and May. Separates from second wife in May. Because of thrombophlebitis in his legs is forced to move to sister Nin's home in North Carolina in June. (Mémêre is already residing there.) On 25 October in New York develops spontaneous writing style -- sketching like a painter, only with words -- as suggested by Ed White, a Denver pal. Borrows money in December and buses to San Pedro, California, for a job on a ship. Later, when job doesn't pan out, goes to San Francisco and stays with the Cassadys.

In December, Mémêre closes the Richmond Hill apartment in New York and moves to daughter Nin's home in Kinston, North Carolina.

1951- Writes or begins work on 16 major books (not in-
1957 cluding On The Road).

1952 From January until May lives in the Cassadys' attic room. Takes bus to Mexico City and stays with Burroughs until June. Borrows bus money and rides to North Carolina. In July leaves again for California and the Cassadys, works for the Southern Pacific Railroad, and stays until December. Drives with Cassady to Mexico and stays there alone; but returns to New York before Christmas.

Daughter Janet Michele Kerouac born on 16 February. John Clellon Holmes' Go is published by Scribner in the spring.

In December Mémêre resumes living in New York City.

1953   Returns to California in April and works again for the Southern Pacific. In June ships out on the S.S. William Carruth, but quits ship in July while docked in New Orleans and returns to New York. Meets "Mardou Fox" in August and falls in love with her. Draws up a checklist on his writing style called "The Essentials of Spontaneous Prose" in November.

1954   Discovers Buddhism. Takes bus to Cassadys' home in San Jose, California, in February. Later, drifts back to New York (April) and continues Buddhist studies. Visits Lowell briefly in October.

1955   In January is in court with Joan Haverty on a paternity suit and non-payment of child support. Moves with Mémêre to Rocky Mount, North Carolina, in February to help build a new home for sister Nin and her family. Is assured in 19 July letter from Malcolm Cowley on Viking's publication of On The Road. Soon after goes to Mexico City and stays with Bill Garver. Leaves by mid-September to meet Allen Ginsberg in San Francisco. Meets Gary Snyder in early October and discusses Buddhism with him. In attendance at the historic Six Gallery poetry reading on 13 October in San Francisco. (Those reading were Allen Ginsberg, Michael McClure, Gary Snyder, Philip Whalen, and Philip Lamantia; Kenneth Rexroth moderates.) In late October goes on a hiking weekend with Gary Snyder and John Montgomery around Yosemite Park. Leaves in December to get home to North Carolina for Christmas.

1956   Visits New York briefly in late January. In North Carolina gets a letter offering a lookout job on Desolation Mountain, Mount Baker National Forest, Washington state. During March, by a roundabout Mexico City route, travels to Mill Valley, California, to be with Gary Snyder in his cabin. Meets Robert Creeley in May. Hitches to job in Washington in June and is over with it by September; then hitches to

Seattle and finally buses to San Francisco. Later, travels to Mexico City and meets with Ginsberg, Gregory Corso, and Peter and Lafcadio Orlovsky; then all travel to New York. By mid-December receives official word from Viking on the publication of On The Road. Goes to Orlando and family for Christmas.

In October City Lights publishes Howl And Other Poems by Allen Ginsberg. In December Mémêre and Nin are living in a new home in Orlando, Florida.

1957   Is in New York again in January: meets William Carlos Williams in Rutherford, New Jersey; visits John Clellon Holmes in Connecticut. In February sails alone to Tangier to visit Burroughs (with Ginsberg and Orlovsky to follow). Leaves during April for Paris and London. Returns to U. S. by ship in May. Later, during May, moves with Mémêre to Berkeley, California; but after six weeks, in July, returns to Orlando. Soon after goes to Mexico City; returns to Orlando in late August, then leaves for New York. On The Road is published by Viking in September. Back in Orlando in October, but by mid-December is in New York again for the Village Vanguard jazz-poetry readings gig.

1957-   Thirteen major works published (not including On The
1963   Road).

1958   Interviews with Mike Wallace in January. Buys a home for Mémêre in Northport, New York, in April (34 Gilbert Street). In November appears at Hunter College in a debate on "Is There a Beat Generation?" along with Ashley Montagu, James E. Wechsler, and Kingsley Amis.

In May Neal Cassady is sent to San Quentin prison on a five-year sentence for possession of marijuana.

1958-   Writes or completes/compiles work on 12 books.
1969

1959   Early in the year is involved with the film Pull My Daisy and spontaneously recites the narrative to it. Interviews with Alfred Aronowitz for the New York Post in February. Begins Escapade column in April.

Flies to Los Angeles in November for an appearance
on The Steve Allen Show and tours The Subterraneans
movie set at the MGM studios.   Meets Lew Welch
and Albert Saijo in San Francisco and all three ride
to Northport in Welch's jeep.

1960   June: New York premiere of The Subterraneans
movie.

In July takes train to San Francisco with plans to
take refuge in Lawrence Ferlinghetti's cabin in Bixby
Canyon, Big Sur.   By end of summer becomes fren-
zied and more alcoholic than ever; has a nervous
breakdown.   Flies to New York in September.

1961   Participates in Timothy Leary's psychedelic drug experiments in January and is administered psilocybin.
Is sued by Joan Haverty for child support in March
in New York.   Moves with Mémère to sister Nin's
home in Orlando in May.   In July goes to Mexico
City and stays the summer.   Goes on a month-long
binge in New York during November.

1962   In March settles in court with Joan Haverty for $12
per week child support payments for daughter Janet
Michele.   In September visits John Clellon Holmes
in Old Saybrook, Connecticut, then goes to Lowell.
Meets Paul Bourgeois in hometown and the two fly
to Florida.   Moves back to Northport with Mémère
in December.

1963   Is visited by Cassady in July.

1964   Moves with Mémère to St. Petersburg, Florida, in
August.   Sister Nin dies 19 September of a coronary
occlusion.

During summer Cassady is bus chauffeur for Ken
Kesey and his Merry Pranksters.   Upon their arrival
in New York, Cassady gets Kerouac to come to a
Prankster party to meet Kesey.

1965   In July flies to Paris to research family genealogy
and to visit Brittany, an ancestral home.   In November visits Holmes in Connecticut and also Lowell.

1965-   Three major works published.
1968

1966 Moves to Hyannis, Massachusetts, in May (20 Bristol Avenue). On 19 November marries Stella Sampas.

   In September Mémêre has a paralyzing stroke.

1967 During January moves family to Lowell (271 Sanders Avenue). Meets Joe Chaput and in the summer the two drive into Canada. In the fall interviews with Ted Berrigan and Aram Saroyan for Paris Review and with Bruce Cook for his book The Beat Generation.

1968 Neal Cassady dies in Mexico on 4 February.

   In March flies with friends to Spain, Portugal, and Germany. During the summer writes "After Me, the Deluge" for the Washington Post. Drives with Chaput and others to New York in the fall to appear on William F. Buckley's television show Firing Line. Visits Burroughs, Ginsberg, and Lucien Carr at this time, also. In November moves family to St. Petersburg with Joe Chaput as driver.

1969 Dies of abdominal hemorrhaging in St. Petersburg on 21 October at 5:30 AM.

1971- Seven works published posthumously.
1977

1973 Mémêre dies on 14 October in St. Petersburg.

C. VIKING PRESS INTEROFFICE MEMOS ABOUT
ON THE ROAD*

Note: The first memo, by Helen K. Taylor, a "Viking senior editor at the time" and the "in-office editor of On The Road," is the more important of the two memos reproduced here (for the first time). It is "good and clear and not too long" and does not "propose to change the style of the book." The second memo, by Evelyn Levine, not a "senior employee" at Viking, is "longer and less clearly thought out."**

MEMO FROM HELEN K. TAYLOR

for MAC from HKT   10/22/53

ON THE ROAD by John Kerouac

I heartly agree with your feeling that this is a "classic of our times." I hope that we will get a book out of it that we will publish quietly and with conviction.

Since I won't see you to talk to Tuesday, I'll make this a conversation piece rather than an editorial report.

The book stirred me for two sets of reasons, operating concurrently. First, Kerouac's bold writing talent: it's lavish, reckless, but for all its rapid jitters and seeming carelessness, it is almost always effective. Moreover, the effectiveness does not lessen, but builds an energy of its own that is all-pervasive by the end of the book. The writing is a torrential force that comes directly out of the material, instead of being applied to it. It is almost as if the author did not seem to exist as an outside agency of creation.

---

*These memos are on file in the Malcolm Cowley archives at the Newberry Library in Chicago.
**The above quotes are by Malcolm Cowley from a letter dated 27 July 1979.

Secondly, the book is a piece of raw sociology. I am
not shocked by this portrayal of the hipster generation as a
portrayl [sic], but by the fact that the generation exists, and
was constantly forced to think of the why of it. I don't say
this in the voice of the YMCA, nor view the book as a piece
of exposure. It is a life slice so raw and bleeding that it
makes me terribly sad. It's the quintessence of everything
that is bad and horrible about this otherwise wonderful age
we live in. The trickles of evil run small and unnoticed
throughout the pattern of life today, and here they come together in a flood, in a bunch of young people who are irre-
trievably gone in the literal sense of the word. There is no
redemption for these psychopaths and hopeless neurotics, for
they don't want any. They believe that the forebrain is sub-
servient to and learns from the violences of sensation. You
don't change such people, but you reflect on the small evils
that have compounded this great human waste.

The figure of Dean is a gargantuan but believably piti-
ful "hero" viewed in these terms. The terms are unstated,
of course, but are implicit extensions from the whole crazy
mass of the book.

It's one of those books that "just is." Except for
some large chunk cutting (for it is too long) it needs only
the lightly touching pencil, for refinement has no place in
this prose. It might be a time-consuming job, but not a
difficult one. I am not too much worried about the obscenity.
I'm sure the whorehouse scene can get by practically in toto.
Not that people won't think it's a dirty book. It's a question
of publishing it quietly for the discerning few, with no touting,
pre-viewing, or advance quotes from run-of-the-mill names.
Not easy, but very challenging.

MEMO FROM EVELYN LEVINE

Having tried for the past few [weeks] to write a comment on THE BEAT GENERATION; I'm beginning to think
that I psychologically don't want to write it ... since I've
found all sorts of legitimate excuses not to. (Truth is - I
don't know how to write it out of my system)

But write it I must because I'm bursting with comment
on it. (1) The novel must be and will be published eventual-
ly. (2) Jack Kerouac is a fresh, new (and fascinating) talent.
(3) The manuscript still needs a lot of work. (4) The novel

must be published even if it is a literary and financial failure.

THE BEAT GENERATION is not a new look at F. Scott Fitzgerald's 20's generation (with a 1950 theme), or any other decade's flaming youth brought up-to-date. I think it's essentially about young people trying to find their identity (and true, a subject of many past and current novels). What I think the author is trying to say - is that Dean Moriarty does not (and probably will never) find his identity and that his friend, Sal, does in the end. But he tries to prove this too hastily and unconvincingly for me - and it's a kind of a sloppy ending - just to have Sal live happily ever after and settle down. He doesn't back up his last chapter - or establish proof (for Sal's settling down) in the beginning (and maybe that's where it should be done). (Also, the section where Sal finds "the old gentleman" with the answer he's [been searching] for. [The] author must explain further.)

All the male characters are for me - very well drawn and convincing - Dean and Sal [,] Ed Dunkel, Carlo Marx, Bull Lee...I dug 'em all (e.g. I understood them and liked the portraits Kerouac painted - good and bad). The girls in the story - are another thing - almost none of them are real...Marylou, Camille...perhaps Jane, Bull's wife, fares better than the rest and becomes a person...and maybe Terri - the Mexican girl Sal loves, is good - but even she is not convincing.

So here are these characters - in search of their identity - and the way they must do it - is by driving all over the U.S. - and the way they are really doing it is by "feeling" life down to its very roots. And they search from plain to city to city. (Incidentally - there are [too] many trips - and I was finally going around circles with all of them - perhaps some of the material from these trips could be condensed into the main ones.' I loved Kerouac's poetic style, and the sense of poetic rhythm in the prose: as they're driving thru the country you can really feel the U.S. passing by, feel the actual speed of the car; throughout there is a Whitman-esque style of expression for the U.S., a feeling that Kerouac communicated - the poetry of the U.S. He also tries to communicate to the reader the feeling of the various cities, Denver, San Francisco, Chicago, N.Y., the California country - with apologies to Steinbeck. The chapter about jazz - reprinted in New World Writing - in this, the style of the prose adds to the descriptive passages about jazz because it sounded exactly like bop music.   I don't know if this [is] great writing - but I loved it.

So here's another lost generation - but this one doesn't run away to Paris - they stay right here - and try to find themselves.   There is a great deal of (what might be called) immorality in the book - use of narcotics, drinking, immoral sexual relationships.   I don't think the author is exaggerating too much - in the search for their identity, they're also try- ing to live life to the fullest; protesting against the older gen- eration's and society's rules.   In other periods, the young people exiled themselves in Paris, participated in revolutions, became radicals, etc.   The Beat Generation searches thru the United States via fast cars.

I like the episode in Mexico, also the episode with Terri in California, right now I can't remember some of the others I liked so much.

Kerouac is not trying for sensationalism - and I think it's a true picture of a some [sic] people - odd as they seem.

Kerouac is a jived-up Walt Whitman - and I loved his picture of America (if you omit the plot of the novel) and I think it's a novel of protest - but I'm not sure what he's protesting about - but that doesn't matter.   It is not a picture of the younger generation as we know it - but neither are they juvenile delinquents.

This isn't really all of what I wanted to say - I'm at a loss trying to write this 3 weeks after reading the ms. but I remember Dean Moriarty, I remember Dean Moriarty [.] In some ways - I think Kerouac is a more honest writer than Saul Bellow (in Augie) maybe that's cause he's younger - I don't mean he's a better writer, though. . . .

D. LAST WILLS AND TESTAMENTS OF JEAN KEROUAC AND GABRIELLE KEROUAC

JEAN KEROUAC*

I, JEAN KEROUAC, a/k/a Jack Kerouac, of St. Petersburg, Pinellas County, Florida, being of sound mind and memory and it being my intention and purpose to dispose of all of my property of every description which I may own at the time of my death, or which I may have the power to dispose of by Will, and not being under undue influence of any character whatsoever, do hereby make, publish and declare this to be my Last Will and Testament, revoking all former Wills and Codicils by me at any time heretofore made.

FIRST: I direct that all my just debts and funeral expenses be paid as soon as possible out of the principal of my estate.

SECOND: I give, devise and bequeath all of the rest, residue and remainder of my estate, real, personal or mixed, of which I may die seized or possessed, or to which I may be entitled at the time of my death, to my beloved mother, GABRIELLE A. KEROUAC, absolutely.

THIRD: In the event my beloved mother, GABRIELLE A. KEROUAC, predeceases me, then I give, devise and bequeath all of the rest, residue and remainder of my estate, as hereinabove defined, to my nephew, PAUL E. BLAKE, JR., of Mountain View, Alaska and of the United States Air Force (29245387) Lackland Air Force Base, Texas.

FOURTH: I nominate, constitute and appoint CITIZENS NATIONAL BANK of St. Petersburg, Florida, Executor of this my Last Will and Testament. I vest my said Executor with full power and authority to deal with my property, real or personal, as it deems necessary and proper in order to carry out my intentions as herein expressed and to do every

---

* Filed for record, 24 October 1969, County Judge, Pinellas County, Florida.

other act and thing necessary or proper to complete administration of this Will.

IN WITNESS WHEREOF, I have hereunto set my hand
and seal and identified the foregoing page and this page of my
Will by signing my name at the end of said page and at the
end of this Will on the 4th day of September A. D. 1969.

Jean Kerouac a/k/a Jack Kerouac

The foregoing intrument was signed, sealed, published
and declared by JEAN KEROUAC, a/k/a Jack Kerouac, as
his Last Will and Testament in the presence of us, the undersigned who at his special instance and request, do attest as
witnesses after said Testator signed his name thereto and in
his presence and in the presence of each other the 4th day
of September, A. D. 1969.*

GABRIELLE A. KEROUAC**

KNOW ALL MEN BY THESE PRESENTS:

That I, GABRIELLE A. KEROUAC, a resident of and
domiciled in St. Petersburg, Pinellas County, Florida, being
of sound and disposing mind and memory, do hereby make,
publish and declare this my Last Will and Testament, hereby
revoking and rendering void any and all wills and codicils
thereto by me at any time heretofore made.

FIRST

I direct that my Executrix, hereinafter named, shall
first pay and discharge any and all debts and expenses of my
last illness and funeral as soon as practicable after my death.

SECOND

I give, devise and bequeath all of my estate, both real
and personal and wherever situate, to my daughter-in-law,
STELLA S. KEROUAC, to be hers absolutely and in fee
simple.

---

* The signatures of the three witnesses are illegible.
** Filed for record, 15 November 1973, Clerk Circuit Court,
Pinellas County, Florida.

THIRD

I nominate and appoint my daughter-in-law, STELLA S. KEROUAC, as Executrix of my Last Will and Testament, giving and granting unto my said Executrix full power and authority to sell and dispose of all or any part of my estate as she in her sole and absolute discretion may deem best. I excuse my Executrix from furnishing any bond for the performance of her duties.

IN WITNESS WHEREOF, I have hereunto set my hand and seal this 13th day of February, 1973.

Gabrielle A. Kerouac

The foregoing instrument was signed, sealed, declared and published by GABRIELLE A. KEROUAC as her Last Will and Testament, in the presence of us, the undersigned, who, at her special instance and request, to attest and have hereunto subscribed our names as witnesses after said Testatrix has signed her name thereto, and in her presence and in the presence of each other this 13th day of February, 1973. *

---

* The signatures of the two witnesses are illegible.

E. "BIG TABLE": THE COURT AND THE
CRITICS; OPINIONS

The Winter 1959 issue of the Chicago Review was suppressed by its parent body, the University of Chicago. This
literary quarterly was to include Jack Kerouac's "Old Angel
Midnight" and ten chapters from Naked Lunch by William
Burroughs: apparently, the two most offensive pieces to the
UC administration. They were alerted to the issue's contents
by Jack Mabley, columnist for the now-defunct Chicago Daily
News. He called it "Filthy Writing on the Midway" in his
25 October 1958 column.

After trying several compromises with the University
executives to get the issue published, and finally being left
without any recourse, six of the seven editors of the Chicago
Review resigned. They took the contents of the entire Winter
issue with them. A corporation was then formed, Big Table
magazine was founded (named by Kerouac, as had been Naked
Lunch), and the first issue, Spring 1959, was printed and
distributed by mid-March 1959.

Soon afterwards, the Post Office Department impounded
and seized Big Table as being nonmailable. It contained material they considered obscene and filthy. A hearing was
held in June - P.O.D. Docket No. 1/150 - and the Hearing
Examiner upheld the initial decision to seize the magazine. *[1]
A short time later a Post Office appeals officer upheld the
examiner's decision. [2]

The matter was brought to the U.S. District Court on
30 June 1960. (Big Table, Inc. v. Carl A. Schroeder, United
States Postmaster for Chicago, Illinois. Case No. 59 C
1382.) The judge was Julius J. Hoffman. Excerpts from

---

*Two appendixes attached to these proceedings consisted of
testimony either stating that Big Table did not have any literary merit (one statement) or attesting that the contents of
the magazine were serious literary works and not obscene in
nature (twenty-four statements). More than half of these
statements are reprinted at the end of this section. See page
198 for Notes to this Appendix.

the proceeding follow:

Action for injunctive and declaratory relief in respect to Post Office order that two articles in a quarterly publication were offensive and filthy and there-
fore nonmailable. Both parties moved for summary
judgment. The District Court, Julius J. Hoffman,
J., held that there was no substantial evidence to
support the post office finding that the articles were
obscene.

The dispositive question in this action is whether
the magazine "Big Table I" is obscene, but a necessary preliminary to that inquiry, as it is raised
here, is a resolution of whether the judicial review
of a Post Office order, barring matter from the
mails on such ground, is subject to and adequately
provided for....

The plaintiff, an Illinois corporation, is the publisher and distributor of "Big Table," a quarterly
publication in the nature of a literary review, of
which the number in suit was the first. The defend-
ant United States Postmaster for Chicago, Illinois,
refused to accept "Big Table I" for mailing pursuant
to a departmental order determining that two articles
contained therein were obscene and filthy and, there-
fore, non-mailable under the statutory declaration
found in... the United States Code.

... The complaint which initiated the present action sought both injunctive relief from the operation
of the order and a declaratory judgment that the
magazine was not obscene or filthy, that the defend-
ant's acts were unauthorized by statute as well as
in violation of the First and Fifth Amendments to
the Constitution of the United States, and that the
seizure and impounding of the publication without
notice or prior hearing did not afford due process
of law....

... The primary evidence in this type of proceeding is, of course, the articles themselves. Ascer-
taining whether the treatment of a given subject is
obscene demands a taxing analysis of both content
and context since it is not merely the use of language or description unacceptable by contemporary
community standards which is forbidden but the material must also be held capable of evoking a prurient interest.

Further, that interest must provide the dominant

theme of the work which may very well necessitate
a dissection of the literary product to determine
whether, even though there be an overwhelming
galaxy of four-letter Anglo Saxon words or other
expressions usually consigned to the category of
obscene parlance, nevertheless, the appeal is to
some other interest than the prurient.

It is presumably for that reason that the courts
have given recognition to the literary setting in
which the attacked expression is found, with references made to the intent of the author, the literary
merit of the work, and the craft requirements of
the styles employed. But, caution must be exer-
cised to avoid relying solely on abstract or academic literary judgments. The legal standard of obscenity is not intended to serve as a protection for
semantic liberalism under the guise of free speech.
It is concerned with the social effect of the language
and, hence, the requirement that dominant theme
be the appeal to the prurient as reflected in the
judgment of the average man, applying contemporary
community standards.

It is by the inclusion of the contemporary criter-
ion that the law of obscenity becomes a vital, living
concept of social freedom, or "ordered liberty."
... Its absence on the administrative record is not
yet decisive of this court's power to review and
render a judgment.

Rather, it must be held, in the absence of a
showing to the contrary, that the official to whom
the function of trier of fact has been assigned by
virtue of the administrative process applied the
contemporary standards which he respects as an
average member of the community. And the court
is competent, likewise, to determine whether his
conclusion could reasonably be drawn from the facts
because the court can stand in the same position,
of an average man, applying the proper standards,
much as it is required to do whenever exercising its
conventional judicial function of deciding whether
reasonable men could differ.

Turning to the record now presented for review,
it must be ruled that "Big Table I" could not be
found obscene, as a matter of law. The two articles said to dominate the publication are works of
prose. The one, entitled "Old Angel Midnight" by
Jack Kerouac, is a bit of construction in the vein

of a "stream of consciousness" technique and appears to be some sort of dialogue between, broadly, God and Man. The contextual scheme is a critique of the world. It is indeed numerically replete with words which are not used, overtly at least, by the average person. But, in the court's opinion, any libidinous effect those words might commonly have could not possibly occur from their present position among other printed characters which sometimes rise to the dignity of a word and sometimes do not.

Obscene material, as stated above, is "material which deals with sex in a manner appealing to prurient interest." The Kerouac article does not deal with sex any more than it deals with anything else. And, surely, the meaning of "manner" in that approved definition implies a method of presentation which is something more than simply using unaccepted words.

In comparison, the other accused article, "Ten Episodes from Naked Lunch" by William S. Burroughs, which is devoted to the days in the life of a narcotics addict, may be termed representational in that there is a purposeful progression of situations, some of which cover topics of sex. But, it must be reiterated, it is the manner of dealing with sex which is to be judged. "Naked Lunch," while not exactly a wild prose picnic in the style of Kerouac, is, taken as a whole, similarly unappealing to the prurient interest. The exacerbated, morbid and perverted sex related by the author could not arouse a corresponding interest in the average reader, as the Hearing Examiner in this case agreed. The dominant theme or effect is that of shocking the contemporary society, in order perhaps to better point out its flaws and weaknesses, but that clinical appeal is not akin to lustful thoughts.

As the foregoing analysis reveals, describing the facts in cases such as this is not an easy task and necessarily requires some characterizations, but that cannot be escaped so long as judicial review is accorded in obscenity matters.

The other evidence contained in the record consists of testimony and exhibits pertaining to literary merit and the serious purpose of the authors. As summarized in the agency decision, a consensus of the views of the witnesses, numbered among whom were respected critics, professors, and authors,

is that the material is within the broad field of
serious literature and that the writers are intent
on literary pursuits.   The merit of their works is
in dispute and not highly regarded for the most
part....

Although having reached the conclusion that the
record does not support a finding of obscenity, the
task of reviewing "Big Table I" is not yet done.
The Post Office also charged that the contents of
the magazine were "filthy, " a separate classification
of non-mailable matter.... The test in that regard
is whether the material has "a tendency to deprave
or corrupt the morals of those who would receive
them...."

That standard... also could not be met by the
evidence in the instant case....

The motion of the plaintiff for summary judgment
is allowed and the order of the Post Office Department declaring "Big Table I" non-mailable will be
vacated and set aside.

TESTIMONY IN SUPPORT OF THE POST OFFICE SEIZURE OF "BIG TABLE I"

I, August Derleth, of Sauk City, Wisconsin, being duly
sworn, do state that as literary editor of The Capital Times
of Madison, Wisconsin, for the past eighteen years, as editor
of Arkham House: Publishers for the past twenty years; and
as the author of 85 published books, some of which have a
modest literary merit, I believe I have at least a minor
claim to some knowledge of what constitutes a work of literary merit.

In my capacity as literary editor of a daily paper, I
obtained and read a copy of BIG TABLE 1.   I read this issue with particular attention because advance publicity con-
tending that the exclusion of this material from a well-known
established literary quarterly had led me to believe that it
might be a) important as a contribution to literature; b) the
object of a regrettable tendency toward censorship, which I
tend both as an author and a gregarious reader to deplore,
and about which I have published several columns in the newspaper of which I am literary editor, usually in vigorous opposition.

I am sorry to have to say that in my considered opinion

the overwhelming majority of the material in BIG TABLE 1 has no literary merit whatsoever. I have here specific reference to the material titled "Old Angel Midnight," by Jack Kerouac; "Ten Episodes from 'Naked Lunch'," by William S. Burroughs; and "Three Poems," by Gregory Corso, which are for the most part undisciplined prose, far more akin to the early work of experimental adolescents than to anything of literary merit. Though two contributions by Edward Dahlberg, "Further Sorrows of Priapus," and "The Garment of Ra," are works of some merit, they occupy so few pages in the magazine as to be negligible in the issue, and do not represent an important contribution to literature.

TESTIMONY IN SUPPORT OF "BIG TABLE I" AS A SERIOUS LITERARY WORK

HAROLD TAYLOR. President of Sarah Lawrence College.

On Burroughs: "a writer of serious intent"; "he manages to make the clinical details of almost every aspect of human experience fairly repulsive, and often very funny."

On Kerouac: "no doubt of his literary intent"; "he is so pretentiously literary and so short of imagination in carrying out his intention that I would question whether it is important enough as literature to be included in a magazine as serious as yours. There are traces of Ted Roethke and second-hand James Joyce but very little of the qualities of mind which makes their work so interesting and important."

JOHN CIARDI. Rutgers University. President, College English Association.

Contents of Big Table 1 are "entirely serious in their search for true values, very deeply concerned with matters of great social importance." "I may confess to some personal disagreements of aesthetic principle here and there in the writing, but in general it must certainly be recorded as work of substantial artistic accomplishment."

NORMAN MAILER. Author of The Naked and the Dead.

"The 'Ten Episodes From Naked Lunch' by William Burroughs are, I believe, the work of a writer with exceptional talents. Burroughs creates the atmosphere of his work by the use of a disciplined chiseled style in which every word seems essential. That this style, lithe, alert to the cadence and nuance of every sound, is still able to create for us the wild, disoriented and fantasy-filled world of the junk addict is part of its considerable achievement. Burroughs is a literary phenomenon almost unique in the history of letters.

"I could go on to talk about the value of this selection as a document, for it offers invaluable insight (not without its medical uses) into the mind of the addict, but I would prefer to offer instead what is for me, the more powerful argument: Burroughs may prove to be one of the most important American writers to be printed since the War.

"Much the same may be said for Kerouac, and his piece, 'Old Angel Midnight.' Kerouac is undoubtedly one of the major young writers in this country, and any passage of experimental work by him is entitled to the dignity of open publication."

ALLEN GINSBERG.

To Whom It May Concern:

My qualifications as a witness: I have a B.A. from Columbia College. I have written book reviews for the New York Herald Tribune, Newsweek Magazine, The Village Voice. I am the author of a book of poems, "Howl," published by City Lights Co. in San Francisco. I have taught a class in creative writing for San Francisco State College. I have given poetry readings--readings of my own and others' poetry--at Oxford (England), Harvard, Yale, Columbia, New York University, Brooklyn College, Muhlenberg College, University of California, San Francisco State College. My poetry has been translated and published or broadcast in Germany, France, Sweden, and Chile. My German publisher is Limes Verlag, my French translator is Alan Bosquet, who consulted me in the preparation of an anthology of young American writers which he is assembling for European use in cooperation with the U.S. Information Service. I have published poetry in various U.S. magazines including The Chicago Review, Partisan Review, Evergreen Review, The Black Mountain Review.

In my opinion the writers Jack Kerouac and William S. Burroughs are the most important prose geniuses to have emerged in America since the last War. In the case of Kerouac, this is not only my own opinion, but also the opinion

of many local and international critics and journalists. He
is considered in France and Germany as certainly one of the
most exciting manifestations of U.S. literary temperament
that they have heard of. Many articles, in almost all countries of Europe and South America, have been devoted to a
description of his writing. Mr. Burroughs' work is less
well known, since very little of it has been published, in
fact, the section of "Naked Lunch" published in the issue of
Big Table under consideration is the first sizeable chunk of
his prose printed in the last 8 years. I think it is the most
significant piece of social criticism that has been published
in America in this century and will ultimately rank, in both
content and prose style, with the work of Dean Swift, author
of Gulliver's Travels and A Modest Proposal.

The question under discussion is whether the works
Old Angel Midnight and Naked Lunch are too obscene to send
thru the mail. I have made the above paragraph of generali-
zation about their literary work in order to emphasize that a
censorship of their work will not be greeted with indifference
by literary figures here in the U.S. or abroad.

The works are in my opinion not obscene at all. Both
are in their mood and conscious intention religious testaments.
Both are concerned with an illumination of consciousness
wherein the Divinity of the soul is revealed. The method of
composition of both works is similar: a transcription of the
inmost & deepest fantasies and insights of the authors, without care for anything but the truth of the reporting. This is
an attempt of great value and could only be attempted by
writers of great human virtue. It is in the tradition of great
Democratic documents, statements of individual realities,
confessions and insights, that includes the work of Thoreau
and Whitman. This literary tradition is the very life-blood
of the individualistic spirit in this country and any attempt to
suppress it by the present government or any of its agencies
would be to me a sign of degeneracy of the Soul of this nation
that has taken place since its founders first agreed that in-
dividuals should be encouraged to explore the divinity within
themselves. One must re-read Thoreau, Emerson and Whitman to understand that they felt that this was exactly the
ideal purpose of America. It is a virtue that has been much
overlooked in recent times, and may even now seem absurd
to the materialistic modern mind.

The specific works in question, Old Angel Midnight
and Naked Lunch are the most advanced pieces of prose composition that the two authors have penned.

In Kerouac's case the principle of spontaneous unrevised
composition (similar to experiments in prose by Joyce & Ger-
trude Stein) has been carried out to its necessary and logical
conclusion. Each section of the work - (49 sections are published here) - is the result of a short session of writing, in
which the author puts down on the page all the actual thoughts
in his mind, uncensored and in the rhythm in which they naturally come. This is an experiment in truthful meditation.
It is a sample of a man's actual mind. If the actual truthful
mind of a man cannot be printed in America, as set forth
after years of competent craftsmanship and practiced art,
then it speaks less well for the official laws of the land than
for the natural laws of the mind. If a man cannot communicate his mind thru the mail then perhaps it ought to be the
mail that is to be stopped, rather than the mind.

The grievance of censorship here is made more unen-
durable by the realization of the religious nature of Kerouac's
meditations. The prose is primarily an exposition of the fact
that an examination of the contents of his mind leads him to
an understanding of a Divinity, an Enlightened One, beneath
his consciousness. This is not in the province of the officials of this government to censor nor would they presumably
censor it if they understood what he was getting at. The officials would probably rejoice and be happy to grant second
class mailing privileges. And deliver the magazine with joy.
Kerouac's piece is called Old Angel Midnight, and that's what
it's about, an angel in the midnight of the meditative mind.

I should add that I consider it his most advanced piece
of writing technically, i. e. it most closely realizes his de-
sire for a near science of prose to transcribe the minutest
variations of inner thought. This is a contribution to American prose which later writers will I think come to value and
learn from. It is a sample of an important prose method.
Its value is, from this point of view, too great to even think
of worrying about its obscenity.

We have very similar considerations to take into account when examining W. S. Burroughs' Naked Lunch. It is
his Word (the title of one section)--his revelation of his own
actual mind. He is a man who is well educated, who has
travelled much, and suffered much, and in his advancing
years (he is over 40) he has come to understand certain
things about himself and society which he wished to express.
Thus the title Naked Lunch. The truth, his truth, is here
naked. One of the main insights of this portion of the mss.
is into the nature of the mass brainwash of individuality that

has come in our century thru scientific technique. (See section 7.) That a prose exposition on this subject of brainwash should itself be censored by an arm of the government is to me proof of the urgency of his message, and the advisability of its being left free to be disseminated to the public thru the mails. What we have in question here, to my mind, is none other than the subtle spread of a mental dictatorship in America which inhibits free individualistic expression of insight into its nature. To censor Naked Lunch in the mail will be an act of political censorship, in its significance.

Burroughs' main prose technique is what might be called a "Routine, "--this is a section of fantasy wherein he takes an idea and carries it out to illogical dreamlike limits. In the course of such mental freedom he often arrives at very useful and entertaining insights. Thus he has described imaginary political parties, brainwash technicians, presidents with obscene dope habits, a whole class of spiritual police, exaggerated nightmare rock and roll riots, etc. etc. These all seem to me to be valid artistic paraphrases of our present human situation. He speaks at length of Junk, or heroin, both literally and as a symbol of habitual dependence on materialistic ideas of selfhood, or false worldly ego. Thus it is quite appropriate for him to extend this fantasy to describe an unnamed symbolic president as a man hung up on symbolic Junk, with all appropriate psychological and sexual abnormalities. I mention this since there I understood that this passage (Section 3) was called into question. I see no reason why an author need hesitate to examine the possibility of a government and its officials being hung up or addicted to false psychological and spiritual conceptions of the world. For that is what that passage means. And censorship of that passage would be treason to democracy.

The whole book Naked Lunch, and the passages printed in Big Table, are very fine, perceptive, dry, comic, nightmarish prose. The writing sometimes approaches a kind of prose-poetry which is found in 20th Century French writing-- notably St. John Perse. To this extent it is also an innovation in American style. It is high class literature, and shouldn't be classed with girlie magazine worries by the P. O. Dept. Why it was ever called into question at all I cannot imagine, except it be the literary incompetence of those officials of the P. O. Dept. to judge such matters. It should certainly be taken out of the hands of people who would censor it; they should be told to leave true Art alone. The artist has enough trouble without having to battle the Govt.

ANTHONY WEST.   Author and New Yorker book critic.

   "patently a serious literary magazine. "   "I do not
think that any contributor to your first issue has succeeded
in reaching the level of great or lasting literature, and I feel
that some of them are exploring what I am convinced are
blind alleys.   But I am quite sure that everything in the magazine is the fruit of a serious attempt to achieve what has
always been, and always will be, the final literary purpose -
that is to tell the truth of man's vital experience as the
writer knows it. "   "I do not believe that any contribution
can be read from its beginning through to its end without ...
that the appeal made is serious, thoughtful. "

ROBERT CREELEY.   Editor of the Black Mountain Review.

   "Jack Kerouac's OLD ANGEL MIDNIGHT makes use of
a device very similar to that which Mr. Joyce used in ULYSSES. "
"Again the terms of the literary work have been forgotten --
terms most clear to one who attempts to understand them;
and only the 'four letter words' so to speak noted. "   "My
respect for Mr. Burroughs, as for Mr. Kerouac, is grounded
on a considerable knowledge of his work since I have had the
good fortune to read a great part of the manuscript of NAKED
LUNCH, from which these sections printed in BIG TABLE
#1 are taken.   I find him a literary artist of great ability,
and I look upon his work as exploring, with great literary
skill and acumen, social problems and areas which are as
real in our society as any I am aware of.   It is surely not
the intention of either man to argue the rightness or wrong-
ness of what their research has in each case discovered;"

ALFRED G. ARONOWITZ.   Author, New York Post reporter.

   "I can report unqualifiedly that the contents of Big
Table 1, including 'Old Angel Midnight' and 'Ten Episodes
from Naked Lunch, ' are intended as serious works of art
and that any attempt to classify them as otherwise is pure
boorishness and/or ignorance.   The Beat Generation is a
serious literary movement of tremendous social significance
and Big Table should be commended, rather than suppressed,
for its initiative in bringing these important documents to
public attention. "

JAMES LAUGHLIN.   Publisher, New Directions Press.

   Describes writers in Big Table 1 as being writers of

"seriousness and caliber. " "These writers whom you have
published are neither purveyors of smut nor sensation seek-
ers; they are sensitive and gifted writers attempting to re-
create in formal terms, the life which they see around them. "

WILLIAM BUTLER. Director, Literature and Drama; Production Director, Radio Station KPFA, Berkeley, California.

"This letter is not meant to constitute any form of
literary appraisal of the contents of BIG TABLE 1, for I
cannot pretend to be in complete accord with the editors of
BIG TABLE as to the value of the literature in their first
issue. There is no doubt, however, that the contents of this
magazine are intended to be, and exists as, seriously inquir-
ing literature. " "There is, indeed, nothing in this magazine
which would be of real interest to anyone except persons
deeply involved in the art and craft and writing, and readers
of much discernment and intelligence; in other words, whether
it is good literature or bad literature, it is highly selective
and erudite literature. "

LAWRENCE FERLINGHETTI. Publisher, City Lights Press,
San Francisco; bookseller and poet.

"In the case of BIG TABLE 1, practically any qualified
unbiased critic would have to admit that there is social importance in all of the material therein and further that the
authors of this material are all well-known, serious writers
in the avant-garde of American literature. "

MARC D. SCHLEIFER. Author and critic, contributor to The
(Greenwich) Village Voice.

MARC D. SCHLEIFER, a frequent contributor to The
Voice, is in another capacity a poet and a friend of the leading "beat generation" writers.

"Readers of 'Big Table 1' (its cover flamboyantly red,
white, and blue) are witnessing not merely another quarterly
birth but rather a thorough literary resurrection. 'Big Table
1' contains the complete contents of the suppressed winter
issue of the Chicago Review. The contributors are Jack Kerouac, Edward Dahlberg, William S. Burroughs, and Gregory
Corso. That the former editors of the Chicago Review have
successfully arranged independent publication can only be taken
as a healthy sign. Literature may yet [survive] the bosomy
bear hug of its official protector -- the Academy.

"The episodes from Burroughs' unpublished 'Naked Lunch' would alone justify 'Big Table's' existence. Writing of a world seen through 'the dead, undersea eyes of junk,' Burroughs' prose flies spear-like at the reader; phrases, images thrown in swift clean motions. The wild humor and mad fantasies possess a quality that Gide described as 'hallucinations of reality' when speaking of Celine. Organized in mosaic form, 'Naked Lunch' earns its own unique continuity through an acute sense of the instantaneous.

"Jack Kerouac's 'Old Angel Midnight' is also episodic. Sadly, there the similarity ends. Not that incoherence is the problem, no matter how hard Kerouac strives for Joycean tone. In the name of spontaneous prosody, Kerouac strains and strains, only to bequeath a sloppy boredom. Pretentious style can never mask dull content, and true spontaneity equates a state of mind, not a narrow technique. In magnificent contrast are Dahlberg's 'Further Sorrows of Priapus.' Dahlberg is one of the last old masters of the article; his rare peers lie buried in back issues of Black Mountain Review. Discussing the Persian tyrants he writes: 'War is the amour of the insane, the voluptuous entertainment of the tyrant. Despotism comes from the insatiable belly and the scrotum...' Dahlberg has also contributed a long and somewhat tedious poem, 'The Garment of Ra,' that still merits reading for its occasional lyrical gems.

"Gregory Corso's appeal has in the past resided in his treatment of prosaic subjects with a paradoxical, wild-gentle, wonderful humor. His three poems in 'Big Table' -- 'Power,' 'Army,' and 'Police' -- are his most ambitious published attempts since his magnicent broadside, 'BOMB.' In 'Power' and 'Army,' however, Corso is unfortunately unable to sustain his special sense of revelation unfolding into greater revelation. Not that any of his images are to be dismissed (those in 'Power' reel the reader); it's rather a problem of movement. But 'Police' is superb in every respect."

KENNETH BURKE. Critic, member of the Institutes for Advanced Studies, Princeton University.

"In my opinion, many passages in this collection are stylistically interesting and valuable. They possess a certain turbulance or saliency that, being attained at times by inventiveness and imaginativeness, are good for literature." "Though the gestures here embodied are a bit obsessive, they serve well to express one motivational strand among the many that should comprise the total dialogue of our civilization."

LE ROI JONES. Editor of <u>Yugen</u> and publisher of Totem Press, New York City.

"The works in question (Kerouac and Burroughs) are unquestionably intended to be artifacts (of one kind or another), 'made' objects; things to be kept & looked at (even learned from) for as long as they have some meaning for (this?) society." "I would say there is not the least erotic intent in either of the works." "but the strange thing is that neither one of the writers in question is a 'naturalist' ... that's a mere front, a vehicle. Both are great romantics with strong penchants for the fantastic." "& on top of all this, the Burroughs piece is perhaps the finest prose work to use America as its jumping off point in some time."

NOTES

1. "The Hearing Examiner herein held that 'Big Table I' was obscene because it went beyond the prevailing limits of candor but he ruled that it could not appeal to the prurient interest." Prurient is equated with a "'shameful or morbid interest in nudity, sex, or excretion.'" And "'the prurient interest is an exacerbated, morbid or perverted interest growing out of the conflict between the universal sexual drive of the individual and equally universal social controls of sexual activity.'" ("Big Table, Inc. v. Carl A. Schroeder, United States Postmaster for Chicago, Illinois," <u>Federal Supplement</u>, Volume 186 [St. Paul, Minnesota: <u>West Publishing</u> Co., 1961], p. 259.)

2. "The Post Office Judicial Officer who rendered the final departmental decision in this case said that he agreed with the Hearing Examiner's conclusion that the material was obscene 'only because' of the Institute's definition of 'prurient.' He then characterized the articles involved as portraying 'sexual matters and subjects in a most exacerbated, morbid and perverted manner.'" ("Big Table, Inc. v. Carl A. Schroeder, United States Postmaster for Chicago, Illinois," <u>Federal Supplement</u>, Volume 186 [St. Paul, Minnesota: West Publishing Co., 1961], p. 259.)

March 23, 1978

Dear Dennis:

Regarding seeming duplications between your text and
the Gifford-Lee book, both of which we read in sequence the
last few days: It may come from reliance on published or
unpublished writing by Carolyn Cassady, or from the habit
Charters, Gifford-Lee, Latham, & yourself developed of relying on Kerouac's novelistic texts for documentation of scenes
and "quoted" conversations. Duplication of documentary
sources, letters, biographical sketches & interviews is inevi-
table, but narrative integration of these sources without using
them as indented documentary-scholarly source matter inter-
leaved visibly in your narrative will cause various confusions.
It may be that you want a smoother prose-reading page, &
not, as in Enid Starkie's biogs of Rimbaud, want to break
the page up with paragraphs or pages of quoted texts reproduced scholar-style. The effect of smoothing it into the page
gives rise to perplexity in reader of seeing familiar or un-
familiar passages from novels, bios by Carolyn, interviews
by me & others, & not know whether it's you writing or you
paraphrasing some source. So for major scenes you describe
you should use quote blocks, or parenthetical phrases to in-
dicate major passages lifted from here & there. It wd make
your book more reliable. After awhile, since you had no
specific footnotes, like real scholar works, but general areas
of footnote including half dozen different references, it was
too difficult (laborious & slow) for me to locate sources, even
tho I'm familiar with much of the source matter.

This is especially true with accounts of scenes derived
from Kerouac's fictionalized account. In those cases you

*The last two paragraphs of this letter appeared in <u>Moody
Street Irregulars: A Jack Kerouac Newsletter</u>, Vol. 1, No.
2 (1978):12. Letter reprinted by permission.

should always warn the reader "This is how Kerouac recalled this scene" or "as Kerouac fictionalized this moment" or "as Kerouac interpreted this in his version of Duluoz etc" or "Kerouac's account in novel form laid it out thus" etc. The reason is simply that K's versions were fictions based on fact, but not at all identical with actual event, part thru novelistic imagination, part thru the specialization of his own views.

So that above is a major critique I have to offer. The genre of fictionalized biography, as Latham did it, is disgustingly inaccurate, & the genre itself delusive & devisive on living people tho it might work for the dead in historical novels--but here you're bordering on fictionalized bio when you integrate Kerouac's accounts into your own, unless you label them as his accounts, or Carolyn's etc. Kerouac made up stuff like an artist remember.

Lucien [Carr] made up a list of sample parallelisms of language or source between your & Gifford-Lee book. I'll try locating some of them so you'll get an idea:

> The bit about arriving on West Coast to ship out with Henri Cru and "as usual there was no job"--maybe you both are paraphrasing Kerouac text? Both books, same phrase.
> The porkchop incident with the Cassadys--maybe Carolyn's mss?
> Ginsberg & psychiatrist--same story repeated with little variation, neither distinguished by accurate context or precise detail, same overgeneralization--source where?
> Second inscription to Carolyn by Kerouac in his book after K. brought whore in house: 'I'll never do it again'--Carolyn's mss?
> Allen as promoter or agent for friends--both books got it from same place, in fuzzy detail & similar (in my opinion--AG).

You can overcome the defect of parallel sources by citing your sources in graceful prose way as part of narration.

Incidentally, in Luanne's document for Gifford--she sez there was no cold cream in reality--just heat, Texas, nakedness sunlight according to Luanne's probably true version I'd guess--so if you take Kerouac's "Road" or "Duluoz" (I don't remember source) version as history, you accept his imagistic hyperbole, acceptable as fiction, and pass it off as fact to unsuspecting reader. You can cover your ass by mentioning where these anecdotes come from, true or embroidered as may be.

Also by using quote marks locally in narrative indicating sources, you can set good example for future biographers; so far Kerouac's biographers have been so overwhelmed by his own narratives that they borrow his elan & method too literally & attempt to compete, rival or parallel him in looseness of reference, for the sake [of] smooth reading.

Lucien & I read the book thru--I skimmed [the] first chapter where I had no info to contribute....I made extensive notations on the margin, which went beyond correction of detail as I knew it, & critiqued a number of your phrasings & generalizations. Lucien's letter goes into that a bit, & he contributed his practiced editor's pencil marks to what I finally called "hyperbole" on your part--feelings "slashing" at the heart, people babbling when they were talking intelligently, shrieking & screaming when they were just writing letters or talking etc. "Overwritten" was the code word I used for marginal comment when I felt the language was excessively naive or hopped up senselessly.

I had dull country pencil so if you have trouble interpreting my notations call me to clarify if need be or useful.

I have a booklet of marginalia-errors I made on first edition hardcover Charters, if that would be useful for you & there's time. It may be too late. I could send xerox.

Criticisms aside, the main thrust of the book intrigues me most in the accounting of K's struggle as artist against opposition & incomprehension. I've written a little note which you can use any way you want, blurb afterword or letter of recommendation. * The assemblage of obstructive reviews is fantastic, just what my heart desired, to see all those jerks lined up against the wall of historic justice on the fields of literary time.

"Slowly the poison the whole blood-stream fills:
The waste remains, the waste remains and kills. "
--Empson?

* Appeared as "A Note On McNally's Kerouac Biography, " in Moody Street Irregulars: A Jack Kerouac Newsletter, Vol. 1, No. 2 (1978): 14.

That's sort of a slogan I've had in head last few months. If
it isn't there you ought to document in footnote, Anatole Broyard chasing Kerouac's corpse with his stiletto in daily NY
Times review of posthumous Visions of Cody, insulting it,
ignoring the great prose experimental energy, the finished
sublime sketches, & also misconstruing my preface so badly
that he told the reader it was "obviously" some kind of dreary
labor of duty I didn't wanna do--when in truth the preface was
reduced from an annotation of the book done as a labor of
love, 3 times the size of the published preface, & printed
later in full by Mulch Press as Visions of the Great Rememberer.

In general in your (worse in Gifford-Lee) book my own
feeling is that not enough respect is paid to the enormity (I
mean penetrant monumentality in beauty, not wishness) of the
work Kerouac did that's known in his last six or seven years,
in the 'sixties--Big Sur is a heroic reconstruction of madness
such as few dying men have ever reconstructed from hallu-
cination & illness. Vanity of Duluoz, standing outside of the
completed romantic legend of youthtime & fame completed by
Part II Desolation Angels, is an "Epilogue in Heaven/Hell"
outside of that narrative time, looking back on the whole
work with justice & true disillusionment, medicine for any
youthful follies, with prose looser, more I-dont-give-shit
free of self-illusion than any before, playful, unguarded, like
mature painter's swift exact unerring brushwork, easy, re-
laxed, unstraining, with strange lyrical flights & condensed
cadenzas, sleight-of-hand rhapsodies & side-of-mouth re-
marks--the tone as maybe nobody was literate enuf to notice,
taken from Melville's late John Marr and other Sailors poems
also addressed to his wife in declining age over a pipe of old
bohee. And Pic, when the last chapter's resurrected, will
combine youth two ways as a little lyrical coda, bringing
early Pic story into retrospective focus with his main heroes
of the road. And only Stella knows what poems & sorrows
& precisions & philosophies are left behind in his last note-
books of seven years--if she knows. And incidental, crucial
to biography, what was his last scribble in his notebook open
on his lap (?) before he went into the bathroom, leaving the
TV set? Can you find out any way? It's important to the
story--maybe some drear illumination.

What more beside health could any of us asked for in
'60's from dying Kerouac--as it is even in that long illness
he outwrote all his peers except maybe Burroughs who was
just getting his wind--certainly Kerouac left as much bulk

and beauty of composition as any writer that decade. Who appreciates that extraordinary work and triumph, 61--67??

OK--Allen Ginsberg

P.S. Floral wreath we brought to funeral home Archam-bault, signed by Holmes, Lucien, Gregory, me & Peter read "GUARD THE HEART."

Numbers preceded by a "p" refer to page numbers; all other numbers refer to citation numbers.